PRIESTS

FOR

TOMORROW

The crisis now being experienced by the Roman Catholic clergy is a major continuing news story; the fundamental questions that are being raised are of the highest ecumenical importance. A growing number of priests are living in painful uncertainty as they ask themselves, "Who am I?" and "What am I doing?" Father Ruud J. Bunnik, a young Dutch theologian, has performed a service for them and the entire Christian community in writing **Priests for Tomorrow,** since he examines the present situation in depth and opens up hopeful perspectives for the future.

Bunnik begins with a description of the priest's uneasiness with his work, the growing "competition" from educated laymen, the possibly dehumanizing effect of priestly formation, and problems of recruitment, seminary training, living conditions, and ministerial function. He then offers a nontechnical presentation of the most important data on ministry, drawing on Scripture, conciliar documents, and some recent encyclicals. Bunnik's emphasis is on the idea of the servant Church, a mystery of salvation that exists for the world, and he insists that the priest should not be reduced to his "role."

Bunnik deals forthrightly with such controversial issues as priestly celibacy, the option to leave the ministry, and the possibility of women priests, and offers positive recommendations for the priesthood of the future, stressing variety, ecumenicity, and professional training. There is no room for clericalism, since Christ is the only true priest of the New Testament, and the specific role of the minister must be built on the general priesthood of all believers.

RUUD J. BUNNIK

PRIESTS
for
TOMORROW

Translated from the Dutch by Frances Wilms

 Holt, Rinehart and Winston
NEW YORK · CHICAGO · SAN FRANCISCO

Designer: Bernard Klein
Printed in the United States of America

1475797

To live is to change, and to be perfect
is to have changed often.

—John Henry Newman

ACKNOWLEDGMENTS

Grateful acknowledgment is made to the following publishers who have so
generously granted permission to reprint from their publications: Darton,
Longman & Todd, Ltd. and Doubleday & Company, Inc., New York, for
excerpts from *The Jerusalem Bible*, copyright © 1966 by Darton, Longman &
Todd, Ltd. and Doubleday & Company, Inc. Used by permission of the publishers; Guild Press, America Press, Association Press, and Herder and Herder,
for excerpts from the Dogmatic Constitution on the Church and the Decrees
on the Ministry and Life of Priests taken from *The Documents of Vatican II*,
published by Guild Press, America Press, Association Press, and Herder and
Herder, and copyrighted © 1966 by the America Press. Used by permission;
Herder and Herder, New York, for passages from *The Church and the Sacra-
ments*, by K. Rahner, copyright © 1963 by Herder K. G.; Newman Press,
New York, for passages from *Lay People in the Church*, by Yves Congar
(Newman Press, 1967) copyright © 1957 and 1967 Geoffrey Chapman Ltd.
Used by permission; Westminster Press, Philadelphia, Pennsylvania, for pas-
sages from *The New Reformation?* by John A. T. Robinson. Published in the
U.S.A. by the Westminster Press, 1965. Copyright © SCM Press Ltd., 1965.
Used by permission.

CONTENTS

✻✻

PART III

The Ministry of the Future

INTRODUCTION

To say that the Church is going through a crisis is like carrying coals to Newcastle: anyone who is not blind and deaf knows this to be the case. But it may not be entirely useless to stress again that the word *crisis* need not arouse any panic. The original meaning of the word is: judgment, consideration, reorientation, a turning point on the way from the past into the future. To speak of a crisis is not in itself the sign of a pessimist, but certainly nobody would use the word if he meant to say that everything was well on board.

To head off all the pessimists, however, it might be better to use the term that Pope John made into a byword for ecclesiastical renewal: *aggiornamento*. It has taken root in the language to such an extent that typesetters no longer put it between quotation marks or in italics. It makes good sense to speak also of *aggiornamento* in regard to the ecclesiastical ministry, if the whole Church is being brought up to date, the ministry cannot be excluded. Here, too, an inventory is needed, a critical evaluation, a reorientation to the future. But updating the ecclesiastical ministry is apparently a rather difficult task, so that the negative meaning of crisis seems to come to mind more readily. If, for instance, as regards the liturgy and ecumenism, one has the feeling of standing at the beginning of a new era, silence still reigns to a considerable extent on the question of the ministry.

How did this come to pass? Why did Vatican II really give comparatively little impetus to any renewal of the ministry? Why do the Council texts on the ministry make so little impression? This cannot be ascribed merely to a lack of time. True, the agenda of Vatican II was too crowded, but in terms of priorities, the ministry might well have come up somewhat earlier and in greater detail than was the case; it was more deserving, for instance, of the time and energy spent on the rather unimportant texts concerning communications or Christian education. Nor would it be quite fair to say that a certain anxiety played a part in the matter. The question of the ministry had several thorny aspects, but Vatican II showed that it had the courage to tackle several extremely sensitive questions. One could perhaps speak of a certain hesitancy, due to a lack of usable material. During the last decade, few important theological works have been published on the ecclesiastical ministry, as compared with the stream of studies on the papacy and the episcopate, minor subjects that were handled not simply out of pure scientific interest, but also because they answered "a need of the times." The premature end of Vatican I had resulted in such emphasis on the papacy that the restoration of some measure of balance between its theological and practical aspects was called for on all sides.

The fact remains that the first schema submitted to the Council regarding the priests was so inadequate that the bishops considered it was not worth debating. The revised text also was only moderately good, and was adopted—by a great majority of votes, even so—more because it was impossible not to say anything at all about and to priests, than because of any real enthusiasm for the actual contents of the document.

Others, however, sociologists and psychologists, have set to work where the theologians had not ventured. The number of publications coming from the former is such that it is almost impossible to review them, and a great deal of useful, necessary spade work has thus been accomplished of which the theologians can now make fruitful use. The problems, seen from every angle, have been carefully itemized; there are piles of statistics and reports on the structures of pastoral care, on the formation of priests, the lack of priests, their role, and the concrete realities of priestly life. This is another invitation to theology to branch out into new activities. The success of the renewal as a whole depends in large part on the proper functioning of the ecclesiastical ministry, and efficiency on the practical level should be supported by and derived from a good theology of the ministry. It is difficult to proclaim the Lord's coming without knowing who his special servants are; it is impossible to draw up projects for the care of souls without knowing what theology has to say about the functions of ministers; and it is also impossible to recruit and to train for a ministry whose characteristic nature has not been made sufficiently clear.

It would indeed be a presumption on my part were I to present this book as an attempt to supply what Vatican II did not. However, it is written in the firm belief that serious thought must be given to a theology of the ministry and in the hope that the quiet work of an industrious free-lance writer may be of some use—if only to challenge others to develop further these beginnings and correct its stupidities as soon as possible.

Many priests are now uneasily asking themselves not only "What am I doing?" but also "Who am I?" Along with many laymen, they are seeking to establish the identity of the ecclesiastical ministry and of the ecclesiastical minister. The traditional formulas are no longer satisfactory because they do not correspond to reality as it is perceived. Many will perhaps welcome a provisional inventory of the problems and a first attempt at interpretation and theological examination, even if they will they may discover that several formulations are not adequately based on explicitly defended theological insights. Others may find that many sacred things have fallen by the wayside. I can only say to them that something is bound to be lost in any reconstruction, but no criticism has been made out of sheer love of destruction or hatred of the past. He who hates the past, hates the womb that bore him. It is equally true, however, that the past is merely a starting point, and that it has real meaning only for the man who also looks to the future. Nor is the present any final criterion of conduct: the man who marks time in the present betrays his historicity and forgets that he is by nature a pilgrim.

The central part of this book is an outline of a theology of the ministry. It is an attempt to set forth in a number of short sections the most important data and problems, examine the tenability of the traditional formulas and see what could profitably be set forth with the help of newer ideas.

A complete treatise on the ecclesiastical ministry would be several thousand pages long. Long historical expositions have inevitably been omitted here: those who are interested can find them elsewhere, but they might be well advised to consider that a book on the ministry is not necessarily better for being larded with references to Funk, Migne, or the *Sources Chrétiennes;* too much attention to the past can also put a brake on renewal, and this is true not only of the theology of the ministry.

Before and after the central part of this book, the reader will find a side panel, each of which is more in the nature of an essay than a rigorously structured disquisition. The first indicates briefly the different elements to be found in the "crisis." It is no exhaustive analysis; it merely pinpoints what any one who is at all familiar with the subject already knows. The other panel, the conclusion, deals with the future and endeavors to develop a few ideas on the basis of the findings given in the central part of the book. I definitely do not pretend to hold the final answers on future developments, but shall be satisfied if something useful may perhaps be found in the conclusion. Whoever finds my ideas too fantastic should remember that imagination is no evil, but a driving force in the history of mankind.

Most of the questions raised about the ministry are those that all Christians are asking everywhere; a theology of the ministry, therefore, must in itself be ecumenical. The non-Catholic theology of the ministry seems to have gone further than the Catholic in many respects, and evolved views on certain problems of which we are still unaware. Use of the results of this research has contributed, I hope, to the improvement of this book.

But is it really possible in our day to speak sensibly about the ecclesiastical ministry? Surely the questions raised seem to be of secondary importance today, when we are wondering whether God is dead and Christendom has come to an end. At a time when our understanding of the Church is changing almost from day to day, will not any study of the ecclesiastical ministry be doomed to obsolescence from the day of publication? The risk is there, but it makes no sense to wait with folded arms until the new ecclesiology has matured; in any case, it can only reach maturity if all its parts grow along with it. The renewal of the faith and the updating of ecclesiastical life are not merely separate and sudden happenings, but also shifts in a gradual evolution. However revolutionary our times may be, its unfoldings are rooted in a stream of continuous changes. The same is true of the ministry; it must be brought up to date day by day; the better it is today, the more easily will it merge into tomorrow.

I should like to offer this book to the past and present residents of Pius Convict at Nijmegen, as a somewhat belated present for its fortieth anniversary. It is in that house, so full of a vigilantly open-eyed love of the Church, that many of the ideas here set down were first formulated.

R.J.B.

Apeldoorn, July 1967

sometimes even contrary, results: fewer people than ever seem ready to be persuaded to practice their religion. Although certain positive developments can also be detected—the promotion of the laity, growing interest in Scripture and the discussion of religious subjects, liturgical renewal, and a new emphasis on interfaith unity, these developments are still recent and seem somewhat erratic, so that they do not fit easily into the traditional structure of ecclesiastical life. Is it surprising that many priests feel uncertain and tired, deriving little satisfaction from their profession and finding it more and more difficult to be enthusiastic about their work?

This sense of crisis is not the monopoly of the minister; he is confronted with the problems that each Christian has to face, but they press harder on him because for him, more than for the laity, ecclesiastical life is both profession and bread. How can he base his life, physically and spiritually, on an altar around which fewer and fewer people gather? What is the use of a church building that apparently is not only in need of inside remodeling, but whose showy exterior seems to be more a traffic hazard in the secular city than an invitation to a meeting, and that has become more a museum for the connoisseur than a public building intended for everyone? The present is unclear for the Church, and her past is not spotless: despite her respectable message of peace and brotherhood, she has taken sides in many wars and organized others; she has not always striven energetically against oppression and racial hatred and has sometimes been guilty of them herself; she has not consistently applied the concept of equality for all; and she has wasted time with paltry domestic problems while the world was clamoring for bread and understanding. Faced with urgent problems arising from new developments like total war and overpopulation, she has been slow to respond because her schools of thought and rules of learning could provide nothing that covered the case.

When a Church has been found so greatly wanting, or is bypassed as irrelevant, what of her minister? Perhaps he would welcome a chance to acquire a fresh understanding of the situation and re-examine his premises. But he finds that a great deal of his time is given over to keeping the traditional routine going, and he rightly hesitates to throw out old ways before he has found new approaches. And to whom will he turn for advice as he recognizes the limitations of his own understanding and competence? His authorities and colleagues are equally uncertain, and he finds it hard to deal with the mass of literature on the relevant subjects. When he does receive an answer, it is often to the effect that the days of general rules and centralized guidance are over, and that one must be guided by the concrete situation. If he comes to a decision according to his own understanding of the matter, however, he may well find himself charged with ignoring dogma and discipline, or with lacking *esprit de corps*. Thus, beside the numberless practical and theological difficulties, he may also be faced with the niceties of balancing authority and freedom. He needs to be faithful to what he holds in pledge—and is thereby bound to the past; at the same time he must renew the face of the earth and turn with confidence toward the future.

A feeling of uncertainty is to be found among all age groups. The younger generation are by nature more familiar with change and relativity; they are not so easily shocked and can always find comfort in the thought that they will live to see the "new times"; on the other hand, they are also liable to lack the wisdom needed to distinguish between essence and form, and their sense of relativity may be such that they cannot decide on a concentrated effort. For the members of the older generation, who are less familiar with the idea of evolution, the future is more unpleasant; the changes in theology, just as in the practical life of the Church and of the society, come upon them unawares and can easily be interpreted as a condemnation of what they themselves have done for so long and with such devotion. Even if they do not stay out of the movement, and try to adopt a fresh approach, they realize that they will never see the new day, and must always work in uncertainty. The young will spare the feelings of their elders as much as possible, but is it surprising that the latter should feel like outcasts, the old guard that is still put up with, but on whose account renewal simply cannot be put off?

2. THE LAITY AS COMPETITORS

Priests used to be the undisputed leaders of the Church. They had the knowledge and the power, and their word was law. The layman was not qualified to judge; his only right was to guidance by the ministry, and his first duty was obedient response to that guidance. If he was outspoken enough to express his own opinion, or to make a practical suggestion, the ministry might obligingly take his idea into account; but it was impossible, structurally, to make such a contribution operative. The assumption was that the ecclesiastical minister knew best, and that his was the ultimate and indivisible responsibility.

This kind of situation is disappearing; the Church is becoming democratic, and to identify the Church with the clergy seems no longer to be a tenable proposition. Knowledge of Scripture and theology is becoming the common property of God's people as a whole, and the obvious fitness of many laymen for tasks traditionally carried out by the clergy, religious instruction, care of the sick and the poor, administration of Church property, is no longer denied but welcomed and put to good use. It is not only a matter of technical assistance in an emergency situation; the idea is growing that the layman, who so clearly stands in both the world and the Church, can make a substantial contribution to the interpretation of religious life and its concrete development. The part he is playing is changing more and more from that of a consultant to that of a qualified equal endowed with the right to make decisions.

A priest will rejoice in these developments because he is prepared to recognize the equal rights of all and to hope that cooperation will yield good results. Nevertheless, these developments will also sometimes depress him. Does he still have the last word, does he still have an exclusive task and a personal responsibility? Are the idiosyncratic nature of the ecclesiastical ministry and the "separate" quality of being a minister no more than historical accidents which, on second thought, must now be eliminated? Will the fact that, increasingly, his work is appraised and, when occasion arises, criticized by laymen shatter the security of his professional performance? Is his traditional "authority" to be imputed simply to his personal abilities, and not to an entirely impersonal mission and grace? Are there any definite limits to the role of the layman and, if so, where do they lie? Besides being a welcome assistance, is the restored diaconate also a Trojan horse that will destroy the clerical stronghold from within? Is there not some truth in Boniface VIII's statement that the laity have always been hostile to the clergy? Even if this "competition" could proceed peacefully, will it not result in driving the minister back to the sacristy, leaving him to defend a narrow holy ground in which the desacralized world is less and less interested? If the need for an explicitly ecclesiastical presence disappears, is not the minister also bound to disappear, or at least to degenerate into a "holy outsider," respected as a person, but no longer considered to be truly useful? These are not academic questions, but involve the very identity of the ecclesiastical minister and of his work.

3. THE MINISTER AS BELIEVER

The issues examined in the two preceding sections lay mainly in the field of professional performance, and consequently entail institutional functional problems. But the minister is also involved in the general problems with which all Christians are personally confronted. Their queries about faith and life are also his: what do I mean when I say that I believe in God? Is Christ the Lord a living reality for me? What does Christ's mes-

sage of salvation mean to our own age? What is the task of the
Church, and what claims may she put forward? Where is the
Church infallible, and where are her doctrine and structure
strongly marked by history? How can a man be justified by
God and yet live in sin and weakness? What is the hope that
inspires me? What do I expect of life here and hereafter? Do I
believe in the Spirit, in a future life, heaven and hell? How do
I associate my loyalty to the historical Church and loyalty to
my own conscience?

These queries are also those of the priest, and rightly so, because he is a human being like anyone else. In fact, he is bound
to take them seriously, even more than others for in his case,
faith permeates the whole of life: his faith is at the same time
his profession, he is a sort of incarnation of belief. A priest must
demonstrate his faith clearly and not let himself slip into a
minimal fringe Christianity. His remaining in the ministry
stands or falls with his faith and his loyalty to the Church.
That is why living with unresolved problems and uncertainties
is even more oppressive for him. As he recognizes how imperfect his life remains, he will wonder increasingly whether
he is worthy of the ministry and satisfactorily fulfills its requirements. By reason of his ministry, he can allow himself no falling
off, no "sabbatical leave"; when he no longer has an instinctive
sense of the divine, his ministry, too, ceases to be self-evident.
At the same time that he detects in himself the general inclination toward secularization, he may feel called, by reason of his
office, to resist this tendency.

Difficulties of this kind are very painful and can leave the
priest torn by doubts about his basic Christian commitment.
Most novels about priests have not yet dealt with these conflicts;
when they do go beyond pathetic elaborations of the "secret of
the confessional," the power of consecration, celibacy, or the
career difficulties of Church administrators, they usually fall
into a simplistic fatalism where doubts almost inevitably lead
to downright apostasy and moral degradation. Reality is differ-

ent: the ecclesiastical minister does not feel like a tragic hero staggering under the burden of the sins of the world, but rather like an ordinary man still searching for truth, while wondering whether he can measure up to his office, which he had assumed so readily and with so much faith, in a life of setbacks and new beginnings.

4. THE MINISTER AS A HUMAN BEING

Whoever studies the actual phenotype of the ecclesiastical minister will have little difficulty in listing its characteristic features. The minister stands fairly high in the social scale. He ranks as a notable and leads a life that in many ways has a style of its own: the clerical life pattern. Its components are, besides celibacy, the wearing of distinctive clothing, exemption, in one way or another, from military service, living in big houses that differ from the usual type, either in cloisters or in official residences, a certain formality in speech and manner, and a fairly marked symbiosis of function and life situation due to which the "loftiness" of his calling permeates his private life: the minister is always a minister.

A phenotype of this kind is practically unknown in contemporary society. There are differences, of course, known and acknowledged, in upbringing, cultural development, standard of living, and functions. But they are all increasingly considered merely incidental to the central and fundamental concept of the equality of all men, and they do not entitle one to greater regard or higher rank. Respect for function or wealth does not automatically result in greater respect for the person, and it is considered a breach of the democratic spirit for someone to cover up or attempt to offset personal failings and deficiencies by bringing up the matter of office or authority. A failure is tolerated, as it is tolerated from every man, but is neither denied nor minimized on the basis that deficiencies of those in high places should go unnoticed. Class distinctions have pretty well disappeared, authority is no longer given by birth, wealth, title, or office; it must be earned by the individual's performance.

The priest, too, lives in this democratic atmosphere. His high office does not compensate for personal idiosyncrasies and weaknesses, nor does professional prestige make up for lack of good manners or knowledge; if he is barely acceptable as a human being, this will have serious consequences for the effectiveness of his work. The same is expected of the ecclesiastical minister as of other people: he must be our fellow man and a citizen of today, not a representative of days gone by. We are not looking for "respectability," formality, studied speech, and a distant friendliness; there is, rather, emphasis on comradeship, a sense of fair play, and the democratic ethos; we want to see a readiness to help, initiative, personal participation, spontaneity, and candor.

Priests themselves seem increasingly to realize the reasonable nature of these objections and wishes. As children of our democratic times, they are less and less happy with the traditional emphasis on being different, with the way in which their person automatically shares in the distinctiveness of their profession, and the uniformity of behavior that is expected of them. They no longer see how being different is really more help to them in their work than being an ordinary fellowman with nothing much to differentiate him from others. They are finding that it is only by establishing contact on the human level that they can reach deeper, and that many well-intended efforts fail because those who come as representatives of "another world" erect a barrier of disinterest and mistrust that neither professional expertise nor good will can breach. Today's ministers respond to the idea that the Word of God and the world of man are one and the same, though they acknowledge that it is precisely their task, even in the face of misconceptions and opposition, to bring out the "relativity" of our earthly existence and make God's self-revelation a living experience, an experience that does not necessarily exclude alienation and suffering.

They know full well that the ministry has requirements which affect their personal life, and have no desire to evade them; but they wish to be personally convinced that these requirements are necessary and unavoidable, and tend to become aggressive when they realize that certain specific "requirements" both endanger their own humanity and good relations with their fellowmen. That is why they insist on their privacy, their freedom, and their independence; they want to carry out their work like adults and on their own responsibility, to develop their own initiative, even, if necessary, against the line imposed on them from above; they want their opinions listened to; they will not be made fools of under an appointments system that apparently considers mutual discussion or any stipulation of terms as a nuisance; and they want payment for their work as a real right, rather than have to speculate about and depend on the liberality of others. Besides, they can no longer believe in a law of celibacy that compels them as a group, and independently of their individual views, to lead an unmarried life, for although they are not a priori unwilling to make this sacrifice, they fail to see why the reasons for it should and could not be left to their own discretion; they wonder why there should exist a near coercion for group life, going beyond the axiomatic need for professional fellowship; and they do not see why they should go about in uniform when they are not manifestly carrying out the duties of their office. Fundamentally, they are asking whether their being ministers must in itself make them somewhat different, and whether their personal life must necessarily be patterned on that of religious who by definition renounce the "normal" life of independence and freedom, marriage and family, comfort and interest in the world of men.

All these questions concerning the humanity of the minister are bound up with those concerning the human nature of the Church. Has the ecclesiastical minister perhaps become isolated because the Church has not dared wholeheartedly to incarnate herself, because, sensing the impossibility of completely "spiritualizing" all Christians, she wanted to have at least a core of "pure" members who could function as a magic alibi for the others? Is that perhaps why the minister had to be a superior being —not only a professional superman, but also a tangible manifestation of a tendency to overdo the "not being of this world"? If so, the community as a whole has a duty to watch and stimulate positive developments because, by its excessive desire for a minister who would always be acting out his official role, the community itself is the sociological and psychological cause of many human problems, and of the "near alienation of the priest of his humanity." [1]

5. THE EXODUS FROM THE MINISTRY

The uneasiness regarding the work of the ministry and the life situation of its members are hardly abstract matters. Naturally, these ministers themselves, whose views of themselves and their work are often blurred, have strong reactions.

Some have broad shoulders and remain optimistic. Without denying or making light of the difficulties, they know how to put up with them, because they also have an eye for the values that remain and for the other good things that new developments will make possible. They do not believe that living in some uncertainty is overly dangerous or inhuman, and recognize that too great a stress on stability and immutability may also present difficulties. Since they know that the final result will not depend upon them, their human insecurity is never fatal, and they see the openendedness of the situation as a goad to creativeness. Although they are the silent strength of the renewal and the pioneers of the Church of tomorrow, they do not see themselves as leading actors, but rather as walk-ons for whom the plot of the play is perhaps not entirely clear, but who know that they are needed for its full resolution.

[1] Cf. L. Beirnaert, "Celibat sacerdotal et sexualité," *Etudes* (March, 1964), p. 372.

Insecurity makes others mark time somewhat passively. Somewhat behind the times, they do not feel called upon to come forward as champions of renewal, because they do not themselves really believe in it; however, they are intelligent enough to realize that an emotional defense of the past does not accomplish much. They hope that the old ways will outlast them, but do not try to prevent others from seeking new ones. Their fondest hope is to be given the chance of remaining aloof. One may wonder whether they are not avoiding their responsibilities to a certain extent, but at least they honestly try to recognize the limitations of their views, and do not pretend, with forced enthusiasm, to be in step. They are not cut out for a pioneer's job, but are perhaps meant to play the devil's advocate: they can be the people who, with sharp—though not unkind—questions and remarks, will force today's enthusiasts to formulate their intuitions and meanings as clearly as possible.

In some, however, the uncertainties and disappointments have led to resistance and anger, even into a feeling of personal humiliation. The man who takes that line is heading not only for black defeatism, but also for a tendency to confrontation, gross denunciation, and inquisitorial activities. Refusing to cooperate, he begins to consider himself a martyr, an unappreciated defender of orthodoxy. He becomes a pitiful character whose complaints are so obtuse that few can consider them seriously. In sulky isolation, tempted sometimes even to downright obstruction and insubordination, he waits for the end.

But it is not always possible to go on enduring the tensions of this now doubt-ridden ministry: one begins to wonder whether it might not be better to turn back and leave. The question is being answered in the affirmative by a growing number of people; in the Netherlands, they amount now to about 10 per cent of the annual total of ordinations. The manner of leaving varies from a panicky and sudden flight to a deliberate and formally correct termination of the engagement. The motivations also are different: sometimes it is a general uneasiness that can hardly be expressed more clearly than by the words "I don't feel like it anymore"; sometimes it is a moral impossibility to adapt loyally to the changes; sometimes one's understanding of the place and function of the ministry has been so radically changed that no room for it seems as yet possible within the Church; and sometimes the problem is not so much an impossibility to carry out one's duties as a loss of affinity for the traditional life patterns imposed on priests. Here, celibacy is naturally the greatest stumbling block, but it is only one aspect of the whole question of the secularization of the person and function of the ecclesiastical minister. As the number of men who leave the ministry grows, the sensational character of the phenomenon seems to subside, and it can therefore be analyzed more soberly; that is not to deny that a tragic aspect is almost always present. It hardly needs saying that the rising number of drop-outs from the ministry is a development that can also undermine the security of those who stay on; for they know that it is not always the least gifted who walk out, and they ask themselves if their own faithfulness does not perhaps hide a certain lack of feeling or simply a spirit of compromise.

6. THE CRISIS IN VOCATION AND TRAINING

The malaise pervading the ministry naturally does not go unnoticed by outsiders; specifically, it is not hidden from those who are thinking of becoming priests.

The ministry is no easy task in itself, but when a growing number of its members find suffering in it rather than happiness, the vocation loses much of its appeal. Intensifying the propaganda is no great help, and can have the opposite effect; when desperate efforts are made to recruit candidates, who can fail to sense that there must be something not quite right with the profession? Its drawing power must arise primarily from concrete, verified, satisfying experience, and not from alluring representations of its pleasant aspects and a glossing over of its difficulties.

Besides, the situation is complicated further by the increasing competition from other professions. Those looking for comfort, social security, and prestige can find them in other fields, and in many of these cases, the proportion between advantages and drawbacks, between sacrifices and satisfactions, is strikingly more attractive.[1] More professions are now open to gifted young men, owing to the greater democratization of education, and there are not many places in which entering the ministry would represent social and cultural emancipation. A family's social standing no longer rises much because it can boast of "a son who is a priest."

In nearly all countries, the number of people attending ecclesiastical training institutions seems to be declining and the number of ordinations is decreasing. In the Netherlands, the total of those entering seminaries seems to have dropped by almost half in the last ten years: from 1772 in 1960-61, to less than 900 in 1966-67;[2] the percentage of candidates for minor seminaries stood in 1953 at 45 per 1,000 boys aged 12-13, and in 1965, at 22. The annual total of ordinations, which stood at over 300 for a long time in the Netherlands, now hovers around 250 and, judging by the present number of those in theological training, soon may be expected to drop to less than 200.[3]

These somewhat discouraging figures bring up the question of whether the continuance of ecclesiastical services could not be ensured by other means. The ordination of older people is beginning to be mentioned, particularly in connection with the

[1] Cf. T. Lindner, L. Lentner, A. Holl, *Priesterbild und Berufswahlmotive* (Vienna, 1963).

[2] This figure, 900, is moreover no longer accurate, because the pupils enrolled in the seminary schools and living on the premises cannot all be considered as "student-priests" anymore.

[3] For further statistical material, see i.e.: *Memoranda* nos. 154 and 159, published by K.S.K.I.; *Pro Mundi Vita*, 1965, no. 4; H. Hendriks, "Priester-wijdingen in Nederland 1965-1995," *Ned. Kath. Stemmen*, 60, 333-346, 1964; *Pastorale Gids.*

part-time ministry, and many activities traditionally carried out by ministers are now being handed over to the laity. Such developments are also part of the crisis, but in a more positive sense: more and more thought is being given to the fact that division of labor and specialization within the ministry might perhaps bring out new possibilities and draw new people into it.

This in turn brings up questions about traditional training methods. The belief in the necessity and possibilities of minor seminaries is diminishing,[4] and one notes a concentration on theological training that promises greater efficiency and better results. Reorganization, however, has so far affected only the more technical aspects; only with a clearer picture of what the ministry of tomorrow can and must be, will a more thorough overhaul become possible. The ministry of tomorrow determines the training norms of today: tomorrow's objective makes the present forms and methods meaningful.

7. THE SHORTAGE OF PRIESTS

The consequences of both the decrease in ordinations and the number of departures from the ministry has been that ever fewer people must do more work, and that vacant posts can no longer be filled, but at the same time also that the need for pastoral services is rising in a world faced with a growing population. Almost unavoidably, therefore, services are falling off, and the demands made on the ministers who are still available are always growing. This can paralyze individual commitment: one feels increasingly unequal to a task that keeps growing, and perhaps begins to wonder whether it is worthwhile to undertake projects which will probably have to be abandoned later in any case for lack of successors. However, the shortage of personnel has been profitable in that it has brought about many

[4] Cf. the articles by O. Thomaasse, W. Stoop, and A. Beekman in *Priesterroeping en Seminarie* (Haarlem, 1964), pp. 41-85.

efforts at improving a division of labor that was sometimes not very efficient; there has also been a transfer of some assignments to laymen, and the main task of the ministry has been pruned to a certain extent. However, the possibilities are not inexhaustible. In this connection, mention should also be made of the "aging" of the corps of ministers. The decrease in ordinations along with the increase in resignations—which, understandably, are more frequent in the younger group—produce a less favorable age structure. In the Netherlands, on January 1, 1965, there were 166 priests per 10,000 men aged 50 to 54, but only 88 per 10,000 aged 30 to 34. The ministers are more and more becoming the presbyters, the elders in the literal sense of the word.[1]

8. THEOLOGICAL PROBLEMS

It is impossible for anyone faced with the various manifestations—positive and negative—of the crisis, not to ask himself what light, if any, the theology of the ministry can throw on them, or, more aptly, whether the changes are perhaps directly bound up with an evolving theological concept of the ministry. With the psychological and sociological identity of the ministry experiencing crisis, how tenable is the traditional dogmatic tract on the ecclesiastical ministry? Is that changing too, and should it perhaps not change within the framework of the whole evolution of theological thought? We shall now touch briefly on some of these points, by way of introduction to the central part of our study which is intended as an attempt at a theological reorientation and inventory.

Is the priest another Christ?

Leafing through old tracts on the ecclesiastical ministry, and especially the "devotional" literature, the reader will often find

[1] The figures appear in *Memorandum* no. 160 of the K.S.K.I.: *"Statistiek van de priesters op 1 jan. 1965."*

that ministers are rather easily identified with the Lord of the Church. They share in his threefold office of king, priest, and prophet; their word is his word and their actions have a kind of divine authority and superhuman efficiency. The history of the Church and her ministry easily accounts for this approach: popes and bishops who ranked as princes of the world, and even claimed more than princely powers, seemed able to do this because they represented the Lord of the world; a theology that sometimes presented the Eucharist as a re-enactment of the sacrifice of the cross turned the priest into an independent sacrificer. The monopoly of doctrinal teaching and infallibility enjoyed by ministers seemed to put them above obedience to the dictums of faith. Protest against such mythologizing of the ecclesiastical ministry was made in particular by the Western Reformation; originally rejected as unfair, it has now come to be admitted more and more within the Catholic community. Among other reasons, this is due to a new awareness, based on Scripture, that an all-too-easy transfer to the ecclesiastical minister of the titles of the Lord (head of the body, bridegroom of the Church, king of God's people, priest of the New Covenant, envoy of God) may cause misgivings.

The ministry as service

No one ever denied that the ministry is a service to the community. But in the actual shaping of the ministry in a Church that developed into a rigidly organized institution with a corps of rulers, a form of leadership came about that looked more like ruling than serving. To this day "the Church," for many people, still means the clergy, its administration, and hierarchical authority. Ecclesiology was often little more than hierarchology, the proper place and role of the laity were seldom mentioned, and when they were, the talk seldom went beyond a description of the various demands of obedience. Now that this actual situation is being criticized on all sides, other questions become urgent: does the fact that the ministry is service not entail a much more radical reshaping of it from below? Does the ministry really have a priori structures, or should it not mold itself much more dynamically on the needs of the community? Should not relationships be declericalized as quickly as possible, so that the laity are given first place within the oneness of God's people? And if this is so, can theology provide the foundations of this intuition?

The structure of the ministry

We have, in the course of time, come to speak quite naturally of the threesome pope-bishop-priest, and of a pyramidal structure of the ministry. But must we not ask: what direct justification is to be found for this development in Scripture? Or could this be to a large extent a coincidental historical development? Alongside a strong emphasis on the basic vertical structuring, should not more thought be given to horizontal cohesion through collegiality? Does the rigidly centralized structure not require as a corrective the counterplay of more independent local Churches? Is there no need for a new formulation of the difference between the power of ordination and the power of jurisdiction? What does it mean that a sacramental character is ascribed to certain functions, and what must we understand by the "indelible mark of the minister"? Can theology show that these questions are legitimate, and can it perhaps even give us fresh answers and suggest new forms?

The relationship between minister and layman

In its opposition to the clericalization of the life of the Church accomplished during the Middle Ages, the Reformation emphasized the scriptural doctrine of the common priesthood, thereby raising penetrating questions about the tenability of the traditional formulation of the difference between layman and minister. The questions are now being increasingly considered in Catholic theology. The simplistic idea of the minister being entitled to a practical monopoly over internal ecclesiastical activities has proved to be indefensible. Every Christian is called to active service in God's kingdom. As this conviction grows, and as the laity become more involved in the apostolate, the need to describe more accurately the specific task and role of the ecclesiastical minister will become more pressing. What are the specifically ministerial forms of ecclesiastical service? Is there a specific field of work with its own physical boundaries, or does rather the ecclesiastical ministry perhaps put its own accent on activities that in themselves are neither lay nor priestly? The theology of the ecclesiastical ministry is at the same time a theology of the laity.

Function and life situation; "priestly spirituality"

The ministerial function is embedded in the whole life of the Christian who has been called to the ministry. This means that certain styles of Christian experience may fit the ministerial calling better than others, and that this calling may properly call for a special shaping of the personal life of the minister. In the course of history, certain forms have evolved: group life inspired by the monastic ideal, clerical garb, celibacy, specified forms of prayer. Were these developments accidental, determined by place and time, by a certain concept of the ideal of Christian holiness, so that they could also be quite different? Or can essential requirements for "priestly spirituality" be established from the basic tenets of the theology of ecclesiastical ministry? Are there nothing but advantages in a formation based on a more or less exclusive professional ideal of sanctity, or does it not also include some disadvantages? Might it be a practical proposition, as an efficient way for the work to be done, and even desirable, theologically speaking, that ministry and life pattern should be separated as much as possible? Questions there are aplenty, and all have some bearing on the crisis in the ecclesiastical ministry.

PART II

**

SKETCHES FOR A THEOLOGY OF THE ECCLESIASTICAL MINISTRY

1. THE ECCLESIOLOGY OF VATICAN II

The theology of the ministry is a part of the theology of the Church. The writer on the ecclesiastical ministry proceeds from ecclesiological viewpoints that he either takes for granted or more or less fully defines and supports. We shall here take a middle course: a fairly short section in which we shall state concisely the ecclesiological themes relevant for a meaningful discussion of the ministry.[1]

Perhaps one of the reasons why so little has been written during the last decade on the theology of the ministry may lie in the fact that ecclesiology has been so deeply stirred. To put it even more strongly: only in the last century has ecclesiology reached a certain degree of maturity. It is really still a fairly young offshoot of theological science. Naturally, there have been throughout the ages discussion and writing about the

[1] For the final text of this book, I have drawn extensively on a collection of articles on the Church of Vatican II, edited by G. Baraúna and published in Dutch in 2 volumes under the title *De Kerk van Vaticanum II* (Bilthoven, 1966). A recent book by H. Küng, *The Church* (New York, Sheed and Ward, 1967), which contains a thought-provoking section on the ministry (pp. 388-480), should also be mentioned; his views prove in many ways to differ only slightly from those set forth in this study.

Church, but no truly fundamental and systematic study has in fact ever been made. There was little need for it perhaps, and little time, during the first fifteen centuries of the Church's history, as men were concentrating on the important problems relating to the person of Christ, grace and justification, the sacraments, and eternal salvation. One could hazard a supposition that the need for a good theology of the Church became acute only after great schisms, particularly of course after the devastating breakup of Christian unity in the fifteenth and sixteenth centuries. In the first, and somewhat negative, phase of ecclesiology, *apologies* for one communion or another have been frequently produced in recent centuries. Moreover, what was actually said about the Church, particularly in the Roman Church, usually pertained to law rather than theology.

Whatever the case may be, ecclesiology is at present the center of interest. It is no exaggeration to say that Vatican II—and its predecessor Vatican I—have been above all ecclesiological Councils. This is not to say that the interest in ecclesiology is a characteristically Roman Catholic phenomenon. It is essentially a subject for our times, now that all the Churches know that they have once more been called to work seriously toward the restoration of the one Church, and challenged by a secular world that is coming of age, to prove the need for their existence and their right to live.

The findings of Vatican II in the field of ecclesiology could be treated together in two points, two themes which in the early days of the Council were described as "the inward Church" and "the outward Church" (*Ecclesia ad intra* and *Ecclesia ad extra*) and culminated in the two great constitutions of the Council: *Lumen gentium,* on the Church herself, and *Gaudium et spes,*[2] on the Church in the modern world.

[2] Council documents and encyclicals are named by the first two words of the relevant Latin text. The citations from the Council texts are taken from *The Documents of Vatican II*, Walter M. Abbott, S.J., general editor (New York, 1966; London 1967).

Of these two themes, the last is without any doubt the most important; it therefore deserves to be considered first.

The Church does not exist in spite of or alongside the world; she exists on behalf of the world. She *is* the world, she *is* the community of men insofar as they have heard the saving Word of God, and through faith and baptism have become the living people of God, the seed and the promise of his everlasting kingdom.

Such a sweeping identification of Church with world has for centuries sounded like heresy in the ears of many, and for some people today it may still do so. Because, poor exegetes that we are, our temporal reality and the "evil world" against which Scripture warns us were treated as one and the same; we imagined that holiness could be achieved only through a radical break with "the world." We thought that the Church of Christ had her own domain, a stronghold that behind heavy walls would ward off the world, an association for the salvation and sanctification of its own members. It is not that we did not take our "mission" seriously, but we thought that our duty was simply to open wide the gates of our citadel, raid enemy territory from time to time, or build new strongholds of salvation elsewhere which would become self-supporting structures in a pagan land.

Indeed, it is not impossible to conceive of the role of the Church in these terms, but it is not how the Lord Jesus spoke about it. He told us in the parable of the sower that the field is the world, and that we Christians must be as salt and leaven; permeating everything, but seldom found in a visible, concrete form. The City of God is identical with the City of man; its wall and borders are the walls and borders of the world itself. There is no place that is not Church, even though the seed has not yet sprung up everywhere. The members of the Church therefore can call themselves not-of-this-world only insofar as, standing in it, they have "related" the world to God, that is, linked it with God, centered it on God. That is why Church and mission are identical. Christians are not people for whom mission is one of their "duties." They *are* a mission. Apostolate and preaching are basic functions of the Church. For Hoekendijk, this feature is so basic that he even goes so far as to invert the order and call the Church a function of the apostolate.[3] This is not quite accurate, for as God's own family, the Church is also the result and source of the apostolate; but this kind of expression can nevertheless clarify our view of her.[4]

The Church is service to the world. The first words of the great constitution of Vatican II on the Church read: *Lumen gentium,* the light of all nations. It is the title with which Simeon greeted Christ when he was presented in the Temple (Lk 2:32), but it is also the basic characteristic of the Church, Christ enduring on earth.

The man who becomes a Christian does not cut himself off from the community of men; he just becomes more of a fellow man. Indeed, he can now detect in himself and in others a new human dimension which makes him richer, and he will feel impelled to try to make others share in the wealth of this joy. The Church is mission, and therefore the Christian is in essence a missionary. A man is not saved and made a Christian by being singled out and withdrawing from the world; living in the world with all the others, he is protected from evil by the Father that he may bear much fruit (Jn 15, 16 and 17:15). Only the man who remains human can develop into a Christian. He who tries to sanctify himself alone, within the inner recesses of the Church, is an individualist and an egoist, and therefore not truly man; and he will eventually discover that his choice has made him poorer and not richer.

[3] See J. Hoekendijk, *The Church Inside Out,* ed. by L. A. Hoedemaker and Peter Tijmes, trans. by Isaac C. Rothenberg (Philadelphia, 1966), pp. 13ff.
[4] Cf. M. Le Guillou, "De missionaire roeping van de kerk," in G. Baraúna, *De Kerk van Vaticanum II* (Bilthoven, 1966), vol. I, pp. 670-686.

Similarly, a Church that is just a Church, and not a world, is a pitiful Church, impoverished by autism and narcissism. A Church that is aware of this danger will humbly recognize that the traditional identifications of the kingdom of God with the institutional Church, of the kingdom of God with a specific ecclesiastical Christian community, are open to criticism. She will recognize and openly confess that she is no more than the transmitter of the Word and the germ-cell of the kingdom. She will want to enter into conversation with a world that she will accept as it is, and she will proclaim that she is concerned about all—*Gaudium et spes, luctus et angor,* "the joys and the hopes, the griefs and the anxieties" of all mankind—the opening words of the Pastoral Constitution on the Church in the Modern World.

This makes it immediately clear that the problems of the internal structure of the Church are not the most important questions facing theology and the general reflection on faith. The real theological and practical problems concern the Church-world relationship. It also means that the validity of the distinction between Church and world is only partial. No complete separation, therefore, can be made between internal and external ecclesiastical matters. The believer knows that those things that at first sight seem purely secular are nevertheless permeated by the divine, and everything that one might be tempted at first sight to consider as purely ecclesiastical seems upon further examination to be only a subordinate part of the one and indivisible divine-human reality.

The Church of Vatican II is busy discovering that Church and world are in the last instance one and the same divine given. They alone can call themselves Christians who, standing in the world, witness to the wonderful deeds of God and to the goodness and love of man and of our savior Jesus Christ, who urges us to repent, to give up exclusively profane desires and godlessness, invites us to a sober, upright, pious life, doing good to all, not only to members of the faith. Nevertheless, even now a group of men can already be distinguished, who are in a special manner *Familia Dei,* God's own household. That is why we may and must also have an ecclesiology of the inner Church.

A remarkable evolution is also taking place in this "branch" of ecclesiology, an evolution which comes to light very strikingly in *Lumen Gentium,* and is also officially acknowledged in that document. We shall mention here briefly a few points that are important for our further study of the ecclesiastical ministry.

One fundamental idea is indicated in the very first chapter: the Church is a mystery, the mystery of salvation. She is the mystery of Christ who lives on in mankind, she is mercy, calling, election, and hope. As the mystery of salvation, therefore, the Church can never be expounded in the words of men, and her form can never be finally structured according to organizational ideas. Law, sociology, and psychology are indispensable for good ecclesiastical life, but they do not make the Church. He who envisages the Church exclusively as an institution misapprehends the deepest meaning of her being; to ask whether the Church is a higher and more perfect community than the state is to waste one's time with an irrelevant conundrum. That is why Vatican II has refused to speak of the Church in the traditional juridico-philosophical language of *societas perfecta.* Ecclesiology is a theological science, not a tract on Church law decorated with a few pious reflections.

This striking and fundamental development is coupled with, and certainly also brought on by, a new understanding of scriptural teaching on the Church and specifically, of biblical symbolism. It could be characterized as a change "from mystical body to people of God." During the thirties and forties, theologians spoke readily of the mystical body of Christ, and the encyclical *Mystici corporis* of 1943 converted the concept into a theme of official doctrine. The image of the mystical body is indeed authentically biblical (Col 1:24) and must therefore have a place in theological considerations of the Church and in practical experience. But it is only one approximation of the mystery of the Church, and an exclusive use of it can lead to distortion. Such an image stresses the oneness of Christ and his Church, but has little to say on the essential difference between them. If it suggests a rich variety in internal ecclesiastical subordinate relationship, it leaves little room for independence and freedom. The image is somewhat juridical and vertical, which is perhaps why it was so popular in a Church strongly inclined to thinking along institutional lines. The fact that Scripture warns us not to spend too much time and energy on weighing the relative importance of each subordinate part (1 Cor 12:14-27) was taken account of mainly by presenting the hierarchical order as an "objective" fact, and insisting that those who wielded authority should remain personally humble.

Vatican II discovered the wealth of implications in the image of the people of God and devoted a whole chapter of *Lumen gentium* to them. Such an image is more likely to appeal to the modern, democratic-minded man who is also jealous of his freedom. But it is also of great value, theologically; it makes greater allowance for the difference between the Lord and his Church and brings out that the underlying unity of the members of the Church is more important and essential than the distinctions between their functions. It is a more "horizontal" image, which does not however reject the need for authority and structure: a people deprived of organization and leadership is not a people, but a horde. At the same time, this image restores to the Church her historical, dynamic, and eschatological character; for a body is primarily a static whole whose functions are internal, whereas a people grows, has external contacts, and stands prepared to spread out and improve.[5]

This development is of the utmost importance for the theology of the ministry and its actual functioning. By emphasiz-

[5] The image also has a much older tradition behind it than that of the mystical body: the whole of the Old Testament.

ing that layman and minister are primarily alike, and that they become different only at a second stage, it prevents making the ministry its own final end, and emphasizes that its nature is to serve. "The inner Church" ecclesiology proves to be much more than a "hierarcheology." It hardly needs saying that this development is also extremely important from the ecumenical point of view, for it was precisely this condensation of the Church into an institution, and of the clergy into a self-sufficient body,. that caused estrangement and separation.

The new insights we have briefly outlined above are still more a matter of promise than realization; they must still grow roots, and in all probability such reforms as will grow out of them will materialize only gradually. Many still find it impossible to give up the idea that being a Christian consists in being concerned with internal ecclesiastical matters; they were happy inside the walls of the ghetto, and dread the wind that they will have to face in the open spaces of the world. The old structures and ways were dear to them, and because they know nothing of evolutionary thinking, they still lack the imagination that might enable them to conceive of a different future. Furthermore,. those in authority are—perhaps not altogether unjustly—slightly apprehensive of the unrest and the practical managerial problems which are the inevitable accompaniment of reforms.

It should also be said that the formulation of the relevant concepts still leaves much to be desired. *Lumen gentium* was not originally conceived of as an exhaustive treatise on the Church; numerous improvements and additions made it tend in that direction, but it never became a balanced synthesis. The theologians still have a great deal of work to do.

A number of points could be brought out in connection with this book. For example, although Chapter 2 of *Lumen gentium* puts great emphasis on the unity of various groups within the Church, and uses the image of the people of God, it contains no thorough re-examination of the traditional groupings and their definition. It would have been useful, for instance, if the call of all men to holiness had been discussed immediately after this second chapter; instead, we do not find the subject taken up until Chapter 5. Nor is it a very happy arrangement that the ecclesiastical ministers are discussed first, and after them the laity (Chapters 3 and 4). Not only would it have been a fine gesture to give first thought to the most numerous group of God's people, it would also have been better theologically; for the ministry exists only as a service to the Church. Ministers cannot exist without the people, and the first place now so royally accorded to ministers indicates a certain clericalism.

In the standard handbooks on dogmatics, the ecclesiastical ministry was usually treated in two places: in the tract on the Church and in that on the sacraments. The first expounded the legal basis of the ecclesiastical ministry, its various ranks, the apostolic succession and related issues; the tract on the sacraments considered the institution of the priesthood, its sacramental nature, the ordination rites, and questions of validity. This division had all the drawbacks inevitable in a theology that chiefly considered the sacraments as individual "means of salvation." As a service to God's people, the ministry is a subject that belongs primarily to general ecclesiology, where it should be treated in substance. Obviously, this in no way impugns the sacramental nature of the priesthood; as we shall see, it is the evolution now taking place in our understanding of the sacraments that opens up new perspectives for synthesis. As for questions of validity and jurisdiction, they belong rather to ecclesiastical law than theology.

2. JESUS CHRIST: PRIEST, KING AND PROPHET

The Epistle to the Hebrews is our best text on the subject of Christ's priesthood.[1] This is because it is addressed to the

[1] Cf. H. Küng, *The Church* (New York, 1967), pp. 363-370.

Christians from among the Jews, who had in their earlier life known the service of the Jewish priesthood and the Temple of Jerusalem, and were now asking themselves whether something positive and meaningful could still be said about these old institutions. The author of the epistle explains that there is a certain continuity, but that there are also changes and developments.

Jesus carries on the priesthood of the Old Testament. That is why the writer gives him the title of *Hiereus* (priest), the name by which, in both Old and New Testament, the priests of the old order were called. The Lord may rightly bear this name for he fulfills all the conditions that a priest must meet: He has been chosen from among men, appointed to act on behalf of men, called by God and sent to offer sacrifices for the forgiveness of sins. He is, like all the priests of the old order, a mediator between God and men (Heb 5:1-5).

However, he is a priest in a different and higher manner. In him, the old priesthood is surpassed and exalted. Christ is not just one among many priestly mediators; he is unique in rank as well as in the efficacy of his deeds.

In rank, he stands above the classic mediators, the angels (1:1-2), Moses (3:1-6), and the levitical priesthood, from which he was not descended (7:1-28). The only priestly type of the old Testament which offers any point of comparison is Melchisedec, the mysterious king of Salem and priest of the Most High, to whom Abraham bowed and by whom he was blessed (7:1-10). In using the analogy, the author of Hebrews links up with Psalm 110 where it was already said of the awaited messiah and king that he was "a priest of the order of Melchisedec and forever." In support of the eternal character of this priesthood, presumably derived, as expressed in Psalm 110, from the idea of the everlastingness of the messianic kingdom, the Epistle adduces an *argumentum e silentio* often used in Jewish exegesis: Melchisedec does not belong to history, for "he has no father, mother or ancestry, and his life has no beginning or ending" (7:3).

This higher rank is related to the personal character of Christ's priestly activity. He offers *himself,* and his sacrifice has such a lasting effect that no more offerings are necessary:

But now, Christ has come as the high priest of all blessings which were to come . . . He has entered the sanctuary once and for all, taking with him . . . his own blood (9:11-12).

And he does not have to offer himself again and again . . . or else he would have had to suffer over and over again since the world began. Instead of that, he has made his appearance once and for all, now at the end of the last age, to do away with sin by sacrificing himself (9:25-26).

And this *will* was for us to be made holy by the *offering* of his *body* made once and for all by Jesus Christ (10:10).

By virtue of that one single offering, he has achieved the eternal perfection of all whom he is sanctifying (10:14).

That Jesus of Nazareth was entitled to the name of priest was never seriously questioned. The Epistle to the Hebrews is too explicit. But one may wonder whether the traditional theology of the ministry, in its treatment of the relation between Christ and the ministers of the Church, has not relied somewhat unilaterally on Hebrews and thereby arrived at a rather pronounced cultic concept of the ministry. Christ's task, after all, was not limited to offering sacrifice.

While the person of the Messiah is seldom described in the Old Testament in terms of priesthood, his kingship is fairly frequently mentioned. The whole of the Old Testament is full of the saving kingship of Yahweh, and hence the Savior sent by God could also readily be seen as the sovereign ruler of Israel; this occurred all the more easily because the Messiah was to be a scion of the royal house of David and so would fulfill the kingship of Israel. Sometimes, as in Psalm 2, he was shown as the awe-inspiring and conquering warrior, but more often he is the solicitous shepherd. Not that this implied any contradiction with his priesthood, for all the rulers of ancient Israel offered up sacrifices and were closely involved in the cult.

Similarly, the Messiah was of royal stature in the eyes of the Palestinian people of the time of Jesus; no wonder, therefore, that those who recognized Christ as the expected Messiah wished to make him king. He himself rejected this for a long time, mainly because the idea of kingship had acquired connotations that were almost exclusively political. But at the end of his life, when his doom was already sealed, Jesus did accept some royal honors when he entered into Jerusalem, and he asserted his sovereignty in his reply to Pilate, although the kingdom he referred to was more of a spiritual nature. In the New Testament writings, this concept of kingship was expressed by the term *Kurios,* a name that was given to Christ even during his lifetime. The Pauline theology showed how, through his death and resurrection, he now shares the sovereign power of God; this power, like the priestly power, is unique.

The Gospels give the impression that Christ himself saw his most important task as that of *prophecy.* On his first visit to Nazareth, he introduced himself by a reference to a prophecy of Isaiah and found from the unfavorable reactions of his hearers that no prophet is ever accepted in his own country (Lk 4:16-24). During the years that he spent preaching in Palestine, he was known as a rabbi, a teacher, the prophet from Nazareth. He taught that the kingdom of God was at hand, urged men to conversion, and explained the Scriptures. When the disciples of John came to ask him, "Are you the one who is to come, or have we got to wait for someone else?" he answered by saying that the prophecy of Isaiah was fulfilled in him: "The Good News is proclaimed to the poor" (Mt 11:5).

Again in this work, he is the greatest, as shown by the authority with which he spoke: "You have heard . . . but I say to you." The Apostle John will later consider this one of the main themes of his theological reflection, and say that the Word who in the beginning was with God was made flesh.

In this way all the functions of the Old Covenant came together in Christ. As Word of God, he is *the* prophet and teacher; as son of God, he is the Lord of the world; as the victim offered on the cross, he has become the perfect priest of the new dispensation.[2]

Vatican II has seen no reason for giving a clear exposition of the triple office of Christ in any of the texts of its constitutions and decrees. Where this classic threefold function is mentioned—for instance, in *Sacrosanctum concilium* (On the Sacred Liturgy), 5-8, *Lumen gentium,* 10-34, and *Presbyterorum ordinis*—it is done in the manner used for questions that are supposed to be well known to everybody. It is indeed an old and undisputed element of Christian belief.

There is, however, much less uniformity of opinion as to the applicability of this threefold function to the ecclesiastical ministry. There are two reasons for this. First of all, it is the function of the entire Church community to carry on this threefold task as the Lord commanded; every form of human servanthood in Church and world is connected with the work of God's pre-eminent Servant, although this is of course particularly the case for the ecclesiastical ministry. And secondly, our concern with this continuity must not make us lose sight of the fact that all participations in the threefold ministry of Christ are

[2] Of the three functions, the priesthood can be least clearly traced to the Old Testament; that is why the writer of Hebrews felt compelled to go into the matter at greater length. From the point of view of Old Testament cult, Christ was a layman, and it is not known that he ever performed any strictly ritual functions. Neither the Last Supper nor the crucifixion were sacrificial acts in the eyes of the Jews. From the moment that the whole life of Christ, culminating in the crucifixion, was considered a sacrifice, the priesthood broke through its old cultic and ritual limitations.

inevitably very imperfect. For his work was unique. No one is a prophet like the Lord; no one is shepherd and king as he is, no one offers up sacrifice as he does.

This also affects the theological presentation of the ecclesiastical ministry and its practical shaping. That is why, in particular, we must say a few words on the fact that the whole gamut of ecclesiastical ministerial services has come to be labeled priesthood. Our brief description of the threefold function of Christ himself has brought out that there are objections to calling everything he did specifically sacerdotal and cultic work. Even stronger objections can be raised in regard to the ministerial functions carried out by men; it might even be asked if the term *priesthood* can be used here at all. Scripture tells us clearly that after the one sacrifice offered by Christ the priest, no further mediatory activity for our salvation is either required or possible; a multiplicity of priests has therefore become superfluous:

Then there used to be a great number of those other priests, because death put an end to each one of them: but this one, because he remains *for ever,* can never lose his priesthood (Heb 7:23-24).

For there is only one God, and there is only one mediator between God and mankind, himself a man, Jesus Christ, who sacrificed himself as a ransom for them all (1 Tim 2:5-6).

The Church-between-the-times knows prophets and shepherds in the proper sense of the word; she can not have priests who are truly mediators and offer up sacrifice for the salvation of mankind. The early Church was conscious of this; she never called an ecclesiastical minister *hiereus-sacerdos,* a name which in Scripture is, with the exception of Christ, reserved exclusively for the priests of the Old Testament and the Gentiles. In the New Testament, ecclesiastical ministers were called bishops or presbyters, and there is not a single indication of the fact that they functioned as officers of cultic sacrifices. However, from about the days of Eusebius—that is, since the end of the third century—ecclesiastical ministers are also named *hiereis-sacerdotes*.

How could this development come to pass, a development that, to say the least, goes counter to the excerpts from Hebrews 7:23-24 and 1 Timothy 2:5 quoted above? It seems pretty certain that it is connected with the then-evolving theory of the Eucharist as sacrifice, a development which can itself be accounted for by the diaspora situation and the competing position of the early Church.

In fact, the author of the letter to the Hebrews had a rather easy task. It was sufficient for him to set forth the priesthood of Christ as the conclusion and sublimation of the priesthood of the Old Testament, and Christ's sacrifice as the final sacrifice for which the other sacrifices only prepared the way. Furthermore, history was on his side: after the fall of Jerusalem, no Jewish Temple survived. But in the Greco-Roman world, with its numerous priests and countless sacrifices, Christians found the situation more difficult. In comparison with the importance attached everywhere to the frequency of cultic ceremonies, Christianity offered only a weak alternative: it could point to only one priest, who long ago and far away had effected one completely adequate sacrifice. What could be more natural than that the Christian ministers should come to be represented as rivals of the heathen priests and the commemoration of the life and death of the Lord as a sacrifice which eclipsed all pagan parallels?

Of course, the official doctrine of the Church and the best theologians have always known how to protect themselves against exaggerations, and never called the Eucharist an independent sacrifice or a repetition of the sacrifice of the cross. But the emphasis shifted. Direct lines were drawn between crucifixion and Eucharist, and it was all but forgotten that the Lord had never demanded a "commemorative" repetition of Calvary; he had only asked that meals be celebrated in memory of all he had done, including his sacrificial death, and had guaranteed that he would be personally present, as the slaughtered and glorified Lord, in the bread that was eaten and the cup that was shared at these meals.

It is understandable therefore that Luther, who was trying to bring theology and practice in line with Scripture, felt compelled to protest against the growing independence that sacrifice and priesthood had acquired. It is a pity that his language was so violent, and that he could not have had an adequate theological terminology at his disposal; because of this, Trent could see little in his words but a complete denial of any sacrificial trait in the Eucharist, and a total repudiation of every form of priesthood. Condemnations were reciprocal, and sensible discussion of Eucharistic sacrifice and priesthood became impossible for centuries.

The gap between points of view that for so long seemed irreconcilable now appears to be narrowing. Catholic theology unreservedly recognizes that the Lord's death on the cross constituted a single and wholly effective satisfaction, and Protestant theology seems generously prepared to acknowledge the existence of the narrow tie linking the sacrifice of the cross and the celebration of the Eucharist, leaving itself open to a new exchange on the subject of the special ministry.[3] A consensus would in all likelihood be easiest to obtain on the pastoral and prophetic functions of the ministry, but a *rapprochement* on matters of cult might also be possible. In the last decade, Catholic theology has given more stress to the Eucharist as meal and has thus already abandoned an earlier one-sided theory of the Mass as sacrifice. It might be worth while if serious consideration were also given once again to the theory of *epiklesis* as held in Orthodoxy; here, the presbyter is not someone who "effects" a transformation by uttering magic formulas, but is the representative of the faithful who recalls aloud what the Lord did during the night of his betrayal, and in their name he asks

[3] Cf. R. Boon, *Offer, Priesterschap en Reformatie* (Nijkerk, 1966).

the same Lord to "charge" this bread and this wine with the power of his presence. Seen in this manner, the presbyter remains the minister who serves salvation; but he runs no risk of being presented as somebody who possesses a real and independent sacrificing priesthood.[4]

However this may be, it is in any case certain that the ministry of the New Covenant cannot be adequately understood on the basis of cult alone. Accordingly, the Greek and Latin words *hiereus* and *sacerdos,* which have this strong cultic connotation, are likely to create confusion rather than elucidate matters and had better be avoided. The terminology of Vatican II points in this direction: in *Lumen gentium* #10 the special ministry is described as "sacerdotium ministeriale seu hierarchicum" (ministerial or hierarchical sacerdocy)—the adjectives are used to distinguish it from the "common priesthood." But in #28, and also in the decree *Presbyterorum ordinis,* the word *presbyter* is preferred, although *sacerdos* is not given up entirely.

As for a number of modern languages, among them English and Dutch, the words *priest* and *priesthood* have a double meaning. They are used to indicate the person and the function of the rank between a bishop and a deacon, but they may also point to the ecclesiastical ministry in its entirety, thus including all ranks and offices; in the former meaning they are a translation of the Greek *presbyter* and *presbyterion;* in the latter they may stand for the Greek *hiereus-hierateuma* and the Latin *sacerdos-sacerdotium.*

In order to avoid misunderstanding we shall, in the rest of this book, refrain from using the words *priest* and *priesthood;* when we speak about the ecclesiastical functionaries of the "second rank" we shall call them *presbyters* and their functions the *presbyterate.* When we intend the ecclesiastical office in its entirety, we shall use the words *minister* and *ministry.* Strictly speaking, the latter terms, of Latin origin, are translations of the Greek *diakon* and *diakonia,* but since these words have their

[4] Cf. H. Bouchette, *Ambt en Mythe* (Bilthoven, 1966), pp. 49-52.

direct transpositions in most modern languages, this will hardly cause confusion.[5]

3. THE COMMON PRIESTHOOD OF THE FAITHFUL

We saw in the preceding section that the only real priest of the New Covenant is the Lord Jesus himself; no other member of the people of God of the New Covenant may bear this title, except by analogy.

However, before we say any more about the ecclesiastical ministers, let us consider briefly what is generally called the common priesthood. Nothing meaningful can be said about the special ministry if the common priesthood is not also considered —indeed, even considered first. For the common priesthood applies to God's people as a whole, and should therefore be discussed before anything can be said about specific groups of the ecclesiastical community.[1]

In the first letter of Peter and in the Book of Revelation, the terms *hiereus-sacerdos* and *hierateuma-sacerdotium* are used, in a collective sense, of the community of the faithful as a whole. We quote the relevant texts:

So that you too, the holy priesthood that offers the spiritual sacrifices which Jesus Christ has made acceptable to God, may be living stones making a spiritual house . . .

But you are a chosen race, a royal priesthood, a consecrated nation,

---

[5] The title of the original Dutch text of this book is *Dienaren van het Aggiornamento* (Servants of Renewal). I chose the Italian word for renewal in honor of Pope John who made *aggiornamento* the catchword for what he looked upon as the main task of his pontificate and his Vatican Council. The word *servants* was chosen because it avoids the ambiguity of the word *priest* and at the same time points to what is the central characteristic of any ecclesiastical vocation and ministry: servanthood to God's world and Christ's Church.

[1] Cf. the articles by E. de Smedt and P. van Leeuwen in G. Baraúna, ed., *De Kerk van Vaticanum II* (Bilthoven, 1966), pp. 446-505; H. Küng, *The Church* (New York, 1967), pp. 33-387; H. Vorgrimler, "Das allgemeine Priestertum," *Lebendiges Zeugnis*, November, 1964, pp. 92-113.

a people set apart to sing the praises of God who called you out of the darkness into his wonderful light (1 Pet 2:5, 9).

He loves us and has washed away our sins with his blood, and made us a line of kings, priests to serve his God and Father; to him, then, be glory and power for ever and ever (Rev 1:5-6).

You bought men for God . . . and made them a line of kings and priests, to serve our God and to rule the world (10:9-10; cf. also 20:6).

The idea that every member of the community of the faithful can and must offer up sacrifices is, of course, no discovery of these New Testament writings. All religions, even those with the most exclusive priestly castes and the most intricate sacrificial rituals, know and teach that no one may appear before the godhead with empty hands (cf. Ex 23:15; 34:20). The difference between priest and nonpriest, therefore, lies not between the capacity to offer or the incapacity to do so, but within the framework of the sacrificial action. For the priest, offering up sacrifice is his *raison d'être* and professional obligation, and a specific mediating power and efficacy are generally attributed to his act.

Taking into consideration all the New Testament texts relating to sacrifice and priesthood, one finds that what is new is not that the exclusive power and function to offer up sacrifice is ascribed to Christ, but that his offering alone is endowed with a real mediating power and efficacy. In the complete, specific, and "technical" sense, the New Testament knows only one priest.

The individual and collective offerings of the faithful are thereby brought into relation with the one authentic and unique sacrifice offered up by Christ. Theirs is an analogous priesthood, different from Christ's, but entirely deserving of the name; their offerings are real offerings.

It follows that it is inadmissible to term "unreal" what Peter in his first letter calls "spiritual sacrifices" (2:5), in order to distinguish them from the "real" sacrifice of Christ. The question here is not one of contrast between a sacrifice that is wholly authentic and other offerings that are merely symbolic, and hence not quite authentic. The word *pneumatikos* used in the basic text marks off the sacrifices of the New Covenant from those of the Jewish Temple and of pagan worship. Because those who offered were sinful men, their sacrifices could only be wanting. The word *pneumatikos* must here be taken in the light of the contrast between *sarx* and *pneuma* so frequently developed, particularly in the works of Paul, between sinful men and men redeemed, between sinful and saving human dealings, and not with the opposition between matter and spirit propounded by Greek philosophy. Every sacrifice that is pleasing to God in the New Order is pneumato-spiritual and utterly real (cf. Rom 12:1). Like many other great theologians before and after him, therefore, Augustine also rejected this distinction between authentic and "figurative" offerings: "The true offering consists of every act we make with the intention of uniting with God in a holy and living communion." [2]

To offer up these real sacrifices is a task imposed on all by baptism. It is, therefore, all the more clear that the authentic-inauthentic antimony cannot be used to separate what is peculiar to the official priesthood from the common priesthood. The common priesthood is a gift bestowed on every believer, including the minister. Consequently, it is not right to say or to suggest that the minister's specific exercise of the cult consists in offering up authentic sacrifices in which the "layman" joins by offering up spiritual—that is, inauthentic—sacrifices. This applies also to the Eucharistic memory of the sacrificial death of the Lord: liturgical tradition shows convincingly that the whole community is actively involved in this commemorative offering, and

---

[2] Augustine, *De Civitate Dei* X, 6 (P. L. 41, 283). It is apparent here too that being a priest has a wider meaning than merely performing ministerial functions pertaining to the official ecclesiastical cult.

from the oldest text on the celebration of the Eucharist, the eleventh chapter of Paul's first letter to the Corinthians, it does not even appear that the minister has any part to play in the offering. We shall later go further into the question of the specific function of the minister in the celebration of the Eucharist. At this point— which links up with our earlier discussion of the unique and exclusive priesthood of Christ—we may say that this function cannot be described in terms of offering up sacrifice.

As we have seen, Christ's activity cannot be summed up by his role as priest; he is also prophet and teacher, king and shepherd. Similarly, the concept of the common priesthood is too narrow to embrace the whole range of Christian activities, for every Christian participates not only in the priestly but also in the prophetic and royal office of Christ. All the members of God's people share in the task of proclaiming the Good News (1 Pet 2:9); we must bear witness, as the Scriptures say so often. We must all sing the praises of God who called us out of darkness into his wonderful light. Every Christian, by his words and example, should make clear to others what impels him: gratitude for the gift of salvation and hope that God's promises will be fulfilled.

We also have a royal task to perform. In 1 Peter 2:9 as in Revelation 1:6 and 5:10, mention is made of a royal priesthood, which is another way of expressing the firm belief that in the kingdom of heaven ruling and serving are identical, that the servant is not inferior to his master, even if their respective duties are different. All the parts of the body are important; if one part is hurt, the whole body is hurt, and the hand cannot say to the foot, "I do not need you." All the members of God's people must contribute to the welfare of the whole, and the personality of each must be recognized and fulfilled.

The second chapter of *Lumen gentium*, speaking of the people of God as a whole and clearly recalling the scriptural doctrine of the common priesthood (#10), considers almost exclusively its strictly priestly aspect. The division into three parts, which is naturally treated very fully in the third chapter, concerning the special ministry, is no less explicitly discussed in the fourth chapter on the laity (#34-36). One may conclude from this that Vatican II wished to attribute to the term *common priesthood* its fullest and richest meaning. Historically speaking, this is an important development, for *Mystici Corporis* (1943) applied the three functions exclusively to the special ministry.

In the course of history, and in particular since the Middle Ages, the hierarchical structure of the Church and the special ministry had been emphasized to such an extent that the concept of the common priesthood was hardly a living reality any longer. The marked development of the idea of the Eucharist as sacrifice—by no means to be rejected *per se,* but which, at the hands of minor theologians, had led to making this Eucharistic offering too independent, and even to adding a touch of magic to its presentation—had secured for the cultic priesthood a very prominent place in the Church.[3] At the same time, her victory in the investiture conflict had given the Church a chance of evolving into a self-sufficient *societas perfecta.* The clergy became a dominating ecclesiastical and social caste, acted as a governing board with absolute power over practically defenseless subordinates, clericalized the liturgy by maintaining the use of an obsolescent cult language, and cut itself off from the community at large by living in isolation with its own rights and usages (immunities, garb, celibacy).

In this atmosphere of weak scriptural theology and strong clericalism, Luther's novel insistence on the common priesthood must have sounded much more radical and far less orthodox than it was in actual fact. The inclination was to see it as an onslaught on the special ministry, and the sometimes infelicitous wording of Luther and his followers played into the hands

---

[3] Nowhere in the New Testament is the Eucharistic meal called a sacrifice. It is only since the *Didache* that theology has known this concept.

of their opponents. Common priesthood and special ministry became antithetical, and neither side succeeded in harmonizing the facts.

The Council of Trent never explicitly rejected Luther's theories on the common priesthood, although it naturally devoted much thought to the justification of the special ministry and its sacramental nature (Denz. 956-968). Later, the Counter Reformation, caught in the bitterness of controversy, went considerably further. The well-known German *Kirchenlexikon* says in its 1852 edition (vol. VIII):

The so-called common priesthood, that hobby-horse of the pseudo-mystics of every age, which is today being used again to batter the rock on which the Church is founded, does not differ from the special priesthood in rank only, but also in nature; it is a projection of the latter, and presupposes it, just as a shadow points to the body by which it is projected, and on which it is dependent.

The *Kirchliches Handlexikon* of 1884, published after Vatican I, states (vol. III):

A priesthood of the laity is a concept that cannot be entertained seriously by anybody. It shows very poor taste and exegetical confusion to deduce anything like it from 1 Pet 2:5 and 9.

Eighty years later, Pope Paul declared in his encyclical *Ecclesiam suam:* "The Christian realizes with joy that he is endowed with the dignity of the common priesthood, the characteristic of the people of God." *Lumen gentium* treated the subject explicitly and even rather fully (#10-12; 34-36).

The common priesthood is a gift granted to every member of God's people. It is not reserved exclusively to the laity, and does not provide justification for theories on any specific character attached to being a layman, or for a distinct "lay spirituality." The doctrine of the common priesthood can indeed lend support to the demand for a more active role for the laity in the Church, but it cannot be used to establish any characteristic manner of being a layman as distinct from being a minister.

That is why any study of the special ministry must necessarily include a discussion of the common priesthood. This creates no confusion, but only makes for greater clarity. It will confuse only those who think that the common and special priesthood are comparable at the same level, and who see the common priesthood simply as a derivative from, and a projection of the ministerial priesthood, or as a psychological stimulant for lay participation in Church activities.

Conversely, one might even hold that the common priesthood is more important than the special ministry since it is a basic category of God's people, while the special ministry is "merely" a functional one. "The power of being the child of God and the right to receive grace is greater—even if also more general—than the power of making the sign of this grace present with a ministerial guarantee of authenticity." [4] Insofar as there can still be talk of an authentic priesthood and real sacrifices in the New Testament, it is one that is granted to all believers. Strictly speaking, it is only by virtue of the common priesthood that the ecclesiastical minister may call himself in a true sense a priest, *hiereus-sacerdos*, together with all his fellow Christians.

It is therefore somewhat unfortunate that *Lumen gentium*, in the chapter on the laity, states that ". . . the supreme and eternal Priest, Christ Jesus, wills to continue His witness and serve through the laity too . . ." (#34). That little word "too" raises a suspicion that the traditional clerico-centered thinking has not completely disappeared. The priesthood of the laity is not a secondary participation in that of Christ, but precisely a primary one.

Hardly any fundamental difference of opinion seems to exist at present between the Reformation and the Catholic theology as regards their respective understanding of the common priest-

---

[4] K. Rahner, *L. Th. K.* VIII, 745.

hood. This is especially promising since, along with the Catholic "rediscovery" of the common priesthood, a new concept of the special ministry seems to be taking shape in Protestantism. Ecumenism will profit from this development, for the theology of ministry and priesthood has in the past been one of the great areas of Catholic-Protestant controversy.

The common priesthood is a source of unity at all levels. It joins the Lord of the Church to all believers; it holds layman and minister together in unity and equality; and it unites Christians who are still separated.

4. THE SPECIAL MINISTRY: INTERNAL SERVICE TO THE CHURCH

Any human community other than a mass or a horde has some internal structure. This structure develops according to the objective which first brought them together. In order to achieve a proper attitude among the subordinates, but even more, effectively to realize the aim of the community, leadership, coordination, encouragement, and discipline are needed; the basic inspiration of the community must be kept alive, its objective must be defined in suitable terms, and the ways leading to the objectives must be ceaselessly opened up and their direction tested for accuracy.

Leadership is a sociological requisite in any community, worldly or ecclesiastical. The structures of authority and the manner of ruling may vary according to circumstances. But although their forms may vary, and however paradoxical this statement may seem, they all spring simultaneously from both above and below. From above, because the aim of the community is always more than the sum of individual purposes and wishes; the dovetailing of these purposes and wishes to the communal objective inevitably requires a leadership that transcends the "ordinary member." Sociologically, an absolute democracy is unthinkable; it would be tantamount to anarchy. On the other hand, authority comes from below, because no rule would be needed if the community and its purpose were not present. Every person in authority owes his position to the fact that he has "subordinates." An absolute monarchy or oligarchy, therefore, is equally unthinkable; either would be tantamount to a dictatorship that makes absolute rulers of those in authority. Authority is present in order to lead and to serve. Authority exists because there must be leadership and service; one leads because one is called to serve, and one serves through leading. Leadership and service co-exist in a perpetual state of interchange and tension.

It follows that authority in any community will always exist to a certain extent in a state of crisis. The balance between leadership and service is always precarious. That is why the history of mankind exhibits such innumerable forms of rule, from tyranny, under which the characteristics of service are practically nonexistent, to a kind of democracy under which there is really no longer any rule, but at most a coordinating tolerance. Those who are not invested with authority always tend to nurse a certain feeling of resentment against those who stand above them, and will watch jealously that their freedom and independence are adequately considered. Those whose task it is to lead can easily forget that their power is intended for service and begin to develop feelings of superiority and isolation.

The existence of tensions can also be fruitful and become a source of great enrichment. A frank recognition of relationships can develop respect, prudence, and a greater ability to make allowances for one another. But any refusal to listen can upset the balance and lead to simplifications that harden existing positions; this in turn may bring about a tightening of the reins and a curtailment of freedom on the one hand; disobedience, unruliness, and revolution, on the other. In ecclesiastical terms: clericalism and anticlericalism.

There must also be authority and leadership in the ecclesiastical community. Whoever admits that the Church of Christ is a community with an objective, admits *ipso facto* the necessity for governmental structure and authorities. Only those who consider Christianity as a doctrine of individual salvation can refuse to recognize the legitimacy of ecclesiastical rule, or fundamentally reject its actual organization.

The faithful have never doubted that the ecclesiastical community also needs leadership; the rejection on principle of any form of Church authority has therefore always been, and still is, a sign of unorthodoxy. A Church devoid of structure and legal system is an unChristian utopia. A Christian is one who recognizes the Lord Jesus as the head of the body, the King of God's people and the Way to life, and is prepared to give an affirmative answer to the question whether, after the Lord's departure, there remained in his Church a ministry of guidance and service, a pastorate which kept the sheep gathered in one fold and led them to the waters of the life-giving Word. The question has been answered affirmatively throughout the centuries; from the earliest times, the Church has had leaders: apostles, bishops, presbyters, and deacons, popes, patriarchs, archimandrites and cardinals, Eastern Orthodox "popes," priests and ministers, members of the synod and vicars-general, catechizers and confessors. In one way or another, they all shared in the leadership of Christ, the Lord of the Church.

The ecclesiastical office, a ministry exercised in a human community, is an unqualified sociological necessity. Again, we may say it springs both from above and below. From above, because the gift of faith is no human attainment, and the expectation of the coming kingdom, no human project. The realization of the aim of this community must be effected from above. The authority of the Church comes ultimately from the Father of all power who appointed his Son Lord of the Church; and through Christ come the calling and the sending of all those who are invested with an ecclesiastical office in the community of the Church. On the other hand, however, the ministry also springs from below. Not only because it is good that the community have its say in the selection and appointment of a minister, but also in the sense that the existence of an ecclesiastical ministry is predicated on the needs of the community and its shape is determined by them. Owing to this dual source of ecclesiastical authority, the Church cannot be regarded either as a monarchy (or oligarchy) or a democracy. A synthesis of both elements must be effected, just as the Lord Jesus called himself both King and brother among brothers. This synthesis is not easy to achieve; it is somewhat like trying to reconcile uncompromising opposites. It is not enough to have a structure which in fact is monarchical or oligarchical, but is coated with a thin layer of democratic mentality among those in authority. It is no solution either to have an essentially democratic structure bestow *pro forma* titles on subordinates who were chosen "from below" in order to suggest a mandate "from above." It is not a question of mentality or terminology, but of the very structures, for these alone guarantee that neither monarchists nor democrats can unduly succeed in carrying out the wishes of their respective groups to the detriment of the whole. This study should gradually make clear that any talk about the "divine authority of the minister" and "the democratization of ecclesiastical relationships" only makes sense, really, and can be saved from sinking toward useless acrimony when the distinction between minister and nonminister has been clearly established.

There will always be a certain antagonism between the person in authority and subjects, even in the Church. By the same token, there will always be a crisis of authority. One should and must continually ask whether the concrete form given to the exercise of the ministry is functionally effective, and—which is perhaps more important—whether it adequately bears the imprint of the example set by the Lord himself, in whom ruling and serving were united in such a wonderful manner (cf. Mk 10:45; Jo 13:12-17). It is worth remembering that the noblest and most zealous endeavors of man may become one-sided and have to be corrected.

After these general considerations on the need for an ecclesiastical office, we must try to determine more closely the characteristics proper to it. We shall, in this section, limit ourselves to two general features, and in the next, examine whether and how far the ministry also has its own characteristic functions. What has already been said suggests that the pastoral function will be emphasized most of all.

The title of this section defines the ministry as an internal service to the Church. Both terms require a brief explanation.

Every ecclesiastical ministry is a *service* to God's people.[1] The gift of the ministry is not a gift to the person of the minister as such, but through him, a gift to the community. Scripture and theology speak almost exclusively in this manner about servanthood, task, office, and ministry. Service to the community is the only reason for the existence of the minister as minister; he is appointed "to act on behalf of men" (Heb 5:1). His personal desire to become an ecclesiastical minister does not entitle him to ordination and appointment. The community calls him, and may do so only if it is in need of his services. The minister can never find within himself the reason to exercise a ministerial function. He takes no initiative, but works in response to the call of the Lord and the community of the faithful. He may offer his services, but he can only exercise his ministry actively if, and for the time, he has been sent; when the community no longer needs him or considers his services no longer suitable, it can dismiss him. Appointment to a ministerial office and dismissal are sober and technical matters. Ordination may, there-

---

[1] On the subject of the ministry considered as service, cf. M. Lohrer, "De Hierarchie in dienst van christenvolk" in G. Baraúna, ed., *De Kerk van Vaticanum II* (Bilthoven, 1966), vol. 2, pp. 9-25; H. Küng, *The Church* (New York, 1967), pp. 388-480.

fore, never be a reward for services rendered, or a means to gain personal prestige; it is not for these reasons that the Lord gave the ministry to his Church.

As long as the fields are white, ready for harvest, there will be little chance of an inflationary increase in the total number of ministers. But history teaches us that at certain times and in certain regions, there can be too many. The practical results of this situation can be that boredom sets in, or morale declines, or that positions which are not of a specifically ministerial nature are gradually clericalized.

But this qualification of "service" by itself does not satisfactorily describe the ecclesiastical ministry, since this concept goes beyond the strictly ministerial. Every Christian is a servant, one who leaves his own self behind, who does not have his own house: "Once again, the house of God is not the Church, but the world. The Church is the servant, and the first characteristic of a servant is that he lives in somebody else's house, not his own." [2] To be a Church is not to look after and save one's self; it means apostolate, mission, turning toward others. The primary apostolic activity, therefore, does not consist in ecclesiastical ministerial functions, but in the labor of all Christians within the community of human beings, in what Schillebeeckx calls "apostolic secularity." [3] This "apostolic secularity" as we shall explain, is the core of the apostolate; it is ecclesiastical service par excellence.

The new ecclesiology does not take the special ministry as its starting point, but the common priesthood of all believers. And this insight implies certain consequences:

It means taking with absolute seriousness "the servanthood of the laity" in the world "not as a nice addition to round off a professional ministry, but as *the* ministry of the Church." The laity are not the

[2] J. Robinson, *The New Reformation?* (Philadelphia, 1965), p. 92.
[3] E. Schillebeeckx, "Dogmatiek van Ambt en lekestaat," *Ts.v.Th.*, 2:258-292, *passim*, 1962.

helpers of the clergy so that the clergy can do their job, but the clergy are the helpers of the whole People of God, so that the laity can be the Church.[4]

Here we begin to get an indication of where the special characteristics of the ministerial servanthood lie. The ministerial office means equipping Christians for service to the world, preparing, inspiring, and guiding their "apostolic secularity." The ecclesiastical ministry means service to the whole world through an internal service to God's people. The ecclesiastical ministry is not a specifically missionary service, and the hierarchy is not the vanguard of the apostolate, but should provide the stimulus for Christian work in the world and for the world. It is *internal ecclesiastical service* to the outward-looking community of Christ, it is the general servanthood in a specific and explicit form, viz. in as far as this servanthood is the organizing principle within the community itself. In the opening sentence of Chapter 3 of *Lumen gentium* (#18) the task of the special ministry is described as follows:

For the nurturing and constant growth of the People of God, Christ the Lord instituted in His Church a variety of ministries, which work for the good of the whole body. For those ministers who are endowed with sacred powers are servants of their brethren, so that all who are the People of God, and therefore enjoy a true Christian dignity, can work toward a common goal freely and in an orderly way, and arrive at salvation.

The last words have a rather individualistic ring, but the first clause makes clear that the ecclesiastical ministry should be considered not only the keeper of the internal life of the Church, but also as the power sparking its missionary impetus. Admittedly, the wording is not quite perfect. The beginning of the chapter on the ecclesiastical ministry does give the impression that the ministry exists more to see to the smooth functioning

[4] J. Robinson, in his *The New Reformation?* (Philadelphia, 1965), citing G. Winter on p. 64 and H.-R. Weber on p. 55.

of the "internal ecclesiastical operation" than to offer service to the whole world through all the faithful. The reasoning still proceeds from the traditional order—of minister, laity, world— whereas it should be exactly the reverse. However, a reading of this text in the light of later documents of Vatican II, like *Ad gentes,* on the Church's missionary activity, and *Gaudium et spes,* on the Church in the modern world, gives a more balanced picture.

The mandate laid on all the faithful is more important than that given to the ministry. The ministry is a means, not an end; it is the closing entry of ecclesiology, not its starting point. That is why the concrete forms of the ministry can never be established a priori. "One should not say: this Church is the true Church of Christ, which has a specific form of ministry, but: that form of ministry is good which best achieves what Christ really meant by the Church." [5] According to Robinson, the fact that the Church is the servant of the world means that "the world must be allowed to 'write the agenda' . . . and that the Church must take shape round the needs of the world . . ." [6] In line with this reasoning, one can add that God's people as a whole, and within it, primarily the laity, should write the agenda of ecclesiastical life, and the ministry should take shape around the needs of the laity.

We call this special form of servanthood, internal; it is not directly missionary in purpose, but indirectly so, because of its apostolic secularity. This does not mean that it is "purely" internal; we have already shown that there are no purely internal ecclesiastical activities, inasmuch as the boundaries of Church and world coincide. The internal life of the Church is a component of the single reality of the world. Nor may the term *internal* be interpreted as restricting the individual minister to such activities as concern the Church's internal life, nor as

---

[5] D. Braun, "Het priesterlijk ambt," in *Priesterroeping en Seminarie* (Haarlem, 1964), pp. 26-40; the above citation appears on p. 28.
[6] J. Robinson, *op. cit.,* p. 92.

suggesting that he is to be the only one active in this field. For the layman also has an active part to play in the internal life of the Church, and every minister is called, as Christian, to break out of his own closed group and witness to the wonderful works of God. However, he does this by virtue of his baptismal consecration to the common priesthood, not by virtue of any specific ministerial mandate. The difference between layman and minister is not identical with that existing between the internal and external Church. Not everything that pope, bishops, and priests do is "ecclesiastical" work, and there is more for the layman to do in the Church than to return as unscathed as possible, after he has had his fling "in the world," to shelter under the protective wings of ecclesiastical ministers.

5. THE SPECIFIC TASK OF THE MINISTER

Whenever in *Lumen gentium* we find a closer definition of the priestly duties of all the members of God's people, it always adheres to the traditional distinction between the respective tasks of king, priest, and prophet. This is brought out very clearly in the section on the bishops' duties (#25-27), less so in the rather short part on those of presbyters and deacons (#28-29), but very explicitly again in the sections on the laity (#34-36). In this manner all the groups are held together by a similar bond to the threefold ministry of the High Priest of the Church. As members of one body and as citizens of God's one people, they all partake in the mission that Christ received from the Father.

The division into three parts may clarify matters, but can also lead to over-simplification. It may, for instance, seem somewhat restrictive to partition the rich variety of Christian activities too rigorously into three categories. Actually, Scripture warns us against this by the flexibility it shows in its terminology: shepherd is often used for king, the words *teacher* and *prophet* are interchangeable. It would be even more dangerous were this partition to suggest that the three functions must always be apparent in the concrete duties of the laity and the ministry. There are bishops who administer much, but prophesy little, and there are laymen who often participate actively in liturgical celebrations, but contribute little to Church management. Owing perhaps to the strictly hierarchical lines of its reasoning, there seems to be no very clear awareness of this danger in *Lumen gentium*, and as a result, it gives the impression of pointing to the existence, among God's people, of a certain subordination, vertical and hierarchical, by virtue of which tasks identical in essence rate, in each category, a lower degree of independence and authority. It is stated repeatedly that there is a real difference between the layman and the minister, but this difference is never actually formulated thoroughly and explicitly.

A certain reserve as regards the traditional threefold partition can be useful. It gives one a better chance to bring out the unique character of the ministry of Christ. His ministry is not simply partitioned into ever-decreasing degrees of participation down to the lowest laborers in the vineyard. It leaves more room also for a flexible shaping of the ministry, adaptable to circumstances. A too easy transference of the threefold ministry of Christ to the ecclesiastical ministry is perhaps one cause of the clerico-hierarchical mode of thinking, which remains so remarkably strong particularly in the Catholic world. The third chapter of *Lumen gentium* is entitled, none too happily, "The hierarchical Structure of the Church." Not only is the word *hierarchy* not scriptural—its credentials are certainly not as good as those of the term minister—but from the beginning, it puts the whole discussion on the relationships between layman and minister in a somewhat juridical atmosphere in which terms like flexibility and evolution are not very appropriate.[1]

In a time when the concept of the relationship between world and Church is changing so rapidly, that of "the ministry" is not immutable either. Accordingly, in studies undertaken under the auspices of the World Council of Churches, demands are

[1] Cf. H. Küng, *The Church* (New York, 1967), pp. 417-420, 436-441.

being made for a definition of the ecclesiastical ministries that is more subtle and more closely based on an inventory of the actual situation. Their suggestion is to give up the expression "the ministry" and to use instead the less pretentious and more dynamic "patterns of ministry." [2] This does not exclude a certain degree of grouping and schematizing, but this would be undertaken only subject to a feeling for relativity on the part of its authors.

Two points should be kept in mind when we endeavor to establish whether and where the ecclesiastical minister has specific duties of his own to perform. They are two fundamental concepts of the relation between layman and minister. In the first place, the distinction cannot be defined in the simple antithetical terms of active and passive; by virtue of the common priesthood he has been granted, the layman, too, is called to active servanthood. Secondly, it follows that the difference lies within the "internal ecclesiastical" field. This derives, negatively, from the fact that the minister, even if he is active in the province of the apostolic secularity, yet has no part of his own to play there; and positively, from the doctrine of the common priesthood, on the basis of which, in the fourth chapter of *Lumen gentium,* a positive role in the life of the Church as such is attributed to the laity.

This is not the place to develop a comprehensive theology of the laity, but we must nevertheless devote some thought to it. The proper character of the ecclesiastical ministry can be described only by contrasting it with the active lay state. We shall make use here of the traditional division into three categories, since we are not dealing now with the concrete duties of the individual layman, but with the tasks which the laity as a group are called to perform.

The whole people of God shares in the *prophetic and preaching activity* of Christ. "Go and teach" is not a mandate given ex-

[2] Cf. *Ministry,* 1965, n. 2, pp. 1-32.

clusively to the apostles and their successors; in the work of proclaiming the wonderful deeds of God, layman and minister do not stand in opposition to each other, but side by side, facing the world. As *Lumen gentium* says,

Christ, the Great Prophet, who proclaimed the Kingdom of His Father by the testimony of His life and the power of His words, continually fulfills His prophetic office until His full glory is revealed. He does this not only through the hierarchy who teach in His name and with His authority, but also through the laity. For that very purpose He made them His witnesses and gave them understanding of the faith and the grace of speech (cf. Acts 2:17-18; Apoc 19-10), so that the power of the gospel might shine forth in their daily social and family life. (#35)

This text stresses mainly the proclaiming to the world outside, but the laity also have an active part to play in making the Word known within, which means inspiring one another and meditating together on the Gospel message. The minister quickens the faith of the laity and deepens their own understanding, but the witnessing faith of the laity is also an inspiration for the minister and their understanding is a matter of importance as regards the further "definition of doctrine." *Lumen gentium* is not explicit on the subject in the chapter on the laity, but turning to the chapter on the people of God as a whole (Chapter 2), one finds this:

The body of the faithful as a whole, anointed as they are by the Holy One (cf. Jn 2:20,27), cannot err in matters of belief. Thanks to a supernatural sense of the faith which characterizes the People as a whole, it manifests this unerring quality when, "from the bishops down to the last member of the laity," it shows universal agreement in matters of faith and morals. (#12)

The sense of faith of the whole people of God, and accordingly, also of the laity, is actively at work in the Church, and is therefore also truly molding opinion. That is why, on the occasion of important ecclesiastical doctrinal pronouncements, reference is often made to an existing unity in religious thinking regarding a specific point of faith.

One should note here, however, that this reference shows to better advantage in matters of faith than of morals. As regards the latter, we are more likely to find abstract reasoning proceeding from theory, general facts, and "natural law" than from the concrete realities of the life of the laity. One could also ask in this connection a most stimulating, and also vexing, question as to whether the voice of the laity cannot also exercise a negative influence. In the matter of dogmatics, he could wonder, for instance, whether diminishing devotion to the Eucharistic presence, or the saints, and also declining interest in virginity and the monastic life, could not be interpreted in terms of a one-sided development which went on in earlier days and now, via a spell of indigestion, is leading to more balanced preaching. As regards morals, he might ask whether the fact, for example, that a large number of believers no longer follow a specific rule regarding Sunday Mass, fasting, or the use of contraceptives because it does not answer (or no longer answers) the demands of their upright ethico-religious feeling, does not indicate that such a rule or prohibition is untenable, and that the indication should be taken seriously? However it may be, the active contribution made by the laity to the formulation of religious and moral doctrine is a reality. The manner in which this contribution is used will vary. It sometimes happens spontaneously and without any great difficulty: in the past, some were made saints by acclamation and bishops often went to councils as the spokesmen of their theologians. Nowadays, what with the spread of ideas of equality and collegiality, there is perhaps a need for organic communications structures. At all events, it remains true that ministers are not the only witnesses to the faith.

Owing to his common priesthood, the layman participates in *the liturgy of the Church and the sacramental celebrations.* He offers up a real sacrifice and consecrates himself and the whole world to God. This theme is discussed in the second and in the fourth chapters of *Lumen gentium* (#10-11 and 34).

A comparison between these two texts shows that Vatican II has hesitated here and failed to come to a well-rounded statement. After the generous statement of #11, the content of #34 is somewhat meager. This might indicate that in the area of liturgy, there was a certain fear of going too far in the equalization of minister and layman. Traditionally, and emotionally, the ecclesiastical ministry has always been strongly, sometimes even exclusively, identified with worship, and particularly with the sacraments. Sacramental celebrations are supposed to be essential moments of the ecclesiastical experience, and the questions of validity, so often raised in connection with the sacraments, put the ecclesiastical minister in the spotlight.

This is not to say that there ever was any desire to clericalize absolutely the whole field of prayer and cult. As a variation on Hamlet: it has always been known that there is more worship between heaven and earth than that rendered according to official liturgical rules and presided over by the ecclesiastical ministers. True prayers are prayed and real sacrifices offered outside of the official liturgical gatherings, and they do not require the presence of a minister. The Constitution on the Sacred Liturgy even states that the layman may obtain the right to administer sacramentals (#79).

But how do matters stand as regards the sacraments in the strict sense of the word: Does the minister here have exclusive duties in the nature of things, or does his position derive rather from historical development and juridical order? A quick glance at contemporary practice and history would lead one to suppose that the latter is the case. In the absence of a minister, the layman may administer baptism, man and woman in fact perform the sacrament of marriage—the minister only witnesses it—and it is apparent from Colossians 3:13 and James 5:16 that every Christian can truly forgive sins to his fellow man. It is difficult to maintain that these are individual and unrepeatable instances of ministerial mission (*ad actum*), and better to say here we have functions which the layman performs by virtue of his common priesthood.[3]

This can also be applied to the Eucharist. Nowhere does the New Testament clearly connect ecclesiastical ministry and Eucharist celebration, and there is no reason to hold that the Eucharist could be celebrated only in the presence of bishops and presbyters, or with bishops or presbyters presiding. In point of fact, the Eucharist was sometimes celebrated by deacons; the Council of Arles, held in 314, condemned this practice, it is true,[4] but there is no reason to suppose that the validity of the sacrament was thereby denied. It is a firmly established part of tradition that the whole community offers up the Eucharistic sacrifice (the *meum ac vestrum sacrificium* of the *Orate Fratres*), and it is really difficult to hold a priori that the possibility of an authentic Eucharistic celebration is totally dependent on the more or less accidental presence of officially empowered ministers. Of course, one could suppose that the question here too is one of "emergency cases" on account of which the lawgiver allows an incidental ministerial mission which normally belongs only to the officially consecrated minister. But, taking into account the fact that the ministry is also generated "from below," one could state just as well that the power to celebrate the Eucharist is bestowed in principle on the common priesthood, but that, for reasons mainly of discipline, it is never, or only exceptionally, exercised by nonministers. Again the variation on Hamlet holds good; more Eucharistic sacrifices are offered up on earth than those that are presided over by bishops and presbyters. Assuming this, it also becomes easier to accept that in Churches where the validity of ordination is dubious (because of questions

[3] Cf. H. Küng, *The Church* (New York, 1967), pp. 379-380.
[4] Denz. 53x; C. Kirch, *Enchiridion Fontium Historiae Ecclesiasticae antiquae* (Friburgi, 1932), p. 373. Cf. F. van Beeck, "Thoughts on an Ecumenical Understanding of the Sacraments," *Journal of Ecumenical Studies,* 3 (1966), pp. 57-112.

relating to apostolic succession) there is room in the Eucharistic celebration for a true, though possibly not the best, commemorative celebration of the life and death of the Lord.[5]

All this, undoubtedly, means a certain "de-mythologizing" of the sacramental ministry. But is this any cause for alarm? For the ministry is there to guarantee an adequate number of sacramental celebrations; it must never become so independent as to detract from the demands of the layman. For the Sabbath was made for man, not man for the Sabbath.

Finally, there is the question of the active contribution of the laity to the shaping of *ecclesiastical life and management*. As we have already indicated in the preceding section, this kind of problem cannot be dismissed merely by saying that "the Church is simply not a democracy"; the question must inevitably come up in a Church which supplements an ecclesiology colored by hierarchism as derived from the mystical body concept with a more horizontal self-understanding as expressed by image of the people of God.

The Church has never been an absolute monarchy or oligarchy. At the Council of Jerusalem, James, who was the bishop at that city, but not an apostle, exercised a definite influence on the decisions concerning the Gentile Christians, and the dispatch of a few men to Antioch to deliver the decisions of the Council was ordered by the whole community (Acts 15:13-22). In 2 Corinthians 2:6 "the majority" exercises disciplinary law. Bishops have frequently been selected by the people and full jurisdictional powers granted to laymen, among them superiors of religious houses.

Following in the footsteps of Pope Pius XII, who acknowledged the case for public opinion in the Church, *Lumen gentium* also made its pronouncements on the active role of the laity

---

[5] The text of #2 of *Presbyterorum ordinis*, the decree on the ministry and life of priests, in saying that through his ordination the priest has the power to offer up sacrifice and forgive sins, states an actual custom more than it gives a strictly theological definition; there is no scriptural argument to show that these tasks are *exclusively* presbyterial.

in determining ecclesiastical management. After describing (#36) the work of the laity in the world as a sharing in the royal power of Christ, the constitution (#37) goes straight into the question of the relationship between layman and minister:

The laity have the right, as do all Christians, to receive in abundance from their sacred pastors the spiritual goods of the Church, especially the assistance of the Word of God and the sacraments. Every layman should openly reveal to them his needs and desires with that freedom and confidence which befits a son of God and a brother in Christ. An individual layman, by reason of the knowledge, competence, or outstanding ability which he may enjoy, is permitted and sometimes even obliged to express his opinion on things which concern the good of the Church. When occasions arise, let this be done through the agencies set up by the Church for this purpose. Let it always be done in truth, in courage, and in prudence, with reverence and charity toward those who by reason of their sacred office represent the person of Christ . . . Let sacred pastors recognize and promote the dignity as well as the responsibility of the layman in the Church. Let them willingly make use of his prudent advice. Let them confidently assign duties to him in the service of the Church, allowing him freedom and room for action. Further, let them encourage the layman so that he may undertake tasks on his own initiative. Attentively in Christ, let them consider with fatherly love the projects, suggestions, and desires proposed by the laity. Furthermore, let pastors respectfully acknowledge that just freedom which belongs to everyone in this earthly city.

These excerpts—the paragraph between them speaks of obedience "to their sacred pastors" and of docility—show clearly, even if the wording is somewhat hesitant, that the laity also can be heard on ecclesiastical activities. The text is nevertheless not very satisfactory; true, agencies are mentioned (to be set up by "the Church"!) but they seem to be considered useful rather than necessary, so that the right to speak out, which is attributed to the laity, is somewhat too simply offset by a moral duty on the part of the leaders to listen willingly to the laymen.

Such hesitations are easy to understand, since these ideas are fairly new in ecclesiology; it is perhaps the first time since the investiture conflict began during the Middle Ages that a conciliar document officially attributes to the laity a part in the inner-ecclesiastical "management." Experience will have to show what the implications of this text are, and how the co-responsibility of the layman can become a living reality. In every human community, there exists an antagonism, difficult to synthesize, between authority and subordinates. But it must be possible to do so, particularly in a Church which realizes more and more that her ministers are servants. In passing, it can be observed that this "democratizing" process will develop more easily once the idea of collegiality, accepted by Vatican II, has also been applied further to internal ecclesiastical management. The final result of this development would be for the laity to draw up the agenda of ecclesiastical life, and which the ministers would then adopt as their program.[6]

But when the layman is able to play an active part in all areas of internal ecclesiastical life—a part acquired not as a favor or for tactical, psychological considerations, but because it is owing to his common priesthood—will there really be any room left for specifically ministerial tasks? Do ministers have a field of action that is properly their own, a scope of activities which

[6] Vatican II recommended the establishment of groups or senates of "priests" and of pastoral councils (*Lumen gentium* #37, *Christus Dominus* #27, *Presbyterorum ordinis* #7), and guidelines for the institution of such bodies are given in the *Motu Proprio Ecclesiae sanctae* of August 6, 1966. They were discussed at the symposium of European bishops held at Noordwijkerhout July 10-14, 1967, and the debates revealed a degree of uncertainty as to the mutual relationships of the groups and their character—whether advisory or decision-making. It would appear, generally speaking, that they will have to be decision-making and that pastoral councils, on which laymen and religious will also be represented, are in the end more important than those made up exclusively of ministers. The life of the Church is the responsibility of the whole people of God. Formal responsibility belongs to the ministers, it is true, but power is not theirs alone to wield. A valid intuition seems to be taking shape in the Dutch experiments with Pastoral Councils constituted by the whole ecclesiastical province. See my article, "Democracy and the Dutch Church," *The Catholic World* (May 1968), pp. 57-60.

they alone and exclusively can undertake, and upon which the layman as such may not intrude? Our reply must be both affirmation and denial. Physically, there are no exclusive ministerial activities, but the work a minister carries out as minister does bear a characteristic stamp. It follows that there is indeed a real difference between layman and minister.

The description of the characteristic stamp of ministerial activities can best be found in Christ's own sending out of the apostles. The Greek word *apostle* is a translation of the Hebrew *shaliach*, the word that Jesus himself must have used when he picked out the twelve (Lk 6:13). The *shaliach* concept derives from Jewish law and does not have in itself the religious meaning it is nearly always given in Christian writings. The *shaliach* is a person who has been entrusted with a mission or instructions, with full powers to act as the representative of the one who sent him. The appointment does not always include a statement of specific activities; the "nomination" is a basic empowering which becomes effective once the nominee performs as such.

The New Testament, as a matter of course, applies this concept to the instrumental mediatorship with regard to salvation, and thereby enriches the concept; but its essence remains: the Lord himself is present in the apostle: he who listens to you listens to me. This representation may assume various styles: in the Acts, the main emphasis is on the fact that the apostles must witness to the life and resurrection of the Lord (1:21-22; 26:16), in the synoptists, they are those who continue Christ's work (Mt 28:18), and in the Pauline writings, particularly in his polemics with the partisans of Judaism, there is a strong accent on authoritative guidance (Gal 1:1; 2 Cor 13:1-3).

The apostles and all those who were later entitled to share in their mission in any way whatsoever are joined to the Lord of the Church in a special manner. They represent him. There is much truth, therefore, in the traditional saying that the presbyter—and a fortiori the bishop—is "another Christ." The very immediacy of this relationship with Christ himself consequently precludes any concept of the special ministry as a mere condensation and intensification of the common priesthood; it is more than that. This "more," however, does not reside in the fact that the minister carries out activities that the layman could not undertake, but that in the speaking and acting of the minister *as such* lies an explicit guarantee that the work is here being performed which the Lord desires his Church to perform.

This, of course, does not mean that the laymen should have any doubts as to his works also being a fulfillment of the will of the Lord. For when two or three meet in his name, Jesus will be there with them. But it is the ministry that formally guarantees this: the overseeing, the *episkopè*, of the ministry stamps the deeds of the Christian community with the formal seal of authenticity. Only those deeds are authentically Christian which can pass the scrutiny of the ministry. This does not require the constant living, physical presence of a minister. In normal cases, in cases when ecclesiastical unity and orthodoxy are not at stake, there will often be little need for outright and formal supervision by the ministry. But the presence of a qualified minister will be required at crucial moments and in borderline cases: being received in the community, formal definition of Church doctrine, and questions of ecclesiastical discipline which affect all the faithful or a large number of them.

There would seem to be no need either for an explicit authentification of a minister's every act. Not all his managerial decisions are automatically covered by the Lord's authority, and not all he preaches is an authentic statement of Church doctrine. The performance of a minister is therefore fully ministerial only when it proceeds from the unity of the corps of ministers whom the Lord has empowered to represent Him. The idea of collegiality makes itself felt as an indispensable element throughout the whole ministry, down to its lowest echelon; just as the minister vouches for the authenticity of the work of the layman, so does the ministry collectively legitimize the acts of the individual minister.

According to the traditional presentation, we can say that ministerial *preaching* strictly speaking means that the college of ministers may and can openly invoke the "Anyone who listens to you listens to me"; as regards *cult,* what is peculiar to the minister is that his *episkopè* ensures the performance *hic et nunc* of a rite "acceptable to God the Father almighty"; the distinctive quality of the *administrative acts* of the ministry is that those subject to the rule of the Church imposed by the college of ministers can rely on a legitimate and effective application of the mandate "Feed my sheep."

The ministry is necessary to the existence of the Church. The fact that the Lord of the Church promised that he would be with his community always, to the end of time, demands that this presence manifest itself and become tangible in persons who are openly and formally called and empowered to be representatives.

The evolution of history and circumstances of time and place will cause one or more aspects of the ministerial office to come out more forcefully or to dwindle in the background. For instance, in a Church strongly inclined to think hierarchically, the king may take precedence over teacher and priest, or conversely, in a freer ecclesiastical system, the evangelist and prophet receive more attention than the shepherd and king; in a Church, concerned primarily for its own sanctification, the priest who offers up sacrifice can be emphasized more than the prophet who thinks as a missionary; in a Church open to the world, the preparation for a proclamation of the Word is considered more important than the internal life and the cultic activities of the group itself. As long as men and Church are living entities, the emphasis will change. To illustrate this, one could point to the fact that some Churches that stress the sacraments, like the Catholic or the Orthodox, see the minister more as a cult person and insist on the separation between him and the layman, while the more "witnessing" Churches, like the Calvinist and the

Methodist, are interested more in the preacher and prophet, whom they tend to see as the leader issued from the community.

A development is now taking place within the Catholic community that could aptly be described as a change "from priest to prophet." [7] It follows logically from the evolution of ecclesiology as a whole and the ending of a more introverted and conservative period of the history of the Catholic Church. A citadel Church behind its walls was interested primarily in ecclesiastical worship and the celebration of the sacraments; in this kind of atmosphere, the minister was first and foremost the priest who offered up sacrifice, especially since the "rival" reformed Churches seemed to ignore the sacraments. Nowadays, there is more emphasis on openness to the world and ecumenical contacts are increasing; consequently, preaching and prophesying are more in evidence. The ministry is turning its attention more to preaching: pondering over the Word inside the Church and preparing to proclaim it outside. It is unlikely that this development will lead to a new kind of one-sidedness. Since Protestantism seems to be growing away from a concern, possibly too exclusive, for the Word alone, and Catholic liturgy is trying to make worship more understandable and livable there is little danger of any atrophy of this part of Christian life.

There are at least two reasons why we should welcome this change.

The ecclesiastical ministry can once again be seen as the continuation of the ministry of the New Testament, in which the main task of the minister was to make known the Word, and in which he scarcely had any specific part to play in the religious rites. The heavy accent on cult came later, at a time when, as we have already indicated, the ecclesiastical ministry had to compete with the pagan priests and pagan sacrificial rites. That is

[7] Cf. F. Haarsma, "Van priester naar profeet," in *Essays en Interviews over de Priester* (Utrecht, 1965), pp. 79-96; "Pastoraal-theologische beschouwingen over de priester," *Tijdschrift voor Theologie* (1965), pp. 272-295, 1965; see in particular pp. 286-295.

why, at the ordination of ministers, and particularly of presbyters, the greatest emphasis came to be laid on the power to administer the sacraments, and why the documents of the Council of Trent concerning the ministry have relatively little to say about the preaching mission. Both *Lumen gentium* and *Presbyterorum ordinis* (#4-6), give almost equal emphasis to prophecy and worship.[8] This frees the ministry from an excessive internal ritualistic isolation. May one hazard a hypothesis here, that such a development is logically linked with the history of the Church during the last century, when, from Vatican I through the campaign against modernism to Pope Pius XII, interest centered so strikingly on the "teaching authority" of the Church?

This shift in emphasis may also help somewhat to lessen the sharp distinction which over the centuries had separated the laity from the ministers. Overstressing the priestly, cultic aspects of the ministry entails the danger of mythologizing both cult and ministry (the *disciplina arcani*), keeping layman and minister farther apart than is good for either the world or the Church. But when layman and minister together turn to Scripture, endeavor in dialogue to grasp the message of the Bible and express it so as to answer the temper of the modern world, they stand side by side more like equals. It surely cannot be entirely by accident that a "Church of the Word," like the Reformed, has been considerably less troubled by the transmutation of ministry into clericalism.

Despite all changes in emphasis, the fact remains whole and entire that each minister is a *shaliach* of the Lord of the Church, invested with his authority. As the twelve apostles were the patriarchs of the new Israel, the Church, the ministers of today are the fully empowered rulers of the Church of our time. Over and above their priestly and prophetic functions stands their pastoral mission. That is their basic and first service to the Church.

---

[8] In *Lumen gentium* #25 as in *Presbyterorum ordinis* #4, the proclamation of the Word is given as the first duty of bishop and presbyter. Vatican II also, therefore, registered a certain degree of the evolution from priest to prophet.

Episkopè constitutes the very essence of the ministry. Whether its system is oligarchic or democratic is a secondary matter; this can and must change with the times.

6. THE DIFFERENCE BETWEEN LAYMAN AND MINISTER

The task proper to ecclesiastical ministers is to make the Lord of the Church present in their ministerial activities. Whereas every Christian must witness to the risen Lord and is responsible for the sanctification of the world, this pertains to the ministers in a special manner because the pastoral task of the *episkopè* devolves on them. It follows that a real difference exists between layman and minister. We shall try here, and in the following section, to identify this difference more closely.[1] It is no simple matter. Unlike "hierarchology," the theology of the laity is still new, and this shows clearly not only in the texts of Vatican II, but in the theological studies of the last decades: their formulations are often uncertain, and their terminology is not always consistent. Besides these difficulties, there are other, more psychological ones. For some, the revaluation of the layman is a potential threat to their own position; others, in their enthusiasm for the rehabilitation of the long-neglected layman, may be trapped into situations and statements that will merely displace, and not remove, the old antagonism.

In any discussion of the difference between layman and minister, their unity must be laid down as a primary factor. They are one in their identical belief in the Lord and their anticipation of salvation. Within the undivided people of God, they are called to brotherly union and love.

Moreover, they are bound, as we have seen above, by the gift granted to each and all of the common priesthood. This common priesthood is a religious feature of God's people as a whole;

[1] Cf. G. Baraúna, ed., *De Kerk van Vaticanum II* (Bilthoven, 1966), vol. 2, pp. 283-362 (articles by E. Schillebeeckx, M. Chenu, C. Koser, M. Gozzini).

it is not a standard of differentiation, but a source of unity: all are called and consecrated alike to strive actively for the coming kingdom and participate in the threefold service of the Church to the world. Layman and minister can therefore never be differentiated on the basis of a direct opposition between common and special priesthood, which implies that a person must exercise one or the other. The common priesthood is indeed the original source of all the active labor of the laity, but it is not the basis of any specific lay apostolate or lay spirituality.

The ever-growing conviction that the ecclesiastical ministry is a service must also keep us from defining the difference between minister and layman in terms of superior-inferior, higher or lower. For a Christian, it should really be meaningless to state the problem in this manner. However, he must, in order not to do so, foreswear a goodly span of the past: the end of the Middle Ages, when the papacy strove with the princes for supreme power over society, when the liturgy was a concern of the clergy who compelled the layman, under pain of mortal sin, to be present as onlooker; the Counter Reformation, whose answer to Luther's somewhat crude attack on the special ministry was a defense of it that precluded any sound doctrine of the laity; the nineteenth century when, for example, attempting to give some information on the laity, the entry for *Laien,* in the 1851 edition of the *Kirchenlexiken,* referred the reader to *Klerus;* and the early twentieth century, when a papal encyclical (*Vehementer nos,* 1906) declared: "The college of pastors alone has the right and the authority to lead and guide all the members toward the goal of the community. The majority have no other right but to let themselves be led, and follow the shepherds like an obedient flock." The only true hierarchical relationship in the Church is that between him to whom the Father has given all power, and the community of the faithful chosen by him and by him enjoined to go out and to bear fruit, fruit that will last (Jn 15:16). In the mutual relationships within the Church, there is no lordship and no slavery, but only brotherhood between equals. To the one who insists on inquiring as to who is "the greatest" one may, if it comes to that, reply that it is the layman; for the minister exists for the sake of the layman: the layman constitutes the service.

Finally, the preceding section brings out another important point. The difference between layman and minister does not lie in the material content, in the characteristic nature of specific internal activities of the Church. For the minister has no activities proper to him as regards their content; he performs the acts which every Christian performs (to offer, to proclaim, to promote the internal life of the Church), but he does so in a characteristic manner, his acts have a different import, a different authority, the authority of the Lord himself. It is this formal aspect only that enables the minister to do things that "the layman cannot do."

Within this unity and basic equality of all the whole of God's people, being a layman appears to be primarily a negative datum: he is the nonminister. Contemporary Church law has this to say:

By virtue of its institution by Christ, ordination bestows on the clerics the authority to direct the faithful and celebrate the sacred liturgy, and in this differentiates him from the laity.[2]

Clearly, from this, the characteristic feature of the layman is a negative one: he is the one to whom the ministerial tasks are not allotted. The specific characteristics of the ministerial tasks are not detailed further here, and, strikingly, no mention is made of the proclamation of the Word. The first paragraph of #31 of *Lumen gentium* gives substantially the same negative definition, although there, by means of an allusion to the common priesthood, we find some reminder of the positive tasks of every Christian:

[2] C.I.C., c. 958.

The term laity is here understood to mean all the faithful except those in holy orders and those in a religious state sanctioned by the Church. These faithful are by baptism made one body with Christ and are established among the People of God. They are in their own way made sharers in the priestly, prophetic, and kingly functions of Christ. They carry out their own part in the mission of the whole Christian people with respect to the Church and the world.

Conspicuous in this passage is the fact that the definition of the laity is doubly negative: he is the nonminister and the nonreligious. The next negative definition comes in the sixth chapter (#43-47), where the religious are again given attention. The addition of the second negative is therefore understandable. On the other hand, it offers this drawback that, besides the difference in *function* (minister—nonminister), it also brings up the question of a different *state in life.* This can create confusion because, according to Church law, every nonminister—and hence, every religious who is not an ecclesiastical minister—is a layman. In addition, it is not quite consistent because in a subsequent section of *Lumen gentium* (#43), it is claimed that one must not consider religious life as an intermediate state between the clerical and lay states; persons can be called from both groups to the way of life of the cloistered religious. The somewhat awkward formulation of the first paragraph of #31 is probably due to the fact that the text of *Lumen gentium* as a whole was revised so often.

Along with these negative characteristics of the laity, *Lumen gentium,* in the same section 31, also contains a more positive formulation. We shall first quote the relevant text:

A secular quality is proper and special to laymen. It is true that those in holy orders can at times engage in secular activities, and even have a secular profession. But by reason of their particular vocation they are chiefly and professedly ordained to the sacred ministry. Similarly, by their state in life, religious give splendid and striking testimony that the world cannot be transfigured and offered to God without the spirit of the beatitudes.

But the laity, by their very vocation, seek the kingdom of God by engaging in temporal affairs and by ordering them according to the plan of God. They live in the world, that is, in each and in all of the secular professions and occupations. They live in the ordinary circumstances of family and social life, from which the very web of their existence is woven.

They are called there by God so that by exercising their proper function and being led by the spirit of the gospel they can work for the sanctification of the world from within, in the manner of leaven. In this way they can make Christ known to others, especially by the testimony of a life resplendent in faith, hope, and charity. The layman is closely involved in temporal affairs of every sort. It is therefore his special task to illumine and organize these affairs in such a way that they may always start out, develop, and persist according to Christ's mind, to the praise of the Creator and the Redeemer.

The description given here is not theological; it is rather, one might say, an itemized list, a typological statement. There is nothing objectionable about this, of course, but the reader who fails to realize it, runs the risk of drawing the wrong conclusions. Our comments are intended merely to put the text in its proper perspective.

It is apparent from the text itself that "those in holy orders" can also "engage in secular activities, and even have a secular profession," but that their specific task is the "sacred ministry." Here we have the official recognition of a fact known to everybody; ministers can also engage in secular work. How far this is desirable need not be considered now; in any case, it is definitely established that the so-called part-time minister is, in principle, a possibility. This leads to an important conclusion: Christian work for the world has no part in the *theological* definition of the idea of the laity. If the minister can also engage in secular activities, it follows that these, although quantitatively characteristic of the layman, do not belong as exclusively to him in the same way that representation of the Lord of the Church is proper to the special ministry. Apostolic secularity is the mission of each and every member of the Church, and implies nothing in regard to the theological differentiation between layman and minister, even if the actual division of labor assigns the larger part to the layman. Apostolic secularity is not the exclusive task of the layman; the minister is also called to it by reason of his baptism and common priesthood. "At a time when the temporal order (or disorder!) has come to hinder or prevent the spreading of the Word, the hierarchy cannot be doomed to inaction by the remission or absence of the Christian laity." [3] That is why missionary priests are not betraying their mission when they build hospitals, teach, or help to improve agricultural methods.

In passing, let us add that the "secular character" is never merely secular. Humanizing the world is not the work of the Christian alone; it is everybody's work. The special task of the Christian, in the words of the constitution, is "to illumine and organize [the temporal affairs in which he is involved] in such a way that they may always start out, develop, and persist according to Christ's mind, to the praise of the Creator and the Redeemer." The Christian's involvement in temporal affairs is aimed at reconciling earth and heaven, effecting the synthesis and symbiosis of the two elements. Define "secular" too narrowly, and the definition will also cover the commitment of the humanist who does not know God, but is devoting himself to the welfare of the world. The Christian's function is broader. While he may not be behind the humanist in respect for, and loving care of earthly realities, as a Christian he must be committed to giving them a different orientation, revealing another dimension.

If one left apostolic secularity to the layman alone, one would be doing the minister an injustice and misunderstand his function. His service is ultimately directed to the synthesis of Church and world. The sacred is no world of its own, completely sepa-

[3] M. Gozzini, "De betrekkingen tussen de leken en de hierarchie," in G. Baraúna, ed., *De Kerk van Vaticanum II* (Bilthoven, 1966), vol. 2, pp. 342-362; the citation occurs on p. 345.

rate from the secular. The minister also lives simultaneously in the Church and in the world, and his person and word are a synthesis achieved, or not yet completed, of secularity and belonging-to-God. To go back again to the words of *Lumen gentium*: the minister also lives "in the ordinary circumstances of family and social life"—there are, after all, married ministers!—and he must "make Christ known to others, especially by the testimony of a life resplendent in faith, hope, and charity"; he also must "work for the sanctification of the world from within, in the manner of leaven." There will be corners of the temporal field in which, as minister, he will not be able to do anything very meaningful; but, as a Christian, he has access to these as well. The following passage from *Lumen gentium* (#33), therefore, seems somewhat doubtful: "Now, the laity are called in a special way to make the Church present and operative in those places and circumstances where only through them can she become the salt of the earth." The text can, of course, be easily defended. Theoretically, it is possible that in certain circumstances and for practical reasons, a specific task is better given to a layman. However, that is only and exclusively a question of practical policy, and a task should never be attributed on the grounds that the minister has no access to any place as a matter of principle. From a theological standpoint, the layman has no specific task as regards apostolic secularity:

The ecclesiastical theological distinction between clergy and layman has consequently nothing to do with the modern concepts of secularity and being-in-the-world, still less with the concepts of the layman in the sense of "layman in the profession," or with not being knowledgeable in religious matters. Being a layman in the Church cannot therefore be defined on the basis of a relation to the innerworldly; it can only be grounded in the inner structure of the supernatural and visible community, the Church—and consequently, only in the kingdom of God, corresponding directly to the apostolic ministry. We may say, however, that secularity, or the innerworldly life function, can be either typical or accidental for believers who are laymen in the theological sense—that is to say, accidental for laymen *as such*, typical for laymen as *Christians* (. . .) The minister keeps himself for the total exercise of his profession.

To this end, granted the scope of his function, he will—to a certain extent—have to forgo secular work in the world, in order to be able to carry out his full-time ministry. Hence, secularity becomes, as it were, typical of believers who are not ministers—that is, of the laity. Nevertheless, apostolic secularity does not thereby become a lay activity *per se* (in the ecclesiastical theological sense). The distinction between layman and clergy does not apply here, except indirectly, as regards their concrete situations.[4]

The apostolic secularity provides no basis for the formal theological distinction between minister and layman; in this field one can point to no task that formally differentiates layman from minister. Nevertheless, is it worth trying to find, in the inner ecclesiastical domain, a specific, positive activity for the layman, one that corresponds directly and formally with the specific task of the minister, representing the Lord? Is there anything to say of the layman, other than that he is not a minister?

One could of course say that being a layman means a total involvement in the active possibilities and tasks that are open to him within the ecclesiastical community. The content of the laity's concrete situation is much richer than the purely negative aspect of not being a minister, but this approach to the question inevitably leads only to making an inventory, rather than giving a theological definition. What a layman does, does not become specifically secular simply because it is not the action of an ecclesiastical minister. As the text of *Lumen gentium* also brings out, the minister may be called to exercise every Christian function; in principle, no field of activity is closed to him.

It appears, therefore, that the *theological concept of layman*

[4] E. Schillebeeckx, "Dogmatiek van ambt en lekestaat," *Tijdschrift voor Theologie*, 2 (1962), pp. 255-269. For further considerations on the so-called part-time ministry, see section 11.

can be defined only negatively; he is the nonminister. The concept is therefore rather narrow, for it is merely relational.

The essence of the ministry in the Church lies therefore in a visible representation of Christ's mediation between the Father and God's People . . . The ecclesiastical ministry is a function by virtue of which the minister, in the performance of the acts pertaining to his office, formally stands over against the People of God . . . Only the bearers of this ecclesiastical ministry are called priests or clergy, and face to face with these ministers, indeed only in correlation with them, the faithful are named laity. It is exclusively in this sense that the distinction between clergy and laity is real, and as such a revealed datum.

Only from this ministerial or non-ministerial point of view can something be called clerical or lay. Being a layman and being a cleric are not, therefore, separate realities that exist in themselves; there is no question here of fundamental characteristics that divide Christian existence, but of ecclesiastical functional concepts. One's state as a Christian is of equal validity from top to bottom; to be a layman or a cleric has meaning only as regards the ministry or ecclesiastical service, and naturally, as regards others.[5]

If the concept of layman in the theological sense can only be stated negatively, the *concept of minister* does have *a characteristic positive content*—namely, *representing the Lord*. But this does not mean that by naming someone a minister one has indicated the whole concrete reality of his person. For he is much more than just a minister; he is also, even primarily, a human being and a Christian. This is a truth that possibly is never denied, but that was perhaps not always envisaged satisfactorily in considering the specific nature of layman and minister. We have seen above that the concept of layman is only relational and negative, and that, in order to give a more complete definition, we must say that he is a Christian, plus a nonminister, plus someone who generally fulfills his mission as a Chris-

[5] E. Schillebeeckx, *op. cit.*, pp. 266-267.

tian in terms of apostolic secularity. In a similar vein, we should say of the minister that he is a Christian, plus a minister, plus someone whose specific function is, generally, to serve the inner Church. Being a minister is in addition to being a Christian an inner-Christian specification.

One more question remains to be considered. If the difference between layman and minister is only one of relation and function within the Church, and if, theologically, one can only define the layman as the nonminister, can the latter be reversed and may we define the minister as the nonlayman? The present section has shown that, theologically speaking, this makes little sense and lands us in a vicious circle. Arguing from the nonminister nature of the layman, one would then define the minister as the non-nonminister, and two negatives cancel each other out.

But in connection with the concrete existence of the person of the minister, the question is valid. It suggests that the Christian who sometimes finds himself in opposition to his fellow Christian laymen, can also be in a situation where he cannot function as a minister because he confronts someone who wields ministerial authority over him. The minister could then sometimes be a nonminister—that is, a layman. This possibility is important enough to warrant special consideration.

7. THE MINISTER IS ALSO A LAYMAN

In one of his sermons, Augustine says to his faithful: "What I should be for you fills me with anguish; what I can be with you is my consolation. Because for you I am a bishop, but with you, a Christian. The first points to my duty, the second, to grace; the first shows the danger, the other, salvation." [1] Besides a feeling of powerlessness, induced by the weight of episcopal responsibility, we note his emphasis on what binds all Christians:

[1] *Sermo* 340 (P. L. 38, 1483).

Augustine is not only a bishop, he is also, and even first of all, a Christian; he is a Christian plus a minister.

Did Augustine fully define himself with these two terms? Most of his hearers probably never asked themselves that question, for they were laymen—that is, Christians plus nonministers; in their eyes, their bishop possessed something that formally placed him over them: he represented the Lord. But what will another bishop, a colleague of those days or of the present time have to say of this definition? Augustine is his fellow Christian, without any doubt. But in regard to him, his colleague, is Augustine also bishop, minister, representative of the Lord? If so, then this colleague is in one respect a nonminister, that is, a layman. If not, then Augustine himself is in a specific case a nonminister, that is, a layman.

Can one say of any individual minister that he is at once a minister and a nonminister, and so a layman? Are the terms mutually exclusive, or can they co-exist?

If we try to analyze what we can state about a concrete human being, we find that there are two levels of classification. One is *disjunctive;* here, concepts and descriptions always come in pairs, of which, however, only one element applies. We must say, for instance, that someone is a man or a woman, black or white, married or unmarried, American or not American; each positive affirmation automatically negates the opposite term of the proposition. On this level also belong the scriptural pronouncements that you cannot be the slave both of God and of money and that a believer is no longer doomed to death but possesses everlasting life. On this level, too, belongs Augustine's word that he is a Christian.

But there exists another group of qualifications. There is a level on which we find properties, and especially functions, whose qualifications are not mutually exclusive, but cumulative. Here, one can be two things simultaneously; a man can even do two things at once, although from a practical viewpoint, that is not so easy. Examples abound: a mayor is also a representative;

a housewife, a seamstress; an insurance agent, a football player; and, in the religious field, a man is *simul justus et peccator!* Augustine's statement to the effect that he is a bishop belongs to this radically different class. To be a bishop is his chief activity, but he can, in principle, exercise another "profession"; Paul, the apostle, was also a tent maker. In the Church today, we have bishops who are also theologians, priests who are workers, and priests who are bursars. Whether these combinations are good is not the point; all we are trying to show here is that they can exist.

One can indeed say of a specific Christian that he is a layman as well as a minister. If it is true that "the essence of the ministry lies in a visible representation of Christ's mediation between the Father and God's People," and that "the ecclesiastical ministry is a function by virtue of which the minister, *in the performance of the acts pertaining to his office,* formally stands over against the people of God," [2] it follows that, in principle, it is possible for a minister not to "be in office" at times, and—whether or not together with other members of God's people—come face to face with another minister.

This is not only a possibility in principle, but clear and perceptible reality. No minister has spent his whole life performing exclusively as a minister; he is often a layman, dependent on another minister, because he is never entirely self-supporting.

This applies naturally to the time preceding his call to the ministry. Through his initiation into the community of the faithful by baptism and while growing to be a mature Christian, he has met men who performed as ministers in relation to him. They gave him the Bread of Life, they spoke the words of absolution to him, they taught him the Gospels and explained them to him, they called him to the ministry and ordained him.

These ecclesiastical functions are still needed after ordination. They are not confined to the strictly personal sphere, but also have their part to play in the mutual relationships within

[2] E. Schillebeeckx, *op. cit.,* p. 266. The italics are mine.

the corps of ministers. This can be explained in the light of the classical threefold division of Church functions mentioned earlier: preaching, guiding, and celebrating the liturgy.

The gift of faith is granted to the Church as a whole, and within the Church it is incumbent on ministers collectively to protect and interpret the treasure of faith. No one minister, however high in authority, can claim such direct and final inspiration that no further confrontation is needed with the sentiment, in matters of faith, of the Church as a whole and of other ministers. Presbyters and deacons can only consider themselves true representatives of the Lord as regards *preaching,* if they are associated with their bishop. The bishop has the duty and the right to test the faith of his priests and deacons and to assign them to further preaching. In relation to the bishop, priests and deacons are nonministers in certain respects. But this also applies for the pope and the bishops. They can be certain of the infallible guidance of the Spirit only when they are sure their own orthodox beliefs correspond to the faith of the apostolic college. They ponder the content of the message of Salvation collegially, and in the course of their joint deliberations, they are each a representative of the Lord for the other.

The same applies to ecclesiastical *guidance.* The ministers stand as a group face to face with the laity as a whole, and as individuals in relation to the faithful who have been entrusted to their personal care. But within the group of ministers we again find this interchange of leading and being led. The bishop has authority over his presbyters and deacons; it is only in association with him that their administration becomes authoritative. But we find this same pattern of giving and of receiving guidance again inside the college of bishops. That is substantiated not only by the fact that the bishops are led by the "successor" of Peter, but also by the relationships of the bishops among themselves, however independent each may be in his own jurisdiction. It has become clear again in our time that the power structures of the inner Church do not follow a simple pyramidal pattern of which the pope is the apex. The bishops collectively wield a real governing authority over, and are responsible for, the Church as a whole. Hence, the bishops working together as a college perform the ministerial governing function for each other, and in a continuous interchange of their roles as ministers and nonministers, represent the Lord of the Church to each other.

Finally, we come to *sacramental and cultic* life. It is possible for a minister to sin, more or less breaking his relation with the Church. Another minister will then have to readmit him in the name of the Church and grant him remission of his sin. The individual minister cannot clear himself, he is no judge of his own case, he cannot dispense himself from ecclesiastical punishments, censure, and excommunication. A striking example of this is provided by Canons 884 and 2367 of Church law which forbid a minister to absolve his "accomplice" in a sin against chastity (the so-called *absolutio complicis*). The transgressor himself cannot redress the harm that has been done; he depends on another minister, and is therefore a layman. The same applies as regards the sacrament of the anointing of the sick: the presbyters of the Church must be called in to pray over the sick minister and anoint him with oil for the purpose of cleansing him from his sins and forgiving them (cf. Jas 5: 14-15).

In connection with the preceding and as a final part of this section, we should like to elaborate on the *relationship of the minister to the Eucharist*. We have already noted that it is not clear, theologically, whether the living presence and the officiating of a minister are always and *per se* required for the celebration of the Eucharist.[3] Naturally, we do not mean to deny that, generally speaking and in normal circumstances, the minister who leads the community of the faithful will also be given the presiding role in the celebration of the Eucharist.

However, there are two forms of Eucharistic celebrations

[3] Cf. p. 58.

that are borderline cases: the so-called private mass, at which no faithful are present, and concelebration, in which several ministers participate, as such, in the celebration.[4] Theologically and psychologically, the idea of "the minister is also a layman" plays a part in both. The fact that they are borderline cases should not make us forget that normally one minister conducts the Eucharistic service for a smaller or greater number of laymen. If, by chance, several ministers are present at the celebration of the Eucharist, then it would be normal for one of them to officiate and for the others to participate as laymen. The question is, how does one interpret, from a theological and pastoral point of view, the cases when the minister officiates alone, or when several ministers conduct the Eucharistic service together?

In the *private mass*, the community of the faithful is reduced to an absolute minimum. There is only one believer present, the minister himself. Layman and minister coalesce here to the extent that any distinction between them is hardly apparent. The minister himself vouches for the fact that the Lord is indeed being commemorated, and sanctifies himself by eating the body and drinking the blood of the Lord. Self-service, in the most sublime sense of the word, is legitimately exercised by the minister. The situation is almost paradoxical.

A theologian could easily point out that the liturgical form of the private mass is far from ideal. The rites and the text both assume that the faithful are indeed present. A drastic reform will be needed if the celebration of the private mass is to remain acceptable from the liturgical and psychological viewpoints. As this unsatisfactory situation can be improved in principle, the theologian cannot claim that the private mass is inherently wrong. He will also tend to reject the argument—which rather strains the imagination—that others are always present "in spirit" at a private mass (those who give the stipend, for instance), and that it is therefore a communal celebration after all.

[4] For material on concelebration and the private mass, see the bibliography at the end of this book.

Moreover, being present in spirit can hardly be called direct and active participation in an event that is visibly taking place.

The meaning of the private mass must therefore lie in the minister himself; it is meaningful because it is a meaningful celebration for the officiating minister personally, though it is truly no easy matter to explain clearly. Some say that this kind of actualization and commemoration of supper and crucifixion has an objective value, and is therefore significant and appropriate. This defense is hardly felicitous, and many people find that they are reminded of prayer mills and the like, and that one might just as well say that showing a film in an empty theater has an objective value. Their objections are understandable. But the latter comparison might help us toward a better interpretation; after all, the projectionist may show the film purely for his own pleasure; he himself then becomes the public, and the subjective need of this minimal public justifies the projection of the film. The objective event becomes significant because it answers a subjective need.

The private mass has meaning only because a personal experience corresponds to the objective event of the enactment of a liturgical rite. The personal devotion of the minister is therefore indispensable. The mystery of Christian salvation is always a personal experience, not something objective and impersonal; building the Church is never to be dissociated from the living human being. If there is no one who can be led to greater holiness through the celebration of the Lord's death, then there is no celebration of this death, but merely the enactment of a lifeless ritual. The private mass offers the possibility, however minimal, of building the Church, and hence the ministry can here become operational. The value of the private mass, therefore, lies in the value it assumes for the minister personally; it has a real subjective value.

The private celebration of the Eucharist must consequently never become the object of legislation, nor can it ever be a criterion of either the devotion or "priestliness" of a minister. In view

of the criticism sometimes leveled at priests who do not celebrate the Eucharist daily, this remark may not be superfluous.
One might even reverse the question and wonder whether the
man who feels that his priesthood obliges him to celebrate every
day does not set his ministry too far apart from the community
by which and for which he was appointed. Too narrow a defense
of the private mass can be a sign of clerical overestimation of
self and concern for function. The minister who considers it
beneath his dignity to take part as layman in a celebration of the
Eucharist makes his office too independent and possibly forgets
that it is a service.

Concelebration is in a sense a counterpart of the private mass,
but at the same time it brings up almost the same points for
criticism. An old custom, particularly in the Eastern Church, in
recent centuries concelebration seldom took place until a short
time ago in the Latin Church, but it has attracted much interest recently, which in turn has led to an expansion of its possibilities. The reasons invoked in favor of concelebration are not
particularly striking, however, and make one suspect that they
are based on a poorly balanced view of the liturgy and appraisal
of the ecclesiastical ministry.

Liturgically and theologically, concelebration is difficult to
defend. This is already clear from the fact that a distinction is
made between ceremonial and sacramental concelebration, and
between chief celebrant and concelebrants. It must be shown
that concelebration can make liturgical celebrations more per-
spicuous and answers a genuine need of the celebrating community. Is this actually the case? One may say, of course, that
the use of several ministers lends the event a somewhat greater
solemnity, something like a celebration of mass with the help
of deacons and subdeacons, but that is not enough. For it does
not answer the question whether the concelebrants actually
bring an added presbyterial contribution to the liturgical event.
If the celebration of the Eucharist requires that someone come
forward explicitly as the representative of the Lord in order to

guarantee that on its occasion the death of the Lord is truly being commemorated, then the functional and formal appearance of one minister is sufficient. The active functioning of several ministers *qua* ministers is not only superfluous, it is even confusing: for if the celebration of the Eucharist is meant to commemorate the Lord's Last Supper, and make it present to us, and if we see the minister who conducts the celebration as the representative of the Lord, then the parallel unquestionably stands much better if only one person assumes the role. The very structure of the Eucharistic service, and the needs of the community as a whole, make it extremely difficult to support concelebration, even though one can adduce in its favor a desire to celebrate the Eucharist with additional pomp on certain occasions. These objections remain whether the celebration is conducted by several presbyters or by a bishop with a group of presbyters.

Of course, one could argue that concelebration manifests the underlying unity of the corps of presbyters and their ties with the bishop. That is true, but this kind of stress on collegial unity simultaneously emphasizes the difference between ministry and laity, precisely when the intention is to proclaim the underlying unity of all believers. Keeping in mind the clear theological principle that the ministry exists to serve the community, every minister might ask himself whether it does any good to try so hard to have the profession given a quantitative emphasis. This could be an indication of a cleric-centered ecclesiology.[5]

Clericalism means to overemphasize and unnecessarily put forward the mission and authority of ministers. It entails disproportionate attention to the difference between layman and minister, and the risk of reducing the laity to a secondary in the Church group. Only the minister who is thoroughly aware

[5] It is, besides, the emphasis of a function that, as we have seen, is not clearly and specifically ministerial. Contemporary liturgy makes the canon a monologue spoken by the minister, even though the text clearly shows him to be the spokesman for the community. Could a canon be devised in dialogue style that would, for instance, let the whole community "consecrate"?

that he is also a layman as well as a minister, will be able to resist this temptation. Our criticism of the concelebration phenomenon constitutes only one application of a principle that is valid in every area of the internal life of the Church. The following section, in which we shall examine further the relation between the ecclesiastical ministry and everyday life, will bring out more clearly the justification for this criticism. There will always remain a difference between minister and layman; but the contradistinction is not absolute. Whoever sees minister and layman as outright and complete contrasts to each other is dealing with a false dilemma.

8. FUNCTION AND LIFE SITUATION: "CLERGY" AND PEOPLE

The preceding sections have led to the conclusion that the difference between layman and minister is one of relation and function, and only exists within the common condition of Christian life; that it is not connected with being active or passive, but in how one is active within the framework of the common priesthood of the faithful, and that the same person can interchangeably have a ministerial and nonministerial relationship with a fellow Christian.

One question remains: when we say of someone that he *performs* ministerial as well as nonministerial acts, can we also say that he *is* minister and layman? What is the relation between *doing* and *being*? The problem is primarily one of linguistics and philosophy, but we should consider it here nevertheless, as a preliminary to a large number of queries about the meaning of what is traditionally called clerical life.

In everyday language, "doing" and "being" are usually identified. For instance, after noticing that someone carries out army work, we go on to say that he *is* an army man. A datum relating to function is shifted to an existential level. This level is not the one described at the beginning of the preceding section as disjunctive, but the existential level of cumulative qualifications. We have no trouble in saying of somebody who *is* an army man that he is also a Dutchman, native of Amsterdam, a married man and the father of two children, a member of the Dutch Reformed Church, and an amateur football player. All these functions and qualifications go together with the qualification "army." In concrete cases, the list can be extended further, but there is a definite limit: two antithetic qualities cannot be attributed to the same person. Nobody is at one and the same time a native of Amsterdam and of The Hague, the father of two and of five children, a member of the Dutch Reformed Church and of the Roman Catholic. That is impossible in principle. But it is possible in principle that somebody perform several functions and have several professions.

Everyday language distinguishes between army men and non-army men, and sometimes terms the latter "civilians." But it is clear to everyone that being a civilian constitutes only a functional distinction: everybody is bound to have the welfare of his country at heart, but it is incumbent upon some to care in a particular manner for the safety and defense of the country. It is only in this regard that the military-civilian distinction applies. From every other point of view, the army man is also a civilian, a member of the national community with civil rights and duties.

Similarly we say of someone who *performs* the work of a minister that he *is* a minister, although we know that the person concerned also does other things and is not only a minister. But in this respect, one notes a certain hesitation, and even resistance: describe the ecclesiastical ministry as a function, a profession, or a task, and you are, for some, using a desecrating language that misapprehends the whole reality of the minister.

What should a theologian do about this kind of "blame"? Should he simply reject it as a survival from the days when minister and layman were too strongly differentiated? Or should he see it as an expression of concern for the preservation of a valid theological principle?

His first duty is to point out that the terms *ministry* and *function* are being used quite correctly. A man is admitted to a special ecclesiastical group because he has been called to, and consecrated for, specific functions. The only reason for his belonging to the ministerial group is that he is available for these functions. The difference between minister and nonminister is functional—we saw this in section 6—and consequently one may, without any reservation, use the terms describing any form of functional human activity. The language of Scripture and the liturgy shows not the slightest hesitation in this respect. The New Testament speaks constantly of the *tasks* that the apostles and their helpers must carry out, and the ordination formularies speak time and again of the assignment of ecclesiastical ministerial tasks and responsibilities. The third chapter of *Lumen gentium* fits in with this, and the same "functional" language appears again in the decree *Christus Dominus,* concerning the bishops' pastoral office, and in *Presbyterorum ordinis,* on the ministry and life of priests. In the last, ample attention is devoted to the personal life of priests, because the calling to the ecclesiastical ministry undoubtedly affects an individual's private life, but that does not deny that being a minister is primarily a functional reality. In studying Scripture, liturgical text, or other ecclesiastical documents, it should always be remembered, moreover, that their language is hardly ever strictly formal and dogmatic, but that it alternates between precise job descriptions, comments on professional ethics, and notes on personal life. The theologian may—indeed, he must—distinguish and separate the various data, never forgetting, however, that *in concreto,* exercise of office and personal life interact. He will, in this way, come to the scientific conclusion that the minister is, formally and primarily, a "functionary."

In doing so, the theologian does not deny that the ecclesiastical ministry is a function of a very special kind, for it does not exist in a series of exclusive activities, but in the special authority with which the minister performs certain internal ecclesiastical tasks. The authority of the minister is closely connected with that of the Lord of the Church, whom he represents. The minister is therefore somewhat more than just an official who carries out certain "technical activities." It is his professional duty to heighten the religious dimension of the human being and bring it to fulfillment, and in carrying this duty out, he is already the embodiment, although provisionally, of a deeper reality of existence. In the ecclesiastical minister, personal life and professional activities are closely bound together, more so than in any chiefly technical profession. An unbeliever, or a man who does not sufficiently practice what he preaches to others, cannot be or remain a minister. It is consequently understandable and acceptable that the faithful should be interested in, and even keep an eye on, the personal life of their ministers.

In most human communities, a distinction is made between the various professional activities of men, and they bear different names. We say that the uneducated worker has a minor job, but the lawyer exercises a profession. By these standards—which obviously must not be taken as any measure of individual worth, integrity, or holiness—the ecclesiastical functionary is undoubtedly a person endowed with a *profession;* this presupposes thorough training and brings great responsibilities—responsibilities connected with fundamental aspects of human existence: belief or unbelief, love or hatred, salvation or damnation, life or death. The ecclesiastical ministry is not just a function that can be assumed or given up at will. No one takes on the work who has not been clearly called to do so (cf. Heb 4:3), and as for giving it up, there is the question of loyalty to be considered, loyalty to the One who called and to those for whom the minister was appointed. Since the ecclesiastical ministry does not function for inert matter, but for living people, it is truly an exalted profession.

Ecclesiastical ministers constitute a specific functional group; they perform certain functions and therefore *are* ministers. In point of fact, this *work-group* also shows itself to be a *life-group*: the clergy. The profession has turned into an ecclesiastical rank and a life situation. The sacred character of the office is extended in a distinctive way of life, certain aspects of which are prescribed by Church law, most strikingly in the Western Roman Church. Among these are mandatory celibacy, the wearing of professional clothing after working hours, a certain degree of clannishness even in social and recreational contacts, a standard of living which generally combine a certain frugality with extensive social and economic security, maintaining a certain distance from certain human habits and interests—although not rejecting these as a matter of principle—particularly in the fields of technology, natural sciences, and recreation.

The theologian whose task it is to study this transmutation of profession into life situation need not reject it in essence, but could and should inquire whether the question is chiefly one of historical and sociological process—which should consequently be judged primarily on the grounds of desirability from the pastoral viewpoint—or of a development that, by strictly theological standards, should be defended and even welcomed.

The concept of *clergy*, as it is treated in traditional theology and Church law, has no basis in Scripture.[1] In the Old Testament, *klèros* meant the part or heritage that befell to the whole people (cf. Dt 4:20; 9:29): the choice of Israel as Yahweh's own people. In the New Testament, in I Peter 5:3, it indicates the "flock of God" entrusted to the care of the presbyterium; here the *clergy* idea has, it is true, some connection with the ministry, but it points only to the group of nonministers. In Acts 1:17, however, the gift of the ministry itself is named *klèros* and this is the starting point of a development that led to naming "clerics" those who have received the ministry as a special grace and a special calling.

[1] Cf. H. Küng, *The Church* (New York, 1967), pp. 363ff., 385-387.

The formal end of this development is to be found in Canon 108 of Church law, under which only those are considered *clergy* who are the bearers of some kind of ecclesiastical authority as regards the powers of ordination or administration, or those who are already clearly set apart as potential bearers of such authority (the tonsured). This last category shows definitely that the *clergy* are distinguished from the laity by more than the possession of ecclesiastical powers: to be a cleric means first to belong to a specific ecclesiastical life-group within which the actual exercise of the ecclesiastical ministry is situated. When *Lumen gentium* states that the term *laity* means all the faithful except those in "holy orders" (*ordo sacer*), it goes along with Canon 108 and suggests that the difference between layman and minister is more than purely functional (#31).

If Scripture indicates clearly that the ecclesiastical ministry bears its own characteristic functional stamp, the change of function into life situation is a development that does not necessarily flow from Holy Writ or can be argued from it. It was settled only later, at the time when the Church fell heir to the Roman Empire with its system of thought that stressed the sense of hierarchy. In the Empire, there was a far-reaching difference between *ordo* and *plebs,* and the familiar difference between the upper layer of society and those largely without rights, which was evident in that social system, became a structural element of the Christian community. Part of the Roman legacy passed over to the nobility of the Middle Ages, but that only reinforced the development of a clerical bloc; since the ecclesiastical and civil legal orders coincided so closely, clergy and nobility often found themselves in competition with one another. The Reformation, occurring as it did when the upcoming bourgeoisie had already altered the status pattern and relativized it, looked at the sociological phenomenon of the clergy in the light of Scripture, and particularly of the "newly discovered" doctrine of the common priesthood. Since the reformers could not find a functional quality pertaining specifically to the ecclesiastical ministry, they had, a fortiori, to reject the development of it into a clerical order. As a result, all the "insignia of the order" disappeared almost completely: celibacy, garb, immunities; only the Episcopal Churches kept something of the older framework.

Taking these biblical and historical data into account, the theologian may wonder whether to interpret this extension of profession into life-situation positively or negatively. At first he may feel much in favor of a positive appraisal. For not only must the minister's functional activities but also the whole trend of his life witness to the faith that actuates him; he must not only do holy work, he must also be holy; he cannot restrict himself to a "professional and technical" representation of the Lord, he must also make apparent in his own person the existential meaning of the Good News, failing which his fellowmen will neither acknowledge nor recognize him. For him, holiness is not only a personal ethical duty, but in a certain sense a professional requirement as well. On this basis, the demand for a typical ministerial life pattern could be understandable.

But this immediately brings up other questions. If the minister must be a "manifest" Christian, does that mean that he, together with his colleagues in the ministry, must choose a "different" and uniform way of life? We will not now examine the feasibility, if any, of blueprinting a typically ministerial life situation, based upon characteristics of the ministry considered as a function (we shall find that the answer to that is negative),[2] but developing and maintaining a specific pattern of clerical life and striving for clerical clan formation can entail a real danger for Christian unity. If the minister's example of sound Christian living is to be followed, it must not be set too far apart. Moreover, this distinctive way of life must not be presented as "higher," for that would mean that Christian holiness is being clericalized. In the eyes of the Lord, all men are equal; there is

[2] Cf. Part II, section 14, p. 145ff.

indeed no one way from man to God, no "higher," no "lower";
the only way to God is Christ the Lord, and it has only one measure: sincere love. Advocating a so-called specific way of life for
ministers also entails the danger of promoting hypocrisy; a minister who can no longer adhere spontaneously to its requirements might feel obliged simply to keep up appearances.

It is highly doubtful that turning a function into a life situation has been—or is—for the good of the Christian community.
The reverse seems to be true; and neither the theologian nor any
other Christian should be upset when he hears it said nowadays
that the difference between layman and minister should be reduced to a minimum. The ministerial performance need not be
endangered; on the contrary, as Bishop Robinson suggests, this
might eliminate some obstacles to the smooth working of the
ministry:

I have no doubt whatever that the Church will continue to require
diversities of ministry—and indeed a much greater diversity than the
few stereotypes to which the Spirit has been confined since the shape
of the ministry hardened in the early centuries. I have no doubt too
that the Church should ordain, set apart, or otherwise acknowledge
with prayer, thanksgiving and authority, those called and commissioned to special functions in the name of its Head and members.
What I question is whether most of the traditional lines of demarcation which run through the ministry of the Church, and which were
accepted by the Reformers without serious question, bear any more
relation to the battles of tomorrow than the trenches of yesterday's
war. In fact they are increasingly becoming a positive hindrance to
freedom of maneuver . . .

The first is the basic division between clergy and laity—what I
called the clergy line—which cuts its way through the diversities of
administration within the Church, often arbitrarily but usually quite
firmly. This is a line of quite a different nature from those distinguishing the various offices or orders of ministry (bishops, priests,
deacons, readers, catechists, etc.) to which the Church under the
guidance of the Spirit has from the beginning commissioned its

members. It is as though somewhere through the middle of these divisions ran an invisible line, marking off those above from those below the salt . . .

We should be ready to recognize that this "clergy line" is neither native nor essential to the Church. It is indeed an alien importation, introduced from the difference between the *plebs* and the *ordo*, the commons and the senate, in the administrative machinery of the Roman Empire. It was entrenched in the Church at the time of its establishment under Constantine, when it became necessary to define the rights and benefits of clergy transferred to it from the heathen priesthood. I believe the whole thing could disappear without loss, together with the medieval concept of indelibility, the mystique, the status, the theology and the legalities by which it has been buttressed and surrounded in our various traditions. The whole differentiation implied in the terms "sacred ministry" and "holy orders" is one that is now destructive rather than constructive of the Body of Christ . . .[3]

For the unity of the faithful community, and because of the dynamics of its activities, the difference between minister and layman should be stressed as little as possible. Opposition to the traditional clericalization of the minister's person expresses an authentic Christian intuition, one founded on the words of Paul, who recognizes the diversity of ministries and charismata in the Church but finds it inadmissible that one part of the body should put itself above another (1 Cor 12:12-31). The Christian of our democratic days is not reluctant to recognize the ministerial authority of the minister; but automatically to extend this consideration to the concrete appearance of the minister and his personal way of life, is a requirement that the Christian will find rather puzzling. A demand of this kind is more likely to turn him away from the minister.

The implications of the people-of-God ecclesiology of Vatican II have by no means yet been established. The declericalization of the idea of the special ministry, which is primarily functional,

[3] J. Robinson, *The New Reformation?* (Philadelphia, 1965), pp. 55, 56, 57.

will take some time, not only because it involves a theoretical theology, but also because it means abandoning an existential situation in which many put great faith. One can only say that it is required by the service of the minister to both the Church and the world.

As a practical conclusion, we can say that the tonsure may properly be abandoned, since it does not entail any ministerial meaning of its own. This also applies to the so-called minor orders, sub-diaconate and the diaconate, unless they are changed and given a truly functional character. Otherwise, they remain a useless clericalization of persons and functions common to all Christians.

9. APOSTLES, BISHOPS, PRESBYTERS AND DEACONS

Christ the Lord is the only one entitled to call himself priest, prophet, and shepherd in the full sense of these words. He rules and administers his Church, is the living Word of God, and offers true worship to the Father. Every ecclesiastical office derives its mission from him, every ministerial act is made "in the name of the Lord Jesus" and through the power of his Spirit.

In the "meantime," pending his return, others act in his place as deputies. Within the circle of their fellow men, they represent the Lord. Their authority derives from his authority, their word is his word. But because their ministry is a mission in a Church on the move through time, every ministry is related to those who first held the office, who were called personally by the Lord: the apostles. *Lumen gentium* plainly refers every ecclesiastical ministry to the apostolic college:

This most sacred Synod, following in the footsteps of the First Vatican Council, teaches and declares with that Council that Jesus Christ, the eternal Shepherd, established His Holy Church by sending forth the apostles as He himself had been sent by the Father. (#18)

That divine mission, entrusted by Christ to the apostles, will last until the end of the world (cf. Mt 28:20), since the gospel which was to be handed down by them is for all time the source of all life for the Church. For this reason the apostles took care to appoint successors in this hierarchically structured society. (#20)

Their ministry was unique. They had known the Lord in the flesh and gave testimony to what they had seen with their own eyes and heard with their own ears (cf. 1 Jn 1:1-3). None of those who came after them can bear testimony with the same force and from the same experience. They are the pillars of the Church, and the fullness of the ministry assumed by men is concentrated in them. Their death brought an end to this absolutely unique ministry. But it did not disappear completely because, before they passed on, they had imposed hands on many and made them share in their own mission; the Lord had also to be made present in the Church after their death, and even during their lifetime the community had spread to such an extent that they could not be personally present everywhere.

The Acts and the letters of the different apostles show most explicitly that the appearance of special ministers was considered as a legitimate and even necessary phenomenon. As regards the concrete shape of the ministry, however, much is unclear, and that is why throughout the ages people have wondered whether and how far the actual evolutionary shape of the ministry was—or should be—in conformity with Scripture. We cannot go fully into the history of the ministries, but should like to state a few general principles which might help us appraise the historical and contemporary structures.

The first principle is that it is impossible, and also unnecessary, to trace back to Scripture, and establish on it, all the concrete forms the ministry has assumed in the course of centuries. It is impossible because the scriptural data are far from complete and clear, and because even when they are clear, they do not necessarily indicate that the structure described is valid for all times and places. The fact that the ministry in the early Church adopted certain forms does not necessarily mean that they are meant to be permanent. It is also unnecessary, because standards for the ministerial structure should be found primarily in the needs and demands of the concrete situation. A close imitation of the form of ministry prevailing in the old Church is no guarantee of its worth; we need forms of ministry that will best ensure the realization of God's plan for the salvation of mankind. Anything that answers this criterion is in accordance with Scripture, even if it departs from the usual. That a certain form of ministry—like the diaconate, for instance—was "reinstated" at a particular time is of interest only to the historian; for the theologian, all that counts is whether it is so structured that it will validly effect the representation of the Lord.[1]

One may well conclude from Scripture—and this is our second principle—that the ministry will always, however, involve both in the centralizing functions of the Church, and those pertaining to participation and assistance. Scripture leaves no doubt on this matter: in the early Church, the twelve took on a very special role, as is shown for instance by the fact that after Judas Iscariot had fallen out, they filled the vacancy in the college (Acts 1:25-26), and that the apostles supervised the whole church. Derivative functions, like those of deacons and presbyters, come into play in a more restricted field: the activity of the latter seems to have been limited by local boundaries; the former, by the scope of their operations. The change from apostolic to episcopal college is shrouded in a fairly thick mist as far as the first century is concerned, but at least by the end of the second century the bishops seem to have become the highest ranking ecclesiastical ministers; all the other ministries are grouped around them. This irrefutable biblical and historical fact still stands as a challenge to the exclusively presbyterial churches. It

---

[1] All such structures can be said to be "of divine right"; it does not seem necessary to offer convincing proof that they are already found in the Bible.

is not enough for them to defend their rejection of the episcopate on the grounds of its monarchical development in later
times. Although a decisive argument in favor of the episcopal
structure is only to be found in the unchallenged situation in
the days of the apostolic fathers, the question nevertheless remains whether the exclusively presbyterial church does not
lack an over-all plan that would bring the local churches together in world-wide unity. Founding world unity on common
adherence to Scripture and confessions of faith only involves a
very abrupt transition from the visible local community to a
purely spiritual universalism; in the early ages of the Church, it
was always understood that the unity should also be embodied
in a visible ruling *collegium*.

A fresh consideration of the question of the episcopate—
which is taking place in a growing number of Reformed
Churches—need not take away from the more "horizontal" idea
of collegiality. Fear of this was justifiable only when the structure of the episcopal Churches was too strongly vertical, hierarchical, and centralized. But those days are over, or at least
disappearing. The Church which, up to now, was the most
centralized and monarchical in structure, the Roman Catholic,
appeared at the Second Vatican Council to be ready to recognize
explicitly that all ecclesiastical ministries, including the episcopate, have a collegial and synodal structure. That obviates one
of the fundamental objections of the Reformation, even if one
must admit that it is as yet a change in theological insight rather
than structures and forms. In the last instance, one will therefore have to say that the episcopal-or-presbyterial alternatives
constitute a false dilemma.[2] The episcopate, the highest form
of the representation of the Lord, is indispensable to the Church,
but this *episkopè* must be exercised collegially. That the college
of bishops should have a head in whom episcopal authority cul-

---

[2] It does not follow from the Scriptures, where a clear differentiation is
suggested between central and participating functions, that this delimitation
agrees with what they say about bishops and presbyters.

minates is not only possible but also desirable and necessary, because to some degree it is thanks to the existence of one head that the multiplicity of visions and longings can be harmonized. On the other hand, however, councils and episcopal colleges are real structural elements of the Church or Christ. The same holds good at the lower level. The bishop is in his own Church par excellence the representative of the Lord and has the final responsibility for the life of that church. But he cannot manage without his presbyters and deacons. He not only needs them because he cannot do the work alone, he also needs them because they, together with him, must embody the unity of the local church.

In conclusion, it can be said that a good theology of the ministry does not allow of any real distinction between "sacred" power and jurisdictional authority.[3] These do not run side by side as competitors, but the latter consists in a closer delimitation—after collegial consideration—of the fields in which the various ministries will perform their threefold task of proclaiming the Word of God, celebrating the liturgy, and guiding the flock. The allocation of the field of work must be done officially by the proper authority, and consequently both pope and the bishop have a special responsibility, the first for the universal Church, the second for the local. However, neither draws for this on a distinct jurisdictional authority, but on the full extent of his "sacred" power.

If, having stated these general principles, we wish to examine the three traditional ministries more closely, we must begin with the *episcopal office*. Since the death of the apostles, the episcopate is the central ministry of the Church. Although its development during the first century can no longer be clearly traced, no one, from the time of Clement of Rome and Ignatius of Alexandria to the presbyterian Reformations of the sixteenth

[3] Cf. G. Baraúna, *De Kerk van Vaticanum II* (Bilthoven, 1966), vol. 1, p. 169; vol. 2, pp. 38, 49, 75, 199.

century, has seriously questioned the right of existence of the episcopal office, and even after the Reformation the great majority of Christian communities have recognized bishops as the "higher pastors" of the Church.

It is also a constant of tradition that this college of bishops is entitled to call itself "successors of the apostles." *Lumen gentium* formulates this belief clearly in section #20, although one must regretfully note the absence of a passage stating that this succession does not cover all the aspects of the apostolic ministry; besides continuity, there is discontinuity as well, because, unlike the apostles, the bishops have not received the call from the Lord's own lips.

The consecration and assignment to this fundamental ecclesiastical ministry is an important Church event and rightly deserves to qualify as a sacrament. There was some doubt about this for ages, but at the Second Vatican Council, the understanding had apparently matured to such an extent that the concept could be formulated (*Lumen gentium,* #21.)[4] This result was achieved thanks to the numerous studies on the theology of the sacraments undertaken during recent years—we shall come back to this briefly in the following section—but it should also be seen in the light of the rejection, mentioned above, of a difference between "sacred" and jurisdictional power. During the centuries that this distinction was admitted, the difference between episcopate and presbyterate was usually described as a difference in jurisdictional competence, and ordination to the presbyterate was consequently considered the focal sacramental event in the ministry. Now, the situation is practically reversed, and the difference seems to be more one of quality than of quantity. This makes the traditional saying that the bishops possessed the "fullness" of the ministry more meaningful: the fullness consists in the explicit and direct relationship with the ministry of the apostles. Moreover, the new insight goes along with a re-

[4] Cf. J. Lécuyer, "Het episcopaat als sacrament," in G. Baraúna, ed., *De Kerk van Vaticanum II* (Bilthoven, 1966), vol. 2, pp. 25-44.

newal, now in process, of theological thinking on the relationship between pope and bishops. A heavy underscoring of the
legal aspect of the authority is liable to evoke a strictly pyramidal
image of the ministry, with the pope wielding a quantitative
maximum of jurisdictional power and the "lower" ministries
participating in it to a greater or lesser degree.

With this we come to another important aspect of the theology of the episcopate. Within the college of bishops, there is a
tension between the practical collegial leadership and the official
head with ultimate responsibility, a tension that must also have
existed in the college of the apostles in which Peter occupied a
place all his own. The variations in this tension go to weave a
fascinating pattern of historical evolution. While in the very
early days, the successor of Peter was first of all a symbol of underlying unity and exercised a moral authority, a more legally
oriented vision developed later, particularly during the struggle
for supreme power waged between pope and emperor. After a
few centuries, it was admitted that efforts to convert the papal
primacy into absolute and supreme rule over the whole of human society were doomed to failure, and after great difficulties
a situation emerged in which the pope was no longer seen or
experienced as head of a social order dominating the national
structures. Within the Church itself, however, the accent was
still on the superiority of the pope over the bishops. There developed a theological trend of opinion which culminated in the
official proclamation of papal infallibility at the First Vatican
Council. After 1870, it was held for a while that councils were
henceforth not really necessary, and that consultations between
pope and bishops were more a question of manners than a requirement of the ecclesiastical structure. The partiality of these
views could not remain hidden or unopposed for long, all the
more so that they were so manifestly out of keeping with the
democratic way of thinking which was taking shape in all
fields of life. In recent decades, theologians have tried anew to
formulate the relationship between pope and bishops, and have

been helped in their endeavor by the widespread present desire for decentralization. Vatican II is an important manifestation of this process[5] which, however, is far from completed, and probably will only be finished when the practice of ecclesiastical leadership has evolved further, along with theoretical ideas. Sections #22 and 23 of *Lumen gentium* and the text of the famous *Nota explicativa praevis* reveal by their involved formulations how difficult it is to unify the data on primacy, collegiality, and personal episcopal responsibility. Much will depend on whether sound structures can be found which would validate for the whole Church the responsibility of the bishops so explicitly recognized, and truly practiced, by Vatican II.

When the duties of the bishops working together as a body are described in *Lumen gentium,* use is again made of the traditional threefold division of the ministries into proclaiming, sanctifying, and pastoral functions (#25-27). The bishops are pre-eminently those who have the authority to render the Lord's Word present in the Church, and under the guidance of the Holy Spirit they enjoy as a body the gift of infallibility when teaching the doctrine of the Church; to them especially is committed, through the apostles, the office of celebrating the Eucharist "in memory," and they are consequently the "priests" par excellence; called to guide the flock of the Lord, they perform their pastoral duties with the Lord's authority. Because the functions of the episcopal office must be carried out collegially, it is not required that each individual bishop be equally involved in the performance of the three tasks. Insofar as the bishop is pastor in charge of a local Church, he must of course be considered as locally the highest-ranking teacher, priest, and administrator. But the episcopal college need not be made up exclusively of the heads of local Churches. It can also include—and this has always been the case—persons who perform some function in the central government of the universal Church or who, be-

---

[5] Cf. the seven articles on episcopal collegiality in G. Baraúna, ed., *De Kerk van Vaticanum II* (Bilthoven, 1966), vol. 2, pp. 45-166.

cause of outstanding personal gifts in theological or pastoral matters, can make an important contribution to collegial episcopal management. The curia bishop is, theologically speaking, defensible, and the same may be said of certain types of honorary bishops, provided that these forms of nonlocal episcopates answer a real necessity and their numbers are proportionate; at the moment, it would seem that too much emphasis is placed on administrative officials and too little on teachers and prophets. Too one-sided a membership hinders the fulfillment of the whole task of the episcopate.

The *presbyter,*[6] as classical theology has it, is the *manus longa,* the long arm of the bishop. He is called and consecrated by the bishop, diocesan or otherwise, to participate in his own tasks:

Although priests do not possess the highest degree of the priesthood, and although they are dependent on the bishops in the exercise of their power, they are nevertheless united with the bishops in sacerdotal dignity. By the power of the sacrament of orders, and in the image of Christ the eternal High Priest, they are consecrated to preach the gospel, shepherd the faithful, and celebrate divine worship as true priests of the New Testament. Partakers of the function of Christ the sole Mediator on their level of ministry, they announce the divine word to all. They exercise this sacred function of Christ most of all in the Eucharistic liturgy or synaxis. There, acting in the person of Christ, and proclaiming His mystery, they join the offering of the faithful to the sacrifice of their Head. Until the coming of the Lord, they re-present and apply in the Sacrifice of the Mass the one sacrifice of the New Testament, namely the sacrifice of Christ offering Himself once and for all to His Father as a spotless victim.

For the penitent or ailing among the faithful, priests exercise fully the ministry of reconciliation and alleviation, and they present the

[6] Cf. J. Giblet, "De Priesters van de tweede graad," in G. Baraúna, *De Kerk van Vaticanum II* (Bilthoven, 1966), pp. 191-215; as it came out later, the decree *Presbyterorum ordinis* was not taken into account in this article.

needs and the prayers of the faithful to God the Father. Exercising within the limits of their authority the function of Christ as Shepherd and Head, they gather together God's family as a brotherhood all of one mind and lead them in the Spirit, through Christ, to God the Father. In the midst of the flock they adore Him in Spirit and in truth. Finally, they labor in word and doctrine, believing what they have read and meditated upon in the law of the Lord, teaching what they believe, and practicing what they teach.

Priests, prudent cooperators with the episcopal order as well as its aids and instruments, are called to serve the People of God. They constitute one priesthood with their bishop, although that priesthood is comprised of different functions. Associated with their bishop in a spirit of trust and generosity, priests make him present in a certain sense in the individual local congregations of the faithful, and take upon themselves as far as they are able, his duties and concerns, discharging them with daily care. As they sanctify and govern under the bishop's authority that part of the Lord's flock entrusted to them, they make the universal Church visible in their own locality and lend powerful assistance to the upbuilding of the whole body of Christ.

In this passage from *Lumen gentium* (#28), and even more so in the corresponding passages from *Presbyterorum ordinis* (#4-6), the traditional threefold division is used to describe the content of the priest's office, as it was for the common priesthood and the episcopate. However, a closer analysis of the texts reveals a few interesting differences.

First of all, they seem somewhat hesitant. They do not have the same clarity as those on the episcopal functions. They contain more of an itemized description of what all presbyters may actually do, than a formal statement of the characteristics of the presbyterial function. The hesitation is understandable, for the difference between the respective tasks of presbyter and bishop is not one of essence, but of form, and then only in a negative, or at least relational sense: the presbyter participates in the tasks of the bishop, but he does not perform them of his

own authority. Furthermore, the concrete content of presbyterial duties varies according to time and place. It was therefore
impossible to refer to any clear scriptural texts, because in the
New Testament, the presbyter is a very vague figure; the New
Testament presbyterate is far less of a prototype of today's, than
the apostle's ministry is of the episcopate of later days. The very
formulation of the text shows that the presbyterate is not at all
as well established theologically as the episcopate. The question
we considered earlier (whether any of the minister's tasks
are of such a nature that they cannot, *per se,* be performed by
the layman) has an even greater significance for the presbyterate.[7]
If the answer is negative, it would mean that, since the laity too
are subject to the *episkopè* of the highest office, and witness
to salvation, the difference between layman and presbyter can
also be described in terms of degrees of "dependence" on the
bishop.

This inference is supported indirectly by another point apparent from the two texts. In the passage from *Lumen gentium*
quoted above, great stress is laid on the task, purportedly proper
to the presbyter, of celebrating the Eucharist. In *Presbyterorum
ordinis,* however, the emphasis is on the proclamation of the
Word:

The People of God finds its unity first of all through the Word of
the living God, which is quite properly sought from the lips of priests.
Since no one can be saved who has not first believed, priests, as co-
workers with their bishops, have as their primary duty the proclamation of the gospel of God to all. (#4)

The emphasis shifts, then, even within the framework of the
same Council, and in such a manner that it actually registers
the movement "from priest to prophet": not only does the ex-

---

[7] We have already shown (footnote 5, p. 59) that there is no scriptural
evidence to the effect that administering the sacraments of the Eucharist and
penance are tasks reserved exclusively to presbyters.

ercise of the cult no longer define the ministry completely, it is even made subordinate to the task of proclaiming. No celebration is possible unless a community has been founded through the Word.

The founding of a community, however, is not a one-sided deed, but a two-way process of offer and response. Degrees, "higher" and "lower," hardly have any part to play here: presbyter and layman stand face to face as equals, under the supervision of the higher pastors of the local and universal Church. One suspects more and more strongly that, theologically speaking, the difference between bishop and nonbishop is more fundamental than that between presbyter and layman. The debates and decisions of Vatican II have sometimes given rise to complaints to the effect that the lower-rank minister has been trapped between the bishops and the laity, who have received so much attention. But on second thought, one could also interpret this fact in a positive manner, as an important step toward the declericalization of the Church: the Church of tomorrow will have many forms of service, many patterns of ministry, but only in the episcopate will this lead to a more explicitly ministerial group formation.

In the light of the above, it can be stated without much further comment that those who share in the episcopal office need not be called to exercise each of the three functions it embraces. It can be argued validly on scriptural and theological grounds that certain members of God's people can be sent to perform particular and clearly specified duties. Various parts of the ministerial work of the Church demand the highest possible technical qualifications. It is not always possible to find persons who are qualified all around: after all, there are few jack-of-all-trades. Dividing the functions would, it seems, best ensure the efficiency of the performance. When Paul describes the variety of gifts and of service in the Church (1 Cor 12:4-10, Eph 4:11), he seems to be welcoming the active participation in ecclesiastical work of as many Christians as possible.

First comes the phrase *to restore* the diaconate. Scripture and Church history show a good deal of change in the work content of the diaconate. According to Acts 6:1-6, it was the need for help in the care of the poor which led directly to its institution, but it becomes evident fairly soon that deacons were also active in the proclamation of the Good News (6:8, 8:5, and 26-40, 21:8). Later, they appear to be working with the catechumens and giving pastoral guidance of a more general nature. They also exercised certain liturgical functions: they assisted the bishop in the celebration of the Eucharist, and sometimes also presided over the celebration; they prepared the penitents, and case of need, could also administer the sacrament of penance.[10] *Lumen gentium* recalls these varied activities, but justifies the reinstatement of the diaconate on the grounds of contemporary needs and motives, and not on account of any compunction its age-long atrophy might have aroused. The diaconate need not exist as such; it can exist only if it is necessary for the Church.[11]

This brings up a more fundamental problem. Can the theologian, however glad he may be from a practical point of view of this broadening of opportunities for ecclesiastical service, rejoice over the institution of a new "hierarchical rank"? When he reads in *Lumen gentium* what tasks are contemplated for the new-style deacons, he discovers that these are in large part duties that were and are carried out by nonministers—those that the Church does not consider specifically ministerial. Should the introduction of the diaconate lead to a stronger clericalization of a number of functions, the development would hardly be cause for any great rejoicing; it would emphasize again the distinction between clergy and people. And as regards the tasks which have until now been performed exclusively by presbyters, one wonders whether it would not have been possible and

[10] Cf. p. 58 and the titles indicated in footnotes 3 and 4.

[11] Quite rightly, therefore, Vatican II did not decide to "reinstate" the diaconate, out of any sense of "unfaithfulness" to *Scripture*, which does show the existence of a diaconate in the early Church.

desirable to entrust them to a larger group of people, without attributing to this group a formal ministerial character. No answer has yet been found to this question.

In *Lumen gentium,* the diaconate is called a *lower* rank of the hierarchy. This is understandable, because it is envisaged as an auxiliary presbyterate, intended primarily to make up for the shortage of priests. It is perhaps worth noting that this kind of legal subordination to the presbyterate, while not impossible, is not necessary. As history shows, the diaconate can also be a direct participation in the episcopal functions. One would even gather from Acts that chronologically, the diaconate was the first participation in the apostolic function, and not a "lower" form of presbyterate; it is certain that later the deacons often constituted their own *collegium* directly around the bishop. This could also be possible and desirable in the future.

All in all, one may say that the "new" diaconate, however useful it may prove to be in the practical pastoral field, is rather green fruit from a theological point of view.

The traditional theology of the ministry states that episcopate, presbyterate, and diaconate are functions "of divine right." This does not mean that the three functions were explicitly instituted by the Lord, and that their institution can be demonstrated from Scripture. All it can mean is that at a certain moment in history, the ecclesiastical community was convinced that this specific branch of the ministry constituted a suitable instrument to promote the work of the Lord. However, the suitability is largely determined by the moment of history. Other times may require a different type of ministry. It is only for the episcopate that the "divine right" seems to be a more valid claim, because sociologically, and therefore theologically also, the representation of the Lord must necessarily have a culminating point.[12]

[12] Cf. footnote 1 on p. 96.

10. VOCATION, APOSTOLIC SUCCESSION, SACRAMENT OF ORDERS

An appointment to ecclesiastical office, whatever its nature, is a specifically ecclesiastical event. For the Lord of the Church becomes present in a special manner in the minister. That is why all Christian communities that have a form of special ministry have a ritual formalizing and celebrating the appointment. That is also why the extent to which it can be established with certainty that a minister truly and validly enjoys ministerial authority is being scrutinized everywhere. The rites, theories, and legal rules will vary, and different concepts will play their part as well: a ministry constituted "from above" or "from below," more closely bound to the fundamental given of the common priesthood, or more detached from it. This is tantamount to saying that the matters discussed in the present section have a markedly ecumenical aspect. This is true of the whole theology of the ministry, but more particularly so of questions concerning the sacramental character of ordination and the content of the concept of the apostolic succession. At the same time, we can suppose that nowadays, when the churches are once again striving for a form of unity, the controversy on these points will not prove as bitter as in earlier times, when a more antithetic system of discussion prevailed in theology. The growing unity of the Churches presupposes a growing consensus of theologians on the concept of the ministry. The Reformation need no longer fear that "Rome" neglects the common priesthood, and "Rome" may find nowadays that the Reformation has adopted a more positive attitude toward the special ministry than used to be feared.

The vocation

No one takes the honor of the ministry on himself, as the Epistle to the Hebrews tells us (5:4-6). As Aaron was called by

God, and Christ made a priest by the Father, so also the ecclesiastical minister does not choose God, but God chooses him, (cf. Jn 15:16). Whatever the manner of the call, whether it is made directly and exclusively by other ministers, or more indirectly in answer to recommendations made by the whole people of God, the voice of those who call is the voice of the Lord.

The call occurs in dialogue form. The invitation is made, the person invited answers and makes himself available. That does not exclude a certain initiative on the part of the latter; he can, long before he is formally called, already feel himself invited and offer his services: to want to be a presiding elder is to want to do a noble work, says the First Epistle to Timothy (3:1). A debate went on about half a century ago that today seems rather academic, but is nevertheless worth recalling.[1] In popular opinion, the feeling of an individual that he was called was the most striking element in the whole vocation process, and it led to the question whether a "right" to ordination could be deduced from this experience. The answer had to be negative. The very word *call* implies that there can be no question of any one-way traffic. Furthermore, it is precisely the service character of the ecclesiastical office and its collegial structure which demand a probing of and adjusting to the wishes of the community. It is impossible, in the ecclesiastical ministry, just "to start on one's own"; the personal desire for the ministry must receive assent and confirmation.

The service character of the ministry, which is service to the ecclesiastical community, also implies that the vocation dialogue should not be seen only as an interpersonal event occurring between God and one man. The ecclesiastical community is involved, and one can even say that its voice and that of God are largely identical, never forgetting, of course, that God is free to call whom he wills and sometimes breaches the line of

---

[1] Cf. J. Lahitton, *La Vocation sacerdotale* (Paris, 1914); A Mulders, *La Vocation au Sacerdoce* (Bruges, 1925); W. Stockums, *Der Beruf zum Priestertum* (Freiburg, 1934).

the established order and prevailing expectations. One can even say that the vocation to the ministry has *per se* a communal aspect, inasmuch as the ministry is a public office. This also accounts for the pressure sometimes exerted on candidates and the pursuit of an active recruitment policy. The histories of Jeremiah and Ambrose show that refusal and fear might have to be overcome at the beginning.

To bring about a vocation, those who already belong to the ministry and the whole community of the faithful both have a part to play. The degree of influence of either group changes. During the very early centuries, one often notes a fairly strong influence of the whole ecclesiastical community: they nominate the candidates, and their proposal is then confirmed by the imposition of hands performed by the ministers. In Acts 1:15-26, we see that Peter specifies the general qualifications required of the successor to Judas Iscariot, that the whole congregation nominated two candidates, and that the one on whom the lot fell "was listed as one of the twelve apostles"; nothing is said about consecration ceremonials or formal installation. The choice of deacons is also done jointly by the apostles and the disciples; the apostles confirm the selection by the laying on of hands (Acts 6:1-6). And when, at the end of the Council of Jerusalem, the decisions must be made known to Antioch, the whole community chooses the delegates (Acts 15:22). On the other hand, it would seem from the pastoral letters that Timothy and Titus were fairly independent in the management of their congregation and could appoint ministers. Later, choice and appointment of candidates became more and more a matter left to the ministers themselves—in particular, to the bishop—although to this day, the community may have a negative word to say: in the ordination liturgy, they are invited to state objections against a candidate. As regards the future, therefore, it is not at all unthinkable that the community of the faithful should again enjoy a greater say in this matter. In recent years several inquiries have been made to find out prevailing wishes, in order to guide the choice of candidates to the episcopate.

Meanwhile, it seems to be fairly unanimously held that the actual assignment of ministerial responsibilities should be made through those who are already in the ministry, or at least with their consent. This brings us to the second point we have to consider.

Apostolic succession

As we saw in the preceding section, any ecclesiastical ministry is connected with the sending of the apostles. Hence the requirement that every minister, if he is to enjoy true ministerial power and be recognized as a representative of the Lord, must stand in the line of the apostolic succession.[2]

This belief is common to all Christian communities. However, numerous and serious disputes have arisen throughout the ages concerning the actual manner in which the link is established. Caught in a situation of estrangement and faction, the Churches claimed each to "possess" the apostolic succession, and in the course of the controversy, often even doubted one another's title to being a Church. One of the causes of this sorry dissension, often due to jurists more than to theologians, is undoubtedly the fact that Scripture gives no very clear indication as to the "technique" of succession, and the fact also that, with the passage of time, the true story of certain separations and schisms became more and more difficult to reconstruct.

A solution to this difficult problem will be found only when it is realized that the matter is not strictly juridical, but primarily theological, and also when the ministry, rather than be considered as an isolated given, is continuously and consistently

[2] Cf. H. Küng, *The Church* (New York, 1966), pp. 354-359, 441-442; N. Lash, "Priestershap, kerkelijk ambt en intercommunie," *Tijdschrift voor Theologie*, 7 (1967), pp. 105-126; see in particular pp. 116-121. For a number of recent articles on apostolic succession, see *Concilium*, 4 (1968), no. 1, pp. 5-107.

studied in the context of the whole of the ecclesiastical life within which it functions.

The Church as a whole is a continuation of the Church of the apostles, and therefore, any Church that has not clearly surrendered a fundamental belief in the Christian confession has an apostolic character. The apostolic character does not disappear automatically and completely if a schism is the result more of juridical and emotional developments and dissensions than of an essential difference in the understanding of the faith. In all the communities in which one finds a true measure of existence as a Church, the word of Christ is indeed proclaimed, true worship is rendered, and guidance is given in the name of Christ. The gift of the ministry is a gift to the Church as a whole, and only after that, a gift to a specific person. Therefore, when in *Lumen gentium* (#15) and in the decree on ecumenism *Unitatis redintegratio* (#3), other communities are recognized as real Churches because the Lord has not withdrawn his Spirit from them, it follows that one must also admit that a real form of ministry exists in these Churches, linked to the office of the apostles. By making the continuation of the ministry depend completely and solely on a correct interpretation of a rite devised by men, one runs the risk of suppressing the Spirit (1 Th 5:19). That Spirit is not bound by the unbroken character of a "genealogy" of bishops; he channels continuity in ways the rigid reasoning of men knows little about. Worthy of mention perhaps in this connection is the procedure applied in papal elections. After the death of a pope, a certain time elapses before there is a new one; there is a gap in the exercise of the ministerial function, and the preceding pope does not hand over his office directly to his successor. The papal power "lives again" after that, through the medium, once more, of the community which chooses a new pope. One may assume therefore that during the interregnum the whole community is the bearer of the highest apostolic office; for it is not reasonable, but a sort of mythologizing of the papal office, to say that a mission is given "purely from above" to each new successor.[3] These ideas can also be applied to other ministries.

This is not to deny that the use of an installation ceremonial manifesting the continuity of the apostolic succession is generally desirable. As a visible community, the Church needs it; a perceptible ritual will give her the assurance that the newly appointed servant truly belongs in the line of succession to the authentic ministry. On the other hand, it would be overestimating the ceremonial to think that unevenness and changes in it could deprive the Church of the ministry. Or course, there must be a moral certainty that a Church which transmits the office is pneumatically and vitally linked to the primitive apostolic community. As this moral certainty varies, so will the "degrees of certainty" of the apostolic succession. In the case of schisms that did not really challenge any fundamental belief in apostolic doctrine, like the split between East and West during the eleventh century, there is no reason to doubt the presence of an authentic ecclesiastical ministry. When this certitude is lacking, partly or wholly, as in the case of the sixteenth-century break, the apostolic quality of the ministry becomes more dubious. The zero mark, however, is reached only when one can no longer reasonably speak at all of the existence of any actual church. Within a certain Church, therefore, the apostolic quality can fluctuate: in times of decline in doctrine and dynamism, it is weak, but grows during periods of reawakening, and the process also governs the possibilities of ecumenism.

Nor should it be forgotten that changes in emphasis as re-

[3] "Pope Paul VI is *successor Petri* and not *successor Johannis XXIII*. He follows John historically, but not formally; that would have required a (legal) transfer of authority. The terms *successio in locum Petri* must therefore be understood in an exemplary sense: as Peter functioned as prototype in the *collegium apostolorum*, so functions Paul in the college of bishops . . . for the Church—the Body of Christ, obeying in faith her glorified Head—concentrates herself in the person of the *successor Petri*, who thus 'receives' his power from the Church, not as a delegation, but by way of a personification of the corporate consensus of the *Ecclesia vicaria Christi*." F. v. Beeck, "Thoughts on an Ecumenical Understanding of the Sacraments," *Journal of Ecumenical Studies*, 3 (1966), pp. 57-112.

gards the three main divisions of the ministerial functions also play a part. Insist on the cultic aspects of the ministry and on the need for the active presence of a minister in order to "validate" the celebrations of the sacraments, and you may find the gap between Churches deepening under the stress of doubts and misunderstandings. That is why Churches that emphasize the sacraments usually find it more difficult to admit of any real ecclesiastical ministry in others.[4] The same applies to Churches that set great store by hierarchical structure and uniformity in doctrine and discipline. Here, efforts at intercommunion are usually up against serious theological and psychological difficulties. But Churches with a ministry more concerned with prophecy can more easily recognize that ministers from other communions also perform real ministerial work. Now that many Churches are changing "from priest to prophet," further possibilities may be found for a *rapprochement* between different communions and recognition of their respective ministries.

Finally, it is also clear that the trend toward a declericalization of the ecclesiastical ministry influences the understanding of the apostolic succession. For once the separation of clergy and people—itself the result of historical developments—has disappeared and the consequences of a fresh insight into the common priesthood have been faced, it will become apparent that the apostolic quality is primarily a distinguishing mark of the whole community, and that it ranks second only as a functional qualification of particular activities of the Church.

Taking contemporary developments into consideration, one may expect and hope that the problem of apostolic succession will gradually be solved, and a situation reached in which the legal aspects of the succession will be considered only of sec-

[4] This seems to apply, for instance, to the question of the validity of orders in the Anglican Churches. The encyclical *Apostolicae curae* of 1896 denies their validity almost exclusively on the basis of a variant understanding of the sacrificial character of the Eucharist. Even if the argument was valid—the historical reconstruction is very difficult—it would still be open to question whether all forms of real ministry are thereby eliminated.

ondary importance, of interest to experts in the history of law and liturgy rather than to theologians.

The Sacrament of Orders

The call to any form of ministry is an important event for those who are called, as well as for the community that calls. The person who is called acquires a new position in the community, and thereby enters into a different, qualified relationship with the Lord of the Church. And the ecclesiastical community fulfills itself again because it opens up new possibilities for ecclesiastical service to the world. It is therefore entirely comprehensible that, toward the end of the first millennium, when the more or less exclusive name of sacraments was bestowed on certain ritual occurrences in the Church, hardly any doubt prevailed as to qualifying the consecration to the ecclesiastical ministry in this category.

It is a known fact that the history of dogma shows considerable fluctuation as regards the use of the word *sacrament*.[5] During the first centuries, all facts and happenings that manifested God's work for the salvation of men were called *mustèrion-sacramentum*. The events occurred in the numinous and always somewhat mystical sphere of the contact of God and man, conversion from sin to sanctity, orientation toward a still nebulous eschaton, and awareness of the Lord's presence. Out of these numerous events of the economy of salvation, a few came to stand out in which it was felt that the Savior was active in a special and explicit manner. From the twelfth century on, their number is put at seven, in the East as in the West, and it remained unchanged until the Reformation. In a sense, Luther was a victim of this narrowing of the sacramental concept. He was unable to trace the origin of the seven sacraments to the Bible and establish their institution by Christ himself, from

[5] Cf. E. Schillebeeckx, *De Sacramentele Heilseconomie* (Antwerpen, 1952), vol. 1. See also *Concilium*, 4 (1968), no. 1, pp. 5-140.

which he concluded that he must deny the sacramental character of five of the traditional seven. In response, but at the same time adhering to the same narrow concept, the Council of Trent found itself obliged to maintain the number and declare that the origin of the seven sacraments lay in their explicit institution by Christ himself. Such a debate cost the exegetes any number of headaches.

In recent years, the theologians are once more using the concept in a broader sense, closer to the language of the Fathers. Vatican II adopted this language and sanctioned its use. *Lumen gentium* states in several places that the Church, the milieu in which the seven sacraments are situated, is herself the sacrament, the sign and means of union with God (#1 and #9), and hence Christ, the living token of God's grace, is also called "the Sacrament of the Encounter with God." [6] The need to found the institution of every single sacrament on Scripture thus becomes smaller:

From the principle that the Church is the primal sacrament it would be possible to see that the existence of true sacraments in the strictest traditional sense is not necessarily and always based on definite statement, which has been preserved or is presumed to have existed, in which the historical Jesus Christ explicitly spoke about a certain definite sacrament. This would have its importance for apologetics of a less anxious and worried kind in the history of dogma, in the matter of the institution of all the sacraments by Christ. A fundamental act of the Church in an individual's regard, in situations that are decisive for him, an act which truly involves the nature of the Church as the historical, eschatological presence of redemptive grace, is *ipso facto* a sacrament, even if it were only later that reflection was directed to its sacramental character that follows from its connection with the nature of the Church. The institution of a sacrament can (it is not necessarily implied that it must always) follow simply from

[6] Cf. E. Schillebeeckx, *Christ the Sacrament of the Encounter with God* (New York, 1963).

the fact that Christ founded the Church with its sacramental nature.[7]

This general principle can be applied to the sacrament of orders. Ordination is an important act of self-actualization of the Church in a situation simultaneously important and determining for the individual. In the ordination service, the Church is present as primal sacrament in a singularizing activity; that is why ordination is a sacrament. It is on this basis that Vatican II explicitly named episcopal consecration a sacramental event (*Lumen gentium,* #21), whereas it had until then been considered mainly as a bestowal of jurisdiction—even though this hardly tallied with the clearly ordaining character of the episcopal consecration ritual. Of course, there was no question of denying thereby the sacramental nature of the ordination of presbyters. The sacrament of orders has several forms: episcopal, presbyterial, and also diaconal. Traditionally, a sacramental character has also been attributed to the consecration of deacons, although usually seen as a sort of partial anticipation of the presbyteral consecration; obviously, the new broader understanding of the sacraments demands a recognition of the fully sacramental nature of consecration to the diaconate; it would, after all, be a little odd to go on saying that deacons, and particularly those who do not become priests, have received only "half" a sacrament. By the same token, all the new patterns of ministry that the future might bring could also be termed sacramental. Some may fear that this would lead to an inflationary use of the idea of sacrament. The danger is not wholly imaginary, but it can be avoided by remembering always that the phrase *sacrament of orders* should be used exclusively in the case of a call to functions that are definitely ministerial in the strict sense of the word, and not to a performance of inherent tasks of the common priesthood.

The broadening of our understanding of the sacrament also

[7] K. Rahner, *The Church and the Sacraments* (New York, 1963), p. 41.

affects the ecumenical discussion of the ministry. The question of the institution of the sacrament *directly* by Christ may be set aside as irrelevant.[8] It is enough to say that as long as a ministry, distinctly recognizable as such, functions in any church, that ministry is also sacramental in nature. There may be honest doubt sometimes as to the fullness of apostolic succession, and there may then be talk of a defective ministry and a defective sacrament. That, however, is a more prudent position and a more positive attitude than an unqualified denial of any authenticity and sacramental value. An unqualified rejection not only produces all-or-nothing attitudes, which preclude any true conversation, it would also fail to show any mature theological insight.

One can apply to the sacramental consecration to the ministry all that is said of the other sacraments. It is a concentrated cultic performance of the Church, and the Lord of the Church makes it a sacrifice acceptable to the Father. The Church, in consecrating a person from her midst to the explicit service of the kingdom of God, in this person consecrates herself to her task in this world. On the other hand, through this sacramental happening, the Lord of the Church becomes present again in his community, and the consecrated minister in particular meets his Lord in a new sanctifying relationship. That is why the ministry is a charism, a blessing by the Spirit, and the minister a charismatic person. Ministry and charism are not opposites, but the ministry is one of the several ways in which the Spirit of the Lord is present in the Church. On the basis of 1 Corinthians 12-14, it is correctly held that the charism of the ministry also implies supervising the other, nonministerial charismata, but the supervision is exercised exclusively with a view to harmo-

---

[8] A side remark, with some bearing on ecumenism, however: Maundy Thursday is traditionally considered as the day of the institution of the ministry because it was then that the apostles were enjoined to commemorate the Lord. It would be wise to realize that the celebration of the Last Supper constitutes a very important part of the ministry, but not the whole of it. The special ministry is much more than the mandate to celebrate the Eucharist.

nizing, and must never lead to thinking in terms of competition. For the ministry is entrusted with the task of supervision only because it is itself a charism and as such transcends its own given structural, legal character. The ministry is a true ministry only when it looses itself in the charismatic. Whoever is prepared to see the ministry as a charism will also realize that to place the ministerial Church and the charismatic church in opposition is wrong, for the disharmony that does in fact exist is no more than human failure, to be explained on historical and psychological grounds. Either the ministry overestimates itself and starts controlling the other charismata too strictly, with the ensuing risk of suppressing the Spirit (1 Th 5:19), or the "free" charismata overestimate themselves and refuse to be integrated in the unity of the undivided Church (cf. Rom 12:3-8; 1 Cor 12: 4-11 and 28-31; Eph 4:11-16).

11. A PRIEST, AND FOREVER?

In the future messianic kingdom, the people of God of the Old Covenant believed, everything would be recovered that was lost through the sins of the fathers: peace and concord in nature, freedom and prosperity, final conquest of enemies, brotherhood among men. And all these blessings—after all the ups and downs experienced in actual history—would be continuous and lasting. Of course, this promise of everlasting happiness was systemized in and symbolized by the person of the Messiah who would reign forever over his people. That is why Psalm 110 attributed to the Lord and Son of David kingship and priesthood encompassing heaven and earth, all times and places, the past and the future, and forever. The royal house of David was itself too unstable to guarantee the realization of this future, but it was known that Yahweh had appointed it as the successor of the kings of old Canaan. And therefore a royal priesthood was ascribed to the Messiah, "of the order of Melchisedec," the legendary king of Salem to whom Abraham paid tithe after his victory over the Palestinian kings allied against him (Gen 14).

The author of the Epistle to the Hebrews, wishing to bring out that the priesthood of Christ surpasses that of the old order, again picks up this theme. It is handled as a kind of Midrash and brings Melchisedec on the scene as the prototype of the everlasting high priest: "He has no father or mother or ancestry, and his life has no beginning or ending; he is like the Son of God. He remains a priest forever" (Heb 7:3).

The special ecclesiastical ministry is a particular form of participation in the ministry of Christ, and therefore a true ministry. But because it is service to the Church "between the times," we should ask whether the permanent character ascribed to the priesthood of the Lord may be attributed also to this ministry of the Church on earth. We need to find out what traditional theology means, or can mean, by "indelible sacramental marks," what the community of the faithful intends when telling their neophytes, "You are a priest forever," and what is the scope of the liturgical, juridical statement that a consecration to the ministry can never be repeated. Are these statements and procedures based on a clear and sound theological proposition, or are they optional historical and pastoral practices?

The doctrine of a sacramental mark does not belong exclusively and uniquely to the Christian Church. The marking of certain persons and things in order to show dependence or possession is a common, widespread human practice. Money is stamped, slaves and cattle are branded, and religious allegiance to a divinity or expulsion from a community is shown in the same manner. We see in the Old Testament how Yahweh put a mark on Cain to protect him (Gen 4:15), and how the Jew is proud of a circumcision that marks him as one of a people whom God chose and to whom he promised a multitudinous offspring (see e.g., Is 44:5 and Ezk 9:3-6). In the New Covenant, these markings in the flesh are changed into pneumatic marks through the baptism which introduces into the new people of God (Jn 6:27; 2 Cor 1:21; Eph 1:13 and 4:30; Heb 1:3; Apoc 7:2-8). Whoever receives baptism is permanently consecrated to God, and even if he breaks faith completely, this primal call is never cancelled. Later, when baptism and confirmation became separated, a mark was also attributed to the latter, through which the two sacraments remained clearly linked together.

Actually this sphragistic character of initiation was never seriously questioned in the Christian Churches, although in times of crisis—like the fourth-century controversy on the baptism of heretics—the validity of baptism could be subject to doubt. One result of these disputes was that the baptismal mark, primarily of a religious and ethical character in Scripture, sometimes came to be interpreted in a rather strict juridical sense.

The person who is called and consecrated to the ecclesiastical ministry also receives a mark of consecration. The whole community recognizes in him someone who belongs to the Lord in a particular manner. The belonging bears an ethical and religious as well as a more legal stamp, because the sacrament of orders is both a charismatic gift to the person and a mandate to act with authority in the visible and structured community.

As regards this spontaneously admitted given of a sphragis, theology puts the marks of baptism and confirmation, and that of ordination, usually on the same level. Augustine calls them two forms of consecration, of devotion to God, and Thomas Aquinas claims that they are two participations in the priesthood of Christ.[1] However accurate in themselves, these formulations do not show sufficient awareness of the idea that baptism and confirmation constitute the basis of Christian existence, but ordination is only a functional specialization of the Christian mission in life. Neglect of this concept led Bona-

[1] Augustine, *Conta Epist. Parmen.*, l.II, c.xiii, n.28 (P.L. 43, 69); Thomas, *Summa Theologica*, III, q. 63, art. 6; q. 66, art. 3 ad 5.

venture to advocate a classification of the degrees of faith; he says that the three marks correspond to a threefold *status fidei: genitae, roboratae, et multiplicatae* (originating, strengthening, and multiplying).[2] The idea is indefensible; it transforms the ministry into a life situation and also suggests that this ministerial status possesses a higher degree of holiness, and stands for a more intensive form of Christian life.

The somewhat facile equalization of the various marks, coupled with the neglect of the difference between the life situation of being a Christian and the ministerial function, has also contributed to making all marks equally lasting. Just as a person was always a Christian, he was also a minister forever. Many theological and ecclesiastical statements on this matter were in a strongly apologetic vein, particularly in the post-Reformation period. Where the Reformation abolished the special ministry, the minister became a layman again, and when in condemning such a step, which could hardly be seen as other than dereliction of duty and heresy (the heresy, of course, of rejecting the special ministry), it was pointed out that a call to the ministry not only could not be terminated one-sidedly, but could not entirely disappear. This is clear, for instance, from the pronouncements of the Council of Trent (sessio VII and XIII; Denz. 852, 960, 964), with its markedly legalistic distinction between minister and layman which failed to bring out that the minister as a person is also a layman. Add to this also—one can see it in particular in Trent's profession of faith (Denz. 996)—widespread cogitation on the proposition that the administration of the sacraments of baptism, confirmation, and orders *may not* be repeated, because repetition would be sacrilegious (cf. also C.I.C., Canon 732).

The opening prayer of the liturgy for a deceased priest reads: "Receive, we implore you, Lord, the sacrifice which we offer for the soul of Your servant N., a priest. In this world You raised

[2] Bonaventura, *IV Sent.*, I.4, dist. 6, p. 1, q. 1.

him to the honor of the priesthood . . ." This text expresses
the conviction that the "perpetuity" of the ministry does not in
any case last longer than the present aeon. This belief is not
simply negative, an admission of our ignorance of what the
end will be, it also has a scriptural and theological foundation.
The minister's task consists in representing the Lord while he
is not with us. But once the Lord has returned, the representation becomes unnecessary because we shall see the Lord "face
to face." Once the Lord is again in our midst, it will no longer
be necessary to remember him as absent; the Eucharistic offer
"in memory" need only proclaim the Lord's death "until the
Lord comes" (1 Cor 11:23-26). The sacrament of penance need
be administered only until the Lamb has finally conquered and
there is no more sin, and no more death as the wages of sin
(cf. Apoc 21:4). The word of man is no longer necessary when
the Word of God is back among us. And the authority of the
apostolic ministry will be replaced by him upon whom the Father bestowed everlasting kingship. Because the Church will
have reached fulfillment in that new aeon, those charismata
will disappear which the Spirit granted in order to build her.
For "if there are gifts of prophecy, the time will come when they
must fail; or the gift of languages, it will not continue for ever;
and knowledge—for this, too, the time will come when it must
fail. For our knowledge is imperfect and our prophesying is imperfect; but once perfection comes, all imperfect things will disappear" (1 Cor 13:8-10).

The minister will no longer be needed in the exercise of his
specific function; he will become a layman once more, a member
of the holy people. The heavenly liturgy possibly has an honorary role in store for him, something like the role so piously fore-
seen by the author of the Apocalypse for the twenty-four elders
(4:4 and 10-11). But he will no longer be indispensable.

Whoever has become a member of God's people through baptism remains that forever. Even if he should for his part cut the

bonds of faith, if he should deny his past, the voice of God has sounded for him, he has been called to a Christian life, the blood of the Lamb has been shed for him. Saved or damned, he is a Christian forever, now and later.

The exercise of the ecclesiastical ministry is, however, restricted in many ways. The limits are set by the physical and moral possibilities of the individual minister and the requirements of the community. The community calls him when it has need of him, and if at that time he is not entirely prepared and fit, it gives him a possibility to develop further until he fully answers the requirements. This same community also dismisses him. Rarely will there be such an abundance of manpower that a certain number must be discharged, but there are cases when a person is no longer fit for the work (sickness, loss of mental faculties, loss of the social acceptability required for the exercise of his function), and like everyone else, ministers reach the age of retirement. No minister can object to discharge on these grounds. In addition, a minister may also hand in his own resignation, not only to obtain an early retirement, but also for other reasons which are valid for himself. The community and its leaders must not reject such a request out of hand, because the personal well-being of an individual carries more weight than their needs.

We shall, in a later section, go further into the question of leaving the ministry.[3] It is enough to point out here that, in the earthly Church being a minister is not necessarily a permanent role. That a person should remain a minister all his life is apparently more a socio-historical *de facto* phenomenon than a theological necessity.

That the sacrament of orders is in fact never administered again is a firmly established datum of sacramental discipline, but theological principles as to why this is impossible in itself are not really clear. One may suppose, therefore, that the texts of the Council of Trent mentioned earlier constitute a record of exist-

[3] Cf. Part II, section 17, pp. 181 and ff.

ing practice, rather than strictly theological pronouncements.

An awareness of the difference between a fundamental aptitude and its actual exercise might shed further light upon the question of the "non-repeatable" quality of the sacrament of orders: a person who has received the sacrament of orders may at a given moment be appointed to a field in which he can actualize his potential qualification. The parallelism with other sectors of social life is obvious: a person who has passed his law examinations can be called to the judiciary, the one who has qualified as a teacher can be called to teach, etc. Let us recall the distinction made above, between *being* and *doing*,[4] and the interconnection between the two: a person remains an engineer even if he has taken a post in the diplomatic service; a person remains a minister even if he seldom or never exercises his ecclesiastical ministry. The case of the minister emeritus perhaps explains the matter best: his established "tenure" has expired, but his essential qualifications for the ministry remain as before and can from time to time be applied if the community requests it. Perhaps one can say that a modified form of difference between sacred and jurisdictional authority can be shown here.[5] It would then only be in connection with the sacred power that one could speak of a permanent quality. Furthermore, it would then become more a question of language and personal feeling when someone whose sacred power is seldom or never actualized still says that he *is* a minister. From the point of view of the theological content of the question, there is finally no difference between the minister emeritus and the minister who has been laicized for other reasons. In cases more closely defined by Church law, both may be recalled to ministerial duties.

In conclusion, we may say that the concept of the ministerial mark must not be rejected out of hand, but that it should be restudied in the light of a fresh theological understanding of the ministry, so as to become actualistic or operational rather than

[4] Cf. pp. 85-87.
[5] Cf. p. 98.

fundamentalist. We might add that theology should compare the marks of ordination not with those of baptism and confirmation, but with the more actualistic sacramental status resulting from the reception of the sacraments of marriage and penance.

In connection with our inquiry into the lasting character of ordination, we should like to submit a few comments on the phenomenon of the so-called *part-time minister*. To begin with, we can say that it has existed from the days of the tent-maker Paul, and continues with the priest-professor and the pastor-emeritus who still hears confession from time to time. We could even go further and suggest that a comprehensive analysis of function would show the existence of some form of part-time ministry in the majority of cases, because the majority of ministers do a great deal of work that is not, strictly speaking, ministerial.

One gets the impression that the present part-time ministry is being justified on the grounds of an emergency caused either by the absence of laymen or by a shortage of ministers. The first of these two reasons seems particularly strange, but it is true. It would be preferable to have the minister completely free to carry out specifically ecclesiastical functions, but because certain social or ecclesiastical activities emerged, for which no laymen were readily available or qualified, ministers were taken away from their proper task. This occurs especially in pioneer situations, teaching, or the care of the sick. A social need produces an abridged ministry. The other form of part-time ministry is now often advocated on the basis of situations of a complementary kind; since there is a shortage of full-time ministers which, it seems, cannot be remedied at the present time, the possibility is being explored of using as auxiliary ministers people who are engaged in other activities, and have them appointed to a kind of week-end presbyterate.

It is not the theologian's business to decide on the practical use of such emergency solutions. But he may well wonder whether the reasoning that prompts them does not proceed too readily from a belief that the ministry should, ideally, be full-time, a position he cannot accept. His own theological findings, on the contrary, might lead him to argue that it is desirable to have as many part-time ministers as possible. The fact that all ecclesiastical work is a service to the world is especially significant here, and also the firm belief that the unity of God's people is best served by reducing to a minimum the differentiation between layman and minister.

It is, after all, the common task of layman and minister to awaken a consciousness of the religious dimension of human existence and, for its own enrichment, to relativize the claims of the world. The task proper to the ministry is indirect, as we have already seen: internal ecclesiastical service to all those who are engaged in apostolic secularity. But when Christians who are also ministers are given the exclusive task of performing internal ecclesiastical activities, the faithful themselves, as well as outsiders, can easily come to feel that these activities make up the supreme ecclesiastical function and that those who perform it constitute the nucleus of the Church. Making ministers a distinctly exclusive group is liable to dim the right understanding how one is to live as a Christian, and to put too great an emphasis on "not being of this world."

An "unadulterated" minister will arouse little interest among most citizens of "the secular city." They may respect him for the enthusiasm with which he delivers his message and for the pious dedication he displays, but he will succeed in gripping them, or have them listen to his message, only if he can be seen as a fellowman who actively and positively promotes human welfare, neither denying nor underestimating it. The man who seems to know about nothing but church will figure at best as a pleasant luxury, a holy outsider, the keeper of an ecclesiastical reservation which one visits merely for its value as folklore, or to relax.

The theologian may therefore express his suspicion that a

part-time minister is not less productive because he is in some measure taken from his own work by "worldly" occupations, but rather that in this way his service to the world might be of better quality. The part-time minister has of course left his rectory and lives as a servant in the house of secular man. It is only because he is admitted as a cohabitant that he has the opportunity to point to the relative character of values, to remind his fellow man that more things lie between heaven and earth than can be seen within the horizon of any earthly human philosophy. Every Christian is a "nuisance value" in the world, a trying person because he shows the relativity of the earthly and thereby unsettles all that is taken for granted, and this is of course particularly true of the minister. But the city of man considers a nuisance value productive only insofar as it is accompanied by a fundamentally positive attitude toward the earthly. It is perhaps not entirely by accident that the great ministers, honored everywhere, are not the full-time liturgists, preachers, and Church administrators, but people who played an active role in science, education, and social work: Vincent de Paul, Don Bosco, Abbé Pierre, Copernicus, Mendel, and Teilhard de Chardin could quite rightly be described as part-time ministers.

The call to the ecclesiastical ministry inescapably means that a person is invited to give up, at least in part, his apostolic secular work. But this renunciation does not follow *from the nature of things,* and the fact that many ministers devote themselves to a large extent to the exercise of their specific ministry is not a theological necessity, but merely a matter of organization and practical pastoral management. The only criterion is the manner in which the Gospel will best be validated in this world. Therefore, when *Lumen gentium* (#31) says that "those in holy orders can at times engage in secular activities," it is stating a situation that has evolved throughout history, rather than appraising the need for or desirability of a continuation of this policy.

Here, too, it becomes clear that the expression "a priest forever" does not cover much of actual reality. For instance, to take an extreme case, when the strictly ministerial activity takes a few hours per year, one can still speak of an enduring call and mark, and the term *minister* still applies to a reality; but ordination is then really not much more than an additional qualification. If one would still claim that he performs all his activities "as minister," we wonder whether such language does not express a clerical overestimation of self which ascribes a more fundamental and more important value to being a minister than to being human and Christian. The work a Christian performs does not become more important for bearing the mark of the ministry.

12. THE PROFESSIONAL IMAGE OF THE ECCLESIASTICAL MINISTRY

Whoever is called to the ministry must answer certain requirements and possess certain skills; after ordination, he should reasonably justify the specified expectations. The person who is too uncertain about what he must do and how to proceed and who does not perform passably is doomed to failure; those to whom he is sent expect professional ability, and if it is lacking, they will find it hard to respect him and will hesitate to trust him. Besides, such a failure is bad publicity for the ministry; the person who is thinking of joining it and is weighing the pros and cons will hesitate all the more to commit himself to a function so uninspiringly exercised by others.

Let us now try to describe the essence of the professional image of the ecclesiastical ministry. We shall have to consider whether and how far this image compares with that of other professions and functions, while bearing in mind what has been established in the foregoing sections about the specific character of the ministry.

The human sciences of sociology and psychology teach us

that many factors are involved in the choice of a profession. Are the requisite qualifications present, do the technical and financial possibilities permit getting the training for the profession? But the important question is, naturally, the degree of satisfaction that can be derived from the profession; it is a matter of more external factors such as remuneration, the extent of free time left after work, and the possibility of keeping function and private life separate, but also of factors directly connected with the work itself, such as possibilities of promotion, enjoyment of the work, and the social status of the profession. The person who is at all free to choose his profession will not easily be led to select one that has many inconveniences to offer and rather one-sided elements of satisfaction. According to the degree of equalization of the distribution of income and wealth, greater emphasis is put on the social recognition granted to a specific function. It is precisely at this point that the image of the various professions differs, and their name projects the difference: we speak of jobs, professions, functions, and offices. Work that can be done by poorly gifted and none too literate people appeals less to the imagination than a function requiring long theoretical and practical training and of which the exercise is surrounded by an atmosphere of authority and complexity, of indivisible responsibility and great professional skill.

These approximations of the behavioral sciences can tell us several things about the ecclesiastical ministry. It can be said, for instance, that the ecclesiastical ministry rates as a leading profession, affording a certain measure of comfort and social security, to which a person is admitted only after careful selection and long training, and which confers great responsibilities and very special, even rather mysterious, powers. To this must be added at once that the ecclesiastical ministry seems to be suffering from a certain loss of status, for reasons both psychological and sociological. There are now many more possibilities, and consequently the competition is greater: whereas before, at least in some areas ecclesiastical ministers constituted the leading class along with civic officials, doctors, and attorneys. There are now many more highly qualified top officials with a better education and a comfortable standard of living, such as authorities in the municipal administration, leaders of industry, and personalities in the field of education, scientific, social, and cultural work. By comparison with these numerous other functions, the ecclesiastical ministry is not particularly impressive, granting even that religion is still considered important in the life of a human society.

The loss of status is also connected with the fact that as the professional work of men becomes more specialized and the *homo universalis* disappears, we are puzzled to see the ecclesiastical minister perform so many different tasks: liturgy, preaching, religious education, business management and administration, personal spiritual guidance, social and psychological counselling of the sick and the hale, the young, the adults, and the elderly. The complicated range of the activities actually carried out by ministers calls up almost a priori an image of amateurism, because it is difficult to conceive that training for the ministry—which, after all, is fairly short—can produce satisfactory expert authorities in all these fields. And a critical look at the facts often confirms the suspicion: the ministry shows frequent cases of failure due to a lack of knowledge of theology and inadequate schooling in the techniques of sociology, psychology, teaching, management, and administration. The ministers themselves know this, and that is why they are increasingly asking for specialization. But others know it too; not only armchair critics, but people whose expert knowledge entitles them to judge.

Obviously, specialization must be taken seriously and faced as honestly as possible. But it will not solve the problem of the characteristic professional image of the ecclesiastical ministry. Only when we have solved this problem, can we ask *how* the professional image can be improved. In section 5, we found that the minister's activities have a special "charge": the avowed representation of the Lord of the Church, the *episkopè* exercised over the service of Christians in and to the world and the

Church. The minister is not the one who does "other things," but the person who, through his supervision, lends the stamp of authenticity to Christian activities in the world.

The crucial question, then, is whether the sociological concepts of expert authorities and professional image can be directly applied to the ecclesiastical ministry. If, materially, there are no properly ministerial acts, it becomes difficult to see the sense of any talk about expert authorities proficient in specific material acts. Not only does it seem fruitless, but it is perhaps even undesirable and likely to create confusion, because it suggests a differentiation between layman and minister that, theologically, is not valid. In other words: an indiscriminate use of sociological concepts is liable to clericalize certain activities pertaining to all Christians.

Another approach is needed for any really tenable and theologically significant discussion of the professional image of the ecclesiastical ministry. We could begin by noting that the intuition of faith has always shown respect for comparatively "stupid" ministers. All centuries have had rather incompetent bishops and presbyters, bad catechists, unbending liturgists, Church leaders without much feeling for the problems of the day, and amateurs bungling pastoral counseling. They are not the ideal, of course, and their kind have perhaps hindered more than helped the Church in her mission, but their behavior did not vitally affect their quality of being a minister. Whoever would make the presence of the Lord totally dependent on the "professional ability" of his representative profanes the ecclesiastical ministry and fails to appreciate its dimension of faith, and whoever does the reverse and sees the Lord of the Church directly active in every detail of the human ministerial performance mythologizes the ministry.

The intuition of faith senses that the minister who is not quite suitable nevertheless represents the Lord and is also convinced that it is better to have ministers who are far from brilliant than none at all. God needs men, and his work is not wholly dependent on the quality of the agent; he can, as the saying is, write straight with crooked lines. The professional image of the ecclesiastical ministry is, first, one of grace and mission, and only secondly is it one of professional ability and expert authority. As to ability, it is always possible in principle for the layman to be superior to the minister: he can be better grounded in theology and be more skilled didactically than many ministers who preach and give religious instruction; he may have a better sense of style, more imagination, and a greater gift of expression than many a person who is now a liturgist; he can have a keener feeling for pastoral guidance than the person by whom he is now being guided. But his place in the Church will always be different because he has not received the charism of the ministerial office. By virtue of his baptism and of the common priesthood, every Christian is called upon to proclaim the message of salvation, to celebrate the death of the Lord, and promote the welfare of the community of the faithful. The greater his technical skill, the more effectively he will perform his task, and the more right he will also have to be brought into the work of the Church. But for all his professional ability, however great, he always remains a nonminister. Professional ability and ecclesiastical ministerial authority are two entirely different matters.

Obviously, there is no denying that a certain measure of technical expertise should be requisite for receiving a ministerial function. That is precisely why so much thought has been and is being given to the quality of the training; it would be ill-advised indeed to consecrate someone who cannot reasonably be expected properly to fulfill his mission as a minister. But qualification is not the source of the ministerial mission, or of the ministerial authority; one does not become a minister owing simply to the fact that he has acquired a specified measure of technical skill. The formal characteristic of the ministry is not technical, but charismatic: the ministry comes "from above" and nestles in the professional ability; as a variation on an old theological maxim: the grace of the ministry presupposes a "natural" fitness, but rises above it; grace brings nature to completion, not by perfecting it on its own level, but by lifting it into another order of competence and service.

Any meaningful discussion of the part-time ministry must take into account the definition of ministerial expert authority given above. Ability is required also for this kind of mission, but it will not have to be as extensive, because the relevant tasks are more limited. This more circumscribed expert authority, however, need not endanger the part-timer's ministerial authority, because the primary source of the latter lies in the charismatic sending as man of God. One might perhaps even say that the part-time minister is in a somewhat more favorable situation as regards his social prestige. For the fact that, owing to his profane occupations, to his involvement in apostolic secularity, he already enjoys a social standing and possesses expert authority, makes it unnecessary, or even superfluous, for him to compete with other professions and offices on the basis of his being a minister: he no longer needs to prove, via his ecclesiastical ministry, that he is socially acceptable and useful fellowman. Rather, his ecclesiastical activity is reinforced by his social prestige, and this social prestige can prepare the way for his moments of ecclesiastical work. One could perhaps even venture to suppose that as more ecclesiastical ministers are recognized as expert authorities in profane matters, many status problems—and financial problems too!—will automatically disappear.

As we have just seen, the grace of the ministry presupposes natural fitness. Although it is perhaps superfluous to point this out again here, fitness implies a definite ensemble of technical qualifications without which a good execution of the ministerial work of the Church cannot be guaranteed. Ministerial activities also require a standard of efficiency: to admit to the ministry, or retain in it, persons who are manifestly unsuitable is not only indefensible from a professional point of view, but could also be a form of presumption. For the work of the ministry is never an isolated episode, but a distinctive accent on human Christian activities; and to achieve that, definite minimum requirements, however much they may vary, will be needed at all times.

But in addition to this more technical substratum another one is needed as well, we might call it religiosity: whoever represents the Lord of the Church, whoever comes before his fellowmen as commissioned, must also witness in his own life to belief in salvation. A vocation is meaningful for the ecclesiastical community only if it is assured that the person ordained to the ministry is grounded in the faith and takes a positive place in the community of the faithful. A nominal Christian cannot be a minister; nobody can be consecrated who is not truly concerned with the kingdom of heaven. The pro-existence of the Lord himself must be recognizable in the minister's person. The concrete form of this criterion is not easy to define, however, especially when so much that was for centuries considered obvious and immutable is now beginning to change. No one, for instance, will wish to dispute that the ecclesiastical minister must be orthodox in doctrine, respect Church regulations, and work jointly with colleagues and superiors. But this does not mean simply that it is his duty *per se* to maintain the *status quo* and uncritically to continue the historical situation he inherited. In an evolving Church, the ministerial function must, in the nature of things, also evolve; for in a changing Church, the insight into the content of the message of salvation addressed to the world also changes. The requirement of religiosity quite rightly set for the minister may develop from day to day. It is not unbecoming for a minister, therefore, to admit his incertitude or, even less so, to be nonconformist and "troublesome" from time to time. The necessary unity will be preserved if every minister, from the highest to the lowest, realizes that the ministerial charism is a collective gift made to the whole corps of ministers and that no individual minister may absolutize his personal ideas as to what is possible, useful, and necessary. Here we see again that the existence of collegiality is a necessary component of the image of "the" ecclesiastical ministry. It holds likewise that being a Christian in common is more fundamental than being a minister: the image of the ministry is a specification of the image of Christian existence.

13. WOMAN IN THE MINISTRY

In the third chapter of his short book *The New Reformation?*, John Robinson wonders whether the Church of today is correct in maintaining the traditional lines of demarcation which divide the ministry from the laity in the whole community of the faithful.[1] They remind him of trenches left over from yesterday's war. He devotes special attention to three of these lines: the clergy line, the professional line, and the sex line. The clergy line draws a functional distinction between minister and layman which extends to one's personal way of life and life situation; in section 8 we tried to show that this division is not very important, theologically or pastorally, and need not be maintained in its traditional form. The professional line converts the ecclesiastical ministry into a specialized profession which can apparently be exercised only by highly qualified full-time practitioners; it has been shown several times in our study (but particularly in section 13) that the ecclesiastical ministry need not, by the nature of things, be restricted to full-time members. In the present section, we will examine more closely what Robinson terms the sex line, the result of which is that until today, the ecclesiastical ministry has been almost always and everywhere entrusted only to men.

Robinson finds that a critical study of this phenomenon is most urgently needed and has this to say about it:

I am increasingly persuaded that this is not the isolated and secondary issue of ecclesiastical controversy that most of our Churches

[1] J. Robinson, *The New Reformation?* (Philadelphia, 1965), pp. 54-77.

would prefer to keep it . . . Unless the Church can show that it is prepared to permit women as full scope for ministry *and responsibility* as ever it gives to men—and as the world is increasingly giving to women—then it has no right to preach to the world a Gospel which declares that "in Christ there is neither male nor female." [2]

Indeed, the question of woman in the ministry is no unimportant detail to be gone into only when all the other "big" questions are settled. It is not enough to ask "whether it would not also be useful to enroll women in the ministerial service to Church and world." There is much more at issue: the evolution of Church structures and services in a changing world, the fundamental equality of all human beings before God and with regard to one another, the admission of important anthropological and socio-psychological data, and an ecumenical problem that should not be underestimated. This amounts to saying that the questions about letting women join the ministry cannot be solved by the simplistic reasoning and the slogans of a suffragette movement bandying about words like *right* and *discrimination.*

A Church whose vocation it is to be embodied in a living world may not ignore the vital developments of this world. Nevertheless, as regards the place of woman, we must point out the marked discrepancy that exists at present between her secular and ecclesiastical status. In ecclesiastical society, she now occupies about the same place as the one she had when the Christian Church was beginning to take shape: during the first century of our era and in the Judeo-Greek milieu of that time. The social changes which have occurred since then need not be described here *in extenso,* nor can they be. Suffice it to mention that the political and legal equality of man and woman is acknowledged in sizeable parts of the world, and that, in the social and cultural interrelations of society, both sexes, each with its

[2] *Op. cit.,* p. 59.

own nature and talents, generally play a proportionate and complementary role.

In ecclesiastical groupings, the equality of man and woman is also recognized everywhere, not only on anthropological grounds, but above all on the basis of their being each called to salvation. One cannot reasonably contend that there is any question of real discrimination toward women in the Churches, but the ministry is a striking exception. Not, of course, that woman is not active in many ways in the internal life of the Church. She occupies an important place in charitable works and religious instruction and, at certain times and in certain places, she goes by the name of deaconess. But her activities have never really qualified as "strictly ministerial," nor does consecration as deaconess ever seem to be accepted as being additional representatives of the Lord. Only in the most recent times does the question of the presence of women in the ministry appear to have been at all significant, and we now see some Churches that have a special ministry make room for them in it. The strength of the traditional idea that women *could* not be called to the ministry seems to have fallen off somewhat, although advocacy of their joining it still arouses much opposition. The times were not ripe, apparently, for any serious discussion of the subject by Vatican II.

In the cultural pattern obtaining at the time of the early Christians, it was hardly conceivable that a woman should exercise a leading ecclesiastical function. Neither Jewish nor Greco-Roman worship had made the idea familiar. One does not gather from Scripture that the question of entrusting the ministerial mission to a woman was ever seriously considered; besides, it should be borne in mind that in the early Church the distinction between ministry and layman was not nearly as formally defined and juridically established as it came to be later. Women were recognized as fully worthy members of the community, and those who were intensively active in Church life could even acquire a certain standing: that of deaconess or widow, as we see in the texts of Romans 16:1, 1 Timothy 3:11; 5:9-16. On the other hand, one does note, particularly in Paul, a certain shrinking at the thought of too active a feminine influence. He does not approve of women speaking at meetings (1 Cor 14:33:35), or holding a conversation with the religious instructor, or otherwise playing an active role (1 Tim 2:11-15); in this last passage, he theologizes on the second chapter of Genesis in a way that was customary at the time, but can hardly be interpreted as a real argument in favor of the proposition that woman *per se* cannot be called to the ministry; his contention is too greatly colored by his concern for order in the community. Biblical scholars are nowadays generally agreed that the exclusion of women from the ecclesiastical ministry cannot be founded clearly and decisively on Scripture.

However, the lack of a really convincing scriptural proof has not kept theologians from seeking other reasons. Special mention should be made here of the strange use made of the so-called symbolic argument, which can be stated briefly as follows: the relationship between Christ the Lord and his Church is like that of husband and bride (2 Cor 11:2, Eph 5:27; Apoc 21:9); as representative of the Lord, the minister is to the Church also a husband; this being-a-husband cannot be represented by a woman, and therefore she is fundamentally unsuitable for ecclesiastical ministry. Obviously, several things could be advanced against this kind of argumentation. First of all, it finds no support in Scripture; for when the relationship of minister to the community is mentioned there, the marriage image is never used, but the symbol of parenthood, not only fatherhood (1 Cor 4:15; 1 Th 2:1; Philem 10) but even motherhood (Gal 4:19; 1 Th 2:7). Secondly, this kind of proposition neglects the fact that a minister is never a minister-and-nothing-more; he is also a member of God's people, and as such he also enjoys the "feminine" relationship with the Lord. The decisive objection is, however, that the image language of the Bible can never be used as criterion for the concrete organization of the life of the Church. Even should Scripture—which is not the case—represent the relationship between minister and community by the image of husband and wife it still does not follow that only persons of the male sex can enter the ministry; symbolic theology, however valuable, is never normative, as Thomas Aquinas has already unambiguously established.[3]

The origin of this theological error is easy enough to trace. It lies in a philosophico-religious reasoning which tries to express the divine being in anthropological terms, and in so doing forgets that the terms have only an analogous meaning. When the culture pattern is strongly patriarchal, when it bestows the highest authority on the man-father, one is inclined to ascribe masculine archetypal traits to the divinity as well. A language of this kind need not perhaps be shunned entirely, but its relative character must be kept in mind. The Old Testament seems to have realized this, for it also likens the love of God to that of a mother (Is 49:15; 66:13) and the writer of Genesis 1 distinctly states that man as well as woman are images of God. Manhood, in the human sexual sense of the word, may not be ascribed to God as one of his attributes, and in Christ, the Son of God and the Second Adam, God did not become a *male,* but a *human being.* Therefore, when the New Testament uses the image of marriage to express Christ's relation to the Church, it does no more than use a readily available and telling symbolism which clarifies but does not formally define the religious reality.

Biblical imagery cannot be decisive in any discussion of the possibility of women being called to the ecclesiastical ministry. Since other variations on the woman's unfitness for holy orders appear also to be mere theologizing of a historical situation, it follows that, to put it as carefully as possible, the access of women to the ministry is not impossible in principle.

[3] Thomas, *I Sent.,* dist. 11, q. i, art. 1, ad. 1.

This negative conclusion does not answer the question of whether the ordination of women is desirable for more practical reasons. We should like to comment on it briefly, precisely because these practical questions are always embedded in a broader anthropological and theological understanding of the relationship between man and woman, Church and world.

One could, to begin with, draw attention to the ecumenical aspect. An increasing number of Churches now make all their ministries accessible to women. As was to be expected, this process is furthest advanced in the Churches that hardly know any special ministry, or else connect it very closely to the common priesthood—that is, Churches of the more presbyterian type. But an evolution is also under way in the Episcopal Churches, more markedly ministerial in style; some Lutheran churches, among them the Swedish and the Dutch, have women ministers, and in the Anglican Communion the question has recently been debated at length. But little development is to be seen in the Orthodox, Old Catholic, and Roman Catholic Churches. Should these groups fail to join the movement, it might raise a new obstacle to unity in the more distant—or perhaps not so distant—future. Now, who is "responsible" for this new obstacle: is it the "fault" of some Churches, because they promote a wrong development, or that of the others, because they wrongly reject the change?

As neither Scripture nor a sound theology of the ministry will yield a clear answer, we shall have to turn to another criterion. It cannot be purely practical or purely quantitative. One could, for instance, advocate the access of women to the ministry as a means to counteract the shortage of ministers. That is a useful, but not a decisive reason. Quality is always more important than quantity. Can it be argued reasonably and perceptively that the quality of the ministerial service will improve whenever women are enrolled in the ecclesiastical ministry? Theories on the matter are appearing in increasing numbers. An exclusively masculine exercise of the ministry can lead to one-sidedness. Masculine thinking and doing tends to intellectual approximation, to "solid" achievement, to asceticism, authoritarianism, and practicing the "hard line"; it often provides little opportunity for spontaneity and improvisation. But mankind and the world cannot do without intuition, imagination, and the development of sensibility:

If a reciprocal complementarity is to be found in all the fields of human existence, why should this not be true also with respect to the ecclesiastical ministry? If the ministry has acquired a form from which any feminine contribution has been excluded on principle, does this form not become problematic also as regards its masculine side? A ministry achieved in an exclusively masculine manner lacks the complementary feminine, so that it does not fully realize its human potential. For a woman will always exercise the function in her own way, without imitating the male ecclesiastical minister. She will in part do work that is different from men's, but mostly she will do the same work in a different way. She will enrich the ministerial function with fresh vision and new *élan,* and animate it with intuition and tact. A feminine shaping carries with it different accents in the ministerial service, which counterbalance the unilaterally masculine performance. The contribution of woman alongside that of man makes the ministry more human. Opposition to the problem of woman in the ministry is sometimes expressed by saying that it is not natural for a woman to exercise a man's office. This misconception of the ministry can be explained by the fact that hitherto we have known only the masculine form of ministerial service.[4]

In-so-far as the ministry is a representation of the Lord, the human sexual polarity is transcended because the Lord himself, he who was sent by the Father, came into this world as an image of the One who is the source of all manhood and all womanhood. Hence, one can neither deduce from the essence of the

[4] R. v. Eyden, "Die Frau im Kirchenamt," *Wort und Wahrheit,* 22 (1967), pp. 350-362; the citation occurs on pp. 351-352.

ministry that it should be exercised by men only, nor that room should also be made in it for women. However, in actual fact, the ministry is incarnate in individuals, and it is performed in a world made up of men and women. That justifies the question of whether the Church can ensure optimal performance when she will not adapt the ordering of her ministry to contemporary views on man and sex, to contemporary social structures and the rediscovered doctrine of the common priesthood. In a phase of culture in which these matters are changing, clinging to an older pattern could entail a risk of making the presentation of the Church as a whole seem outdated. A Church with a ministry "for men only" can be suspected of refusing to incarnate herself wholly in a changing world, to accept the actual reality for which her message is intended.

Seen in this light, the question of woman's presence in the ministry acquires a deeper perspective. It is not a question of right (are the rights of women being denied?) or of pastoral efficiency (should the one-sidedness of an exclusively masculine performance of the ministerial function not be compensated?); it is a matter of *kerygma*—or, if you will, of *secularization*: is the Church prepared to go and live in the city of man and to take this human being as the starting point of her ecclesiastical order and service?

Meanwhile, it would be unfair to suggest that the Church has in the past completely ignored woman and given no consideration whatever to the feminine element. There were and are a wealth of opportunities for women to contribute in the field of charities and teaching; monasticism often flourished among them; continence, especially of the virginal, maidenly type, was held in high esteem; and varied devotions to the Mother of God developed among them. Still, it is hard to dismiss the feeling that all these manifestations were casual and compensatory, consciously or not, rather than manifestations of balanced theological understanding and mature anthropological psychological perception.

In this connection, it is good for us to be aware of the fact that the Catholic Church, with its masculine hierarchy, can also be seen as an historical patriarchal phenomenon. This communion has not stopped calling itself Mother Church (despite the fact that the title is not biblical), just as it has greatly encouraged the devotion to Mary. Possibly, the ineradicable pull of the feminine, which put the *Hail Mary* next to the *Our Father,* has softened somewhat the manly appearance of this Church by pointing, however safely upward, to woman. The Marian devotion diminishes as woman secures a more fitting place in the Church, and the change harms neither the Mother of God nor the female sex.[5]

One might add that, along with the changes described above, (and probably not by accident,) the problems attaching to the celibacy of ministers have very much come to the fore. This is, of course, particularly true as regards the Catholic Church. As long as celibacy was revered almost like a dogma, and the idea that a minister could be married often caused an emotional disturbance in many, it could not be expected that people would be prepared seriously to consider the possibility of having women ministers. The questions are mutually related, and both are factors and test-cases of the whole problem of the symbiosis of Church and world.

14. SPIRITUALITY: MINISTRY AND LIFE PATTERN

Christian spirituality is, as the words themselves indicate, the whole of various facets in which a Christian's life acquires its concrete form under the guidance of the Spirit. This concrete form feeds on the existential situation of character and natural ability, time and milieu, possibilities used or left untapped. There are, therefore, as many spiritualities as there are Christians. For no two people are identical, and for each there can be an entirely personal way of serving God and being religious.

[5] Th. v. d. Linden, "Naar een nieuw matriarchaat?" *Dux,* 32 (1965), pp. 295-304; the citation occurs on p. 301.

However, this does not exclude the possibility of effecting a qualified ordering and grouping. The form of the existing possibilities can to a large extent be similar, and a knowledge of this can ensure the establishment of groups and the further elaboration of a specific life pattern. One finds, as a result, spiritualities bearing a characteristic stamp: active and contemplative, secular and monastic, Eucharistic, liturgical and devotional, Benedictine, Franciscan, and Ignatian.

Spiritualities are gifts of the spirit, charismata. Some have a highly individual character; they are granted for a person's own sanctification. Others have a more explicit social aspect; they are gifts to serve the Christian community and through it the world as a whole. The leaders of the Church have the right and the duty to exercise their *episkopè* as regards both kinds of charismata, particularly, of course, those of a more social nature. The authorities must always see to it that order reigns in the community, which means, among other things, that they must be in a position to give the community the assurance that certain gifts are "from God" and that others cannot, or not so clearly, be identified as such. A degree of institutionalization of the charismata is possible and necessary, especially when the similarity of the charismatic gifts leads to the formation of groups within the community.

The exercise of this kind of *episkopè* is an extremely delicate task. Maintenance of order must go hand in hand with respect for individual freedom. Individual or collective idealism must not degenerate into harmful highhandedness and lack of balance. On the other hand, charismata also have a part to play in the critical analysis of existing structures.[1] The Spirit of the Lord is not bound by historical human insight as concretized in the existing order. The same Spirit who has granted a gift of leadership to those in authority can also challenge this ministry by bringing to life more spontaneous and freer charismata. Those

[1] Cf. K. Rahner, "Das Charismatische in der Kirche," *Stimmen der Zeit*, 82 (1957), pp. 161-186.

in authority and the guardians of the pledge committed to their care are almost inevitably inclined to idealize existing situations and structures, and mistrust any rumor of evolution or revolution as a source of unrest. Paul's warning applies to them: never try to suppress the Spirit (1 Th 5:19). Structures, organizations, and rules of life exist to serve man and the community; they have no claim to independent existence, or to be indiscriminately cultivated and continued as they are.

When we say that the ecclesiastical ministry exercises a regulatory supervision over the charismata, we are also saying that the ministry can neither *constitute* nor *continue* the charismata. As to the first, there is little doubt: as mouthpiece of the Lord and of the community, the ministry can only acknowledge and authenticate what the Spirit has brought to life, and tend it with pastoral care; but the ministry is not itself the source of those gifts of grace, and therefore it cannot impose any form of spirituality on individual Church members or on groups, and certainly not require from anyone that the choice of a way be sealed by promises and vows. Making promises or taking vows is not unacceptable in principle, but only as a manifestation or confirmation of a decision freely made. The question of continuing in the spiritual way selected earlier is more complicated, particularly in practice. Man can be a weak and fickle creature, and great difficulties impeding the execution of his plans can make him decide prematurely that "it doesn't work any more." In such a case, it may be a useful thing that a person has bound himself in relation to others and is held by them to his decision. Luke's ethical imperatives (9:62) may apply here: "Once the hand is laid on the plough, no one who looks back is fit for the kingdom of God." But this does not solve the problem of loyalty, and even less that of the competence of the ecclesiastical ministry in the matter of adherence to a charismatic choice of Christian life pattern. Man is a historical and contingent being; he grows inwardly and is influenced by external factors. He can therefore develop away from a period during which he could do nothing but cultivate the form of spirituality he selected, toward a situation and a condition in which it has become impossible to do so, and in which he wishes to tread a different path. This can be a wrong step and a disregard of the voice of the Spirit, but it is just as conceivable that the Spirit is calling to another way of living for God. The person concerned may not exclude this possibility *a priori* and bind himself absolutely and irrevocably to the choice he once made; he would then be contending that he holds his own future completely in his own hands and can anticipate it. However, this belief also distinctly limits the rule of the ecclesiastical ministry over charismata. For neither can the ecclesiastical ministry affirm with certainty that the call of the Spirit to a specific way of life is a permanent call. This applies especially—a fact that has always been admitted—to the more accidental variations in spirituality; but it is valid also as regards the more formal, juridically regulated monastic state of life. Absolutely and permanently binding monastic vows cannot exist, because if they did, they would fetter the freedom of the Spirit and the freedom of man. Recognition of this has sometimes been difficult to obtain—hence the protest of the Reformers—and to this day, we still have the curious legal provision that makes the taking of solemn monastic vows a diriment impediment to marriage, a prohibition which quite evidently exceeds the powers of the ecclesiastical ministry.

This last point is related to a frequent tendency to classify the various modes of spiritual life into higher and lower—a classification in which sexual abstinence is considered a higher way of life than marriage. It has long been said of those who followed the evangelical counsels that they lived "in a state of perfection," Thomas Aquinas seems to mean that those who live according to the counsels can reach a higher degree of perfection than the others,[2] and the Council of Trent also expressed itself in this sense, reacting to Luther's simplistic attack on mo-

---

[2] Thomas, *S. Th.,* II-II, q. 184, art. 2-3.

nastic life.[3] Clearly, these comparisons of higher and lower are not only meaningless, but even dangerous. Meaningless, because it is not up to man to judge personal holiness. Only the Spirit of the Lord knows how attractive is the content and compelling the power of his own gifts. In every serious human life, God is served and honored; and even if one can say that some ways of life are in appearance more directly turned toward God, and others lean more toward man and the world, it does not mean that, in the latter, God is any less sought after and found. God does not compete with his creatures,[4] and from them to him there is no single way, straight or winding. The only connection comes "from above" as a grace, sovereign and free. But besides being a waste of time and energy, this thinking in terms of competition is also dangerous. For it can lead to pharisaical behavior which distinguishes between perfect, less perfect, and sinners, and so threatens Christian unity and exercises on the individual a moral pressure to select or keep to a way that was not freely and responsibly chosen. Vatican II seems to have realized the danger: religious life is still sometimes mentioned as "the easier way," but the expression "state of perfection" is not used in any of the Council texts.[5] Every Christian is, by his baptism, called to serve the Lord his God with his whole heart, mind, and strength, and to be perfect just as his heavenly Father is perfect (cf. Mt 5:48). The exclusivism of love of God must never be at the expense of the love of fellow men or creation. The characteristic of the love Christ brought is precisely that it knows no measure or bounds, and that it does not separate, but unites.

[3] Conc. Trid., sess. 24, can. 10 (Denz. 980).
[4] Cf. P. Schoonenberg, "God concurreert niet," *Th. en Z.,* 61 (1965), pp. 1-10.
[5] Cf. *i.a. Lumen gentium,* ch. 6 and the decree *Perfectae caritatis* on the religious life. This is not saying that Vatican II has completely and consistently kept clear of the old way of thinking. The comparisons between marriage and virginity contained in the recent encyclical *Sacerdotalis caelibatus* on celibacy constitute in fact, a very distinct return to the old patterns of thought.

As for the spirituality of the minister, we must first remark that here, too, there are as many spiritualities as there are ministers; for every minister has his own character, his own existential situation, and he is personally guided by God's Spirit. It is also clear that the similar nature of activities can, particularly among those who belong to the ministry, bring about a certain resemblance in the patterns of spiritual life.

Can these ways of spiritual life be defined more closely and can one even say that the suggestions or demands for the establishment of specific forms lie in the ministry itself? In the past, this question was answered without much hesitation. Links were supposedly found to exist between the ecclesiastical ministry and the monastic way of life. Both the ministry and the monastic life was seen—to a certain extent, legitimately—as the expression of a special concern with the kingdom of heaven. It is easy to understand that, in the course of centuries, ministerial spirituality adopted specifically monastic traits: community life, religious clothes, the breviary, celibacy. This approach is still very apparent in Vatican II's decree *Presbyterorum ordinis*. But many people have realized that this sweeping identification of the ecclesiastical ministry with the monastic way of life was somewhat simplistic. They realized that the monastic way of life could not always be practiced, and also began to doubt whether a monastic pattern of spiritual life, or a spirituality inspired by monastic life, really possessed such a superiority that it must be assumed by the minister. It is difficult to say which of the two factors, the practical or the more theoretical, played the greatest role, but in the last decade much has been written and said about the spirituality of the secular minister. That he should have been given special attention can also be explained by the fact that the regular minister was presumed to receive his pattern of spiritual life from the religious group to which he belonged, whereas no such foundation was found for the secular.

If further reflection on the spirituality of the minister is to bear fruit, we must first of all consider that the eventual spirituality is not only a consequence of the vocation to the ministry, but that the presence of a certain form of spiritual life is equally a condition of this vocation. The person called to the ministry is an adult Christian, and therefore already has a spirituality. This spirituality, theologically and chronologically, precedes his being a minister. The ordination liturgy bears out this thesis. When the bishop who calls them to the ministry tells the candidates that they are expected to lead a life of piety and faith, of devotion to duty and righteousness, of chastity and discipline, he is saying that their life hitherto has shown the beginnings of these qualities and raised the expectation that the candidates would develop them in the office they were about to receive:

The consecration is no absolute zero point, no starting point. But the ordination prayer says that the priest's personal life with God will receive a new coloring, a finer shading through the ministerial service. Hence the exhortation to the candidate: "Know what you are doing, and fulfill in your own life what you carry out in your ministry." Proximity to the holy, living with God's Word, will mark the spirituality of the priest (which is presupposed) with a distinctive stamp. The candidate can see in the prayer he is listening to an invitation to perform his ministerial function with the whole of his person; and also, an assurance that his service will have a new effect on his spirituality and his striving for holiness. In other words, the priesthood is not the basis of spirituality, it does not give holiness; it shades, gives a special character, a new profile to what is already there in the man.[6]

We are once more reminded of the fact that the difference between layman and minister is not as great as is often thought. As person and work do not overlap completely, every detail of the minister's spiritual life is not necessarily "ministerial." In other words: it is impossible to describe the spirituality of the Christian

[6] F. de Grijs, "De geloofsbeleving van de priester," in *Essays en Interviews over de Priester* (Utrecht, 1965), pp. 55-78; the citation occurs on p. 60. The author gratefully acknowledges that he made use of the ideas contained in the aforementioned article in writing the present and the following sections of this book.

who is a minister on the exclusive basis of his office. Minister and layman are both called to sanctity of life: both are guided by the Spirit who bids them choose, freely and responsibly, their own "better way"; let the grace of God grow in them, and become perfect as their heavenly Father is perfect.

That is also why the spirituality of the minister is not fixed and unalterable given, but changes and develops. The whole person of the minister is planted in the evolution of the living community of God in this changing world. Just as his service is shaped by and changes according to the needs of the community, so also his spirituality evolves along with the developments occurring in the spirituality of all the faithful. Should ministers reject this and consider themselves irrevocably bound to the life pattern they have once selected, they will be disavowing in their own lives what they impress upon others: that the Christian must keep himself available to follow the new ways the Spirit shows him, that he must be ready, as Abraham, to be drawn away from the established and trusted situation. If the minister refuses to accept this dynamic, and clings to a hardened and formalized life pattern, his attitude can be detrimental to his ministerial activities. People will come to see in him a figure out of a dated era, the representative of a past that is over and done with. Here lies perhaps the most important cause of the loss of contact between minister and layman. For it is hard to believe that this loss of rapport is due exclusively to a sudden drop in ministerial ability and zeal for souls. It would seem legitimate to ask whether, for many Christians in the world of today, the person of the minister speaks with sufficient power to the imagination to release in them a desire to follow.

We must never forget that the spirituality of the minister must be exemplary, an example so structured that its attractiveness leads others to imitate it. The minister should live before men the ideal of Christian holiness, but in ways that can be imitated; there is no point in gaining respect by departing too much from the ordinary to act as a direct stimulus. Church law stipulates that the ecclesiastical minister must excel *prae laicis* in the inner and the visible holiness of his life (Canon 124). This cannot be read simply as a call to "greater" holiness; for everybody is called to optimal and maximal holiness, and furthermore we do not have the criteria by which to gauge this "more"; again, this kind of language could entail a risk of pharisaism: the measure of participation in Church life and the strength of the love binding a person to God are not identical. But the expression becomes meaningful if we think in terms of a living image:

Then the words *prae laicis* [translated as "more than laymen"] do not mean that the priests must be more or better than the faithful, more intensely devout and holy; they must be holy in a manner that other people can adopt. For what does example mean? In my opinion, a Christian, human, adult, and believing manner of life is exemplary only when it is what it is, motivated and justified in itself. The setting of an example may not be the motive actuating a priest's life: it would empty his existence of meaning and formalize it, robbing it of any drawing power as an example. Priests must strive for holiness because they themselves are intimately convinced that such is their human, personal duty; to the extent that their life in this way becomes more authentic and individual, its pull as an example will become greater.[7]

We begin to see, therefore, that the acquisition of a specific spirituality is more a norm of selection than a professional duty deriving from the ministry; the specifically ministerial traits which are going to develop within this spirituality are secondary, because they cannot exercise any exemplary function in the presence of the nonminister. It may also be concluded that there is really no reason to say that the spirituality expected of a minister should necessarily found itself on the special charismata of the monastic life pattern. Insofar as the spirituality of a minister does have its own peculiar traits, this is more a matter of strictly personal "devotions," or of elements belonging to what one might

[7] F. de Grijs, *op. cit.*, pp. 58-59.

call professional ethics, rather than of spirituality. We could perhaps even go a step further and say that precisely because he must *be* an example, it is more difficult for the minister to indulge in many "special devotions," because by doing so he would show too particularized an image of Christian life.

In attempting to give a more positive description of the spirituality of a minister, one would have to say, among other things, that it should revolve around the *great general spiritual themes of the Church:* Holy Scripture, the Eucharist, liturgy in general, the person of Christ, and the Mother of God. The exemplary minister must above all be an expert in the crucial aspects of Christian spirituality. His spirituality will also always have to have an *ecclesiastical social aspect;* the task imposed on him invites orientation toward the themes of redemption together and being "sent" together. We have already remarked that a nominal Christian is hardly suitable for the ministry; one might add that along with concern for his own spiritual welfare, the minister is deeply concerned for the well-being of God's people as a whole, and that the ecumenical dimension of that concern should not be forgotten. The social ecclesiastical dimension can also be gauged from the standpoint of the ministry experienced as service, an aspect of the ministry so greatly emphasized in our current biblical renewal. An altruistic attitude is indeed indispensable for an exemplary performance of the ministerial function. The classics on the spirituality of the ministry always call it the ethos of the *Good Shepherd,* and in doing so clearly link it to the priestly ethos of the Lord Jesus himself. Since the shepherd image is somewhat paternalistic, the social coloration of today's spirituality should stress the democratic ethos, the idea that God's people in the final analysis, know no rank or status, but that the individual worth and personal responsibilities of each member of the Church should be generously acknowledged.

The factors mentioned above show that it is often very difficult clearly to set the respective limits of the spirituality of the minister, his professional ethos, and his occupational ethics.

This is perhaps not a serious problem, since Christian and minister are one and the same person. Professional ethical requirements, after all, are no more than the general demands that must be made of anyone to whom a task has been allotted, although admittedly the stresses vary according to the concrete cases concerned. One may say that the ecclesiastical minister should see that he acquires the necessary theological understanding and keeps refining it, that he is always ready to improve his "technique," that he learns teamwork and knows how to defer to the leader, that he is tolerant and allows for differing opinions and usages, that he is conscientious and can see the relative quality of his views and experiences. All this is valid for everybody. As for the specifically ecclesiastical ministry, the most one can say is that it possesses an extra stimulus to disinterestedness and charismatic commitment.

Finally, the concrete ministerial assignments clearly may call for different criteria as regards the choice of a spirituality and, after ordination, lend a different color to this spirituality. In practice, this means that in a religious community, for instance, a personal affinity with the monastic life pattern may be expected of the minister, but a person whose spirituality has been formed in the sense of religious community life is not automatically qualified for a workers' parish. Generally speaking, it can be said that the minister should be someone drawn from the community he will serve; this is the best guarantee that he will set an effective example. Naturally, the situation of the part-time minister is again distinct. His limited ministry will have few repercussions on his personal life pattern, and his spirituality will be based primarily on the profane situation in which he finds himself "as layman." Monastic ways of life can hardly be expected to fit in with his activities and will often be undesirable, because they can be conducive to isolation. That these ideas have implications for our discussion of ministerial celibacy is already clear, and must be developed further in another section.

15. SECULAR AND REGULAR

One of the most striking forms of Christian spirituality is that of people who, finding they were akin in spirit, unite to live in a spiritual community ordered by rules of a more or less fixed character. These forms of life are usually called canonical or regular; "religious life" is a somewhat vague, and therefore less useful description, because religious feeling, the love of the Lord and his Church, and a readiness to worship and serve him should mark the life of every serious Christian.

The rule governing this "regular" religious life can vary a great deal, and its form can therefore range from the eremitic to that of the secular institutes. Usually, however, the "regulars" have committed themselves to following expressly the so-called evangelical counsels of detachment, sexual continence, and community life (in popular but sometimes misleading terms: poverty, chastity, and obedience). The scriptural credentials of the three counsels, however, are not very convincing. Nowhere do they appear together as a more or less clear-cut pattern of spirituality, and independently they are put forth with differing emphasis: evangelical simplicity is often mentioned; Paul alone (1 Cor 7) really recommends a life of continence, and then only as his personal opinion; and a text directly advocating community life is really not to be found. Nevertheless, living according to the three counsels has, in the course of centuries, proved that it can yield a most important and fruitful form of Christian spirituality.

We have already shown in the preceding section that classifying the various spiritualities as "higher" and "lower" is a senseless waste of time, because the power of God does not allow itself to be tied to human categories, and because no man is entitled to pass a real judgment on holiness. It is also worth clearly repeating that canonical life cannot be qualified as a "higher way." Even if it can eventually be argued that in the structures of this canonical life, which entails a certain renunciation of specific earthly values (independence, possession, marriage), one may see a special proof of the primacy of the Lord over all creation, it does not follow that, in general or in concrete instances, the religious is more deeply steeped in the love of the Lord than the Christian living "in the world." It makes no sense either to hold that the life of the regulars is more of a foretaste of the life to come after the present. Our human competitiveness certainly does not extend beyond the boundaries of death; only love does that, and love pays little attention to rank or result, position or achievement. God cannot be reached by any way devised by man; the only way to him is the Lord Jesus, who came to redeem all men.

From a very early date in Church history, the belief has prevailed that the men who had committed themselves to this canonical life would be suitable candidates to a ministerial mission; canonical spirituality seemed to guarantee good ministerial performance. The expectation was not unwarranted, for one can reasonably hope that persons of this kind will be keenly interested in the life of the Church, and that their education and training for the canonical way of life will endow them with a number of qualities and skills which positively answer the requirements of the ecclesiastical ministry. To this must be added that in the times preceding the Council of Trent, secular ministers were hardly trained, and that many of them apparently did not satisfy the none too exacting prevailing requirements, either professionally or spiritually, or as regards discipline. Naturally, one must beware of idealistic exaggerations here; there were excellent seculars in earlier days too, and there have always been weak brothers among the regular ministers. The literature of the Middle Ages gives the impression that the dissolute monk was more the object of criticism and derision than the stupid, cheating, and fornicating pastors and the worldly bishops with their princely lives; perhaps we should remember here that pride goes before a fall, *corruptio optimi pessima?* However it may be, it was thought that the minister's being "taken from among men" went with the regular's "not belonging to the world." The monastic community life which Augustine led together with his clergy undoubtedly strengthened this view, and any possible remaining doubt disappeared almost completely during the Middle Ages, when it was found that the urge for renewal sprang mainly from the cloisters, and an increasing number of religious were appointed to posts in the administration of the Church. Even the minister who did not actually follow the canonical rule seemed to be well advised in patterning his life as closely as possible on the monastic, of which certain aspects (clothing, breviary, celibacy) even became mandatory. Education and training also conformed to it; the seminaries instituted by Trent were— and often still are today—hardly to be distinguished from cloisters. This is particularly true of the preparatory seminary, which could, of course, give no professional training, but which had as one of its most important objectives the practice of a monastic type of religious worship: lengthy and sometimes somewhat esoteric celebrations of the liturgy, including parts of the divine office, meditation, days of recollection and retreats, periods of silence, personal spiritual direction, and much emphasis on the community idea. Naturally, the literature also projected a ministerial spirituality inclining strongly to the monastic, and as we mentioned earlier, the same emphasis is still definitely to be seen in Vatican II's decree *Presbyterorum ordinis:* uniformity in the style of living, the community idea, the significance of the three traditional evangelical counsels.

It is still expected that candidates should not only be interested in the ministerial service, but also have a certain innate feeling for this monastically colored life-ideal and be prepared to develop it further. At certain times, the regular ministry seems to be very popular; in the Netherlands, for instance, the total number of ordinations of regulars has for a few decades been higher than that of seculars. But this should not be ascribed exclusively to any marked sympathy for monastic radicalism; one reason at least as important lies in the fact that the phenotype or, if you will, the professional image was much more varied: the field of action of the secular ministry was fairly restricted, whereas the regular ministry offered extra possibilities such as, for instance, missionary activities, special spiritual care, teaching, and further study.

As soon as one attempts any theological evaluation of this century-old phenotype of the ecclesiastical minister, he confronts the rivalry between secular and regular. Rivalry, up to a point, is not unwholesome; differences in life situations can bring out a fruitful play of action and reaction; but sharpen the distinctions and make them absolute, and an atmosphere of petty, piddling competition is created.

We must, however, compare this phenotype of the minister with the theological data we have found in the course of this study. Is its development necessary or accidental, useful or harmful: can or must other forms also be possible?

First, we should note that there is nothing in theology that binds the ministry to any specific form of spirituality whatever. The mold of any personal spirituality cannot be deduced from theological data on the ministry as such, and it therefore can never be said a priori that the ecclesiastical ministry demands a monastic life pattern. The fundamental reason for this is that the ministry is a function, and being a religious is a life situation. The two quantities are on a line but their comparability is not in the same plane. It may be desirable, in a concrete situation, that religious be called to the ministry or seculars advised to adopt a quasi-monastic life pattern, but the ministry, of its nature, does not demand it. This can best be seen if we realize that the ministry is not an immutable and uniform given. Since the representation of the Lord is the formal characteristic of each ministerial function, we can in fact only speak of *ministries to,* and concretely molded by, the needs and wants of the community. The predilection for the regulars' life pattern developed at a time when the ministry had been condensed into a life situation. From this point of view, the connection is understandable: if one starts with the idea that a person is a minister twenty-four hours a day, and that his being a minister actually stamps all his activities, it is indeed entirely comprehensible that he begins to talk about a "priestly" life situation and wonder whether this situation should not have a monastic bent. We saw in the preceding sections, however, that the minister is also a layman, that a part-time ministry does in fact exist, and that the ministerial mission is not by nature permanent or for life. The inevitable conclusion is that there cannot be a required relationship between "incidental" ministry and the permanent monastic life situation. One can eventually claim that for practical reasons even the part-time minister must adopt a monastic or quasi-monastic life pattern—the proof will be hard to establish—but it will always be impossible to say that this requirement is inherent to the nature of the ministry.

Of course, this argument does not constitute a condemnation of the religious-minister. Anyone familiar with the history of the Church knows that he has, in the course of centuries, done a great deal of good. But this historical experience is only a relative given, not an imperative. The ministerial charism can, at least theoretically, reside in other spiritualities than the monastic, and history shows that this has in fact happened. Conversely, it can also happen that a minister's spirituality, originally monastic, or of monastic inspiration, begins to develop in a different direction. As we saw in the preceding section, this kind of development should not be hampered or made impossible by the ecclesiastical community and its authorities; the supervision exercised by the Church over the charismata does not apply to their continuation.

The monastic life pattern is not a "professional" duty of the minister, deriving from the ministerial office. It can at most be used, for more practical reasons, as a selection criterion, as a prerequisite for entrance to or maintenance in the ministry. As such, it is used by different Churches in different ways. The Reformation Churches have hardly any regular ministers, Eastern Orthodoxy holds them in high esteem and considers them the most suitable (even the only suitable) candidates for the episcopate, and the Latin Western Church has so great a predilection for the monastic life pattern that she actually has no real secular ministers:

The classic systematization of the sanctification of the priests who are, so disputably, called "secular" also derives from monastic spirituality and practices. Fundamentally, clerical life as it has been progressively fixed in the West, which has been adorned by so many holy men since the Council of Trent, is a reduced monastic life too. There are no "secular clergy" such as those of the East: married priests with no daily Mass or Breviary obligation, sharing closely in the life and work of the village and its people, essentially responsible for the spiritual guidance, maintaining Christian discipline and ministering the sacraments. Here in the West since the Middle Ages, and especially since Trent, the ideals and means of priestly holiness have been borrowed from monachism, adapted from a spirituality that is monastic, or at least "religious" in the technical sense.[1]

Theologically, what can one say about this preference? If it were founded purely on practical reasons, the answer would have to be that the theologian as such can express no opinion on the matter. However, it is closely connected with the concept that the "religious" life is somewhat superior. We have already indicated in the previous section that this superiority thesis is hardly tenable, and that Vatican II has in some measure kept away from it. It becomes a legitimate question then, whether the clear predilection for the "monastic minister" is indeed desirable from a *kerygmatic* point of view. One finds in the new ecclesiology a growing realization of the fact that the task of the Church

[1] Y. Congar, *Lay people in the Church*, tr. by D. Attwater (Westminster, Md., 1957), p. 390.

does not consist in being a community alongside other communities, or a ruler among other rulers, but that she must be the yeast that will leaven the world, incarnating herself in the secular world in order to enrich it both from within and without. This ought also to be manifested in the concrete shaping of the ecclesiastical ministry.

The monastic life pattern, however, does not stress this incarnational approach; renouncing the human values of possession, marriage and independence places the monk "beyond"[2] this world. That is not a complaint against someone leading a monastic life; he is needed in a world sometimes too much inclined to see itself as the end of all things, and it is his proper function not-to-be-of-the-world and to bring out the transitory nature of this aeon. The question is, however, whether this aspect of Christianity is not being unduly emphasized when all, or nearly all, ecclesiastical ministers concentrate in their personal lives on this other-worldly style. Their spirituality should "set an example" to the community in which they perform their function, and ought, therefore, to assume a form which will not only invite respectful admiration, but above all, also incite others to follow. The specific drawback of monastic spirituality is that it cannot be a direct source of inspiration for the Christian living in the world, whose "way" consists precisely in a commitment to earthly values which must be considered in a positive manner, such an appraisal leading to a determination of their relative worth and new dimensions. A minister truly living as a secular justifies in his own person this approach to God through creatures and takes the lead himself.

Much more is involved here than the question, rather petty and difficult to answer in general terms of whether the minister who leads a monastic type of life knows enough about what the world has to offer to be able to give useable, practical advice. (That question, too, is valid, considering the growing uneasiness

[2] Cf. D. Thalhammer, *Jenseitige Menschen. Eine Sinndeutung des Ordensstandes* (Freiburg, 1953)

about, let us say, marriage ethics propounded by celibates or the monastic type of meditation and prayer of the *Imitation of Christ.*) But the point at issue is more important: is the ministry as such, and are the ministers as a corps, fully doing justice to the world-related and human quality of being Christian and members of Christ's Church, and thereby ensuring an optimal performance of their task? In other words, is the efficacy of the ministerial charism bestowed on the Church not being hampered by being "incarnated" exclusively in forms used, or closely resembling the forms used, by regulars? Add to this the practical aspect that the imposition of a monastic style on the life pattern of ministers may make recruitment more difficult. Whoever is now wondering whether to apply for the ministry must not only ask himself if he is equipped to carry out ministerial functions, but also if the style of life required at present of all ministers is sufficiently congenial to him. It is possible that opposition to this "other-worldly" style of life is weightier—and, consequently, the life pattern a greater handicap to vocations—than the workload of the ministry itself. The drop now apparent in the number of vocations must not be separated from the waning interest in the life of the regulars in general. Of course, the requirement of celibacy is a prime factor; we shall return to it again in the next section.

There will always be ministers whose spirituality will take a monastic cast, and it will always be possible to find suitable candidates for the priesthood among those who lead a monastic life. The ministerial charism and the charism for life according to the evangelical counsels go well together. But the combination is not a mandatory requirement of the ministry itself, and for kerygmatic as for practical reasons, it would seem best not to give too much stress to the combination as a selection criterion. There are more suitable spiritualities than the monastic or quasi-monastic types, and a spirituality definitely oriented to the secular might be the answer for many ministers who must set an example of Christian living in the secularized world of today. The minister-religious need not disappear; he should simply be complemented by colleagues who have a different spiritual outlook, so that the multiplicity of Christian possibilities may also be seen within the corps of ministers.

Moreover, it will not be necessary, it might even not be good, to assign the religious-minister exclusively to the monastic field of work. It is perhaps his primary ground, because there he can also exemplify the specific aspects of his personal spirituality. But he can be called to other tasks too, and there is no need for him to remain shut up behind cloister walls. His living in community offers possibilities for specialization and collaboration that can also be made fruitful in a wider field, and the fact, in particular, that he is unmarried makes for dynamic employment rich in possibilities of interchange; in actual fact, the minister-religious often does pioneer work, while the secular is more sedentary. True enough, these practical considerations do not constitute the essence of his monastic ministerial spirituality, but they are by-products worth noting. Finally, it should be added that it is important, from a kerygmatic point of view, that some ministers also emphasize the "not-of-this-world" aspect. The religious has a specific nuisance value precisely because, by relativizing earthly values, he impresses on everybody, in a striking manner, the primacy of the Lord and draws attention to the fact that there is more between heaven and earth than human philosophy dreams of. This particular way of "disturbing the peace," provided it is not used excessively and at the expense of other means, can enrich the total picture of "the" ecclesiastical ministry. There is room in the ministry for "other-worldly people" too, as long as their presence does not dominate so as to give the impression that real Christian holiness is a privilege of the monastic Christians. The danger of overemphasis will dwindle as more room is made for an authentic secular ministry. It is, above all, to the development of the latter that we shall have to attend at this juncture.

In the eighth section we showed that the ecclesiastical ministry is primarily and formally a functional given. Without modifying this statement in any way, we may add that this functional given is very closely connected with the personal life pattern and spirituality of the minister. The minister performs various services, but because these services are so closely bound up with the fundamental human Christian values of faith and redemption, love and hope, the strictly functional is exceeded in the person of the minister who, in the community, represents the redeeming Lord in his whole life. What can and must be separated in a formal study on the ministry constitutes, in actuality, an indivisible whole. Understandably and reasonably, some people find that an overly "functional" analysis of the ministry is difficult and even dangerous, because it can sometimes fail to do full justice to the fact that, *in concreto,* person and ministry are very intimately interlocked. On the other hand, they cannot deny that the distinction between function and life pattern must be taken seriously, because by rejecting it, they would be hindering a shaping of the ministry at once dynamic and developmental.

16. THE CELIBACY OF THE ECCLESIASTICAL MINISTER

The communion in which John Robinson exercises his episcopal function gives him little cause to include "the regulars" in his summing up of the demarcation lines running through the ecclesiastical ministry; the Anglican Church is as unfamiliar with a strongly developed monastic life as the other Churches belonging to the sixteenth-century Reformation, and seldom knows the regular minister. Quantitatively speaking, monastic life and monastic ministry are a characteristic of Orthodoxy and the Roman Catholic Church.

There is another line that is no great problem for the Reformation Churches, but is for the Orthodox, and even more so for the Roman Catholic Church. It is a variation on the "sex line": many, or almost all ministers belong to the group of the unmarried. This line coincides in part with that of the "regulars," but then cuts once more right through the secular group, although in different ways. While the Orthodox Churches admit celibates and married persons to the ministry and reject marriage only after ordination, the Roman Catholic Church has such a marked preference for celibate ministers that she consents to the ordination of married persons only in exceptional cases (the possibility is greater in the "reinstated" diaconate). She forbids celibates, under pain of dismissal from the ministry, to marry after ordination, and recognizes the validity of a marriage contracted after dismissal only if an explicit dispensation has been granted to the persons concerned, to whom, despite their release, the law of celibacy still applies.

This preference for the unmarried minister implies the belief that the spiritual life pattern of the celibate—a religiously motivated and positively directed celibacy, of course—or, to put it in more legal, formal terms, the life situation of virginity is a good criterion for the selection of candidates to the ministry (unmarried persons are admitted by preference), and that the ministry once received also demands continuance of celibacy (no marriage is desired after ordination). The connection between ministry and celibacy is considered to be so strong as to constitute the grounds of legislation. To the religious-minister who has vowed to adhere to the evangelical counsel of continence, the celibacy law is merely an extra obligation imposed from outside; for the secular minister it is the only suprapersonal reason for his being unmarried.

The preference for unmarried ministers is justified on the basis of a number of arguments which can be roughly divided into theological and practical. We cannot here go at length into the practical arguments.[1] Suffice it to say that they are not un-

[1] Cf. R. J. Bunnik, "The Question of Married Priests," *Cross Currents*, 15 (1965), pp. 403-431; 16 (1966), pp. 81-112, esp. pp. 81-95.

founded—especially the advantage of greater availability—but are not strong enough to serve as a basis for a general law. Their relative value is now generally admitted, which explains the striving, apparent in official pronouncements as in the studies of theologians, for the more idealistic argument of the inner connection or, as it is often called nowadays, the "affinity" between the ecclesiastical ministry and the charism granted to not-being-married "for the sake of the kingdom of heaven."

What is the foundation of this affinity theory? And how can its content be formularized? [2] We speak of a "formularized content" deliberately, because it may be that all formulations are possibly only poor expressions of a concept of faith that cannot be fully put into words; a purely intellectual and theoretical approach cannot grasp the essence of an underlying religious given. However, we should add at once that a distinction must be made between the idea of affinity itself and its application by law: the charism of virginity is a given of salvation which passes human understanding and conceptualization, but a law on celibacy is a human enactment concerning which it is impossible to invoke, expressly and directly, the word of the Lord, and which stands or falls along with the validity of the human arguments adducible for it.

When we consider this affinity theory in itself, a few negative observations are inevitable. To begin with, an inner connection between ministry and celibacy cannot be demonstrated in any way directly from Scripture. Where a positive value is attributed to being unmarried (Mt 19:10-12—hardly a real counsel, 1 Cor 7—a rather idiosyncratic position of Paul), it is not related to the ecclesiastical ministry, and it is apparent from the texts concerning the early Church (1 Cor 9:5; 1 Tim 3:12; Tit 1:6) that the majority of ministers were married, and that the unmarried constituted rather an exception to the rule.

[2] For a more detailed study of this problem, see R. J. Bunnik, "De theologische studie van virginiteit en ambtscelibaat," *Tijdschrift voor Theologie,* 6 (1966), pp. 148-182. See also my article, "Theology of Celibacy," in G. Frein, ed., *Celibacy, The Necessary Option* (New York, 1968), pp. 73-86.

The lack of a clear scriptural reference is the reason why—and that is our second point—the affinity theory has never been collectively held by Christianity as a whole. The scarcity of available data relating to very early times precludes any precise information as to when the theory first made its appearance and how widespread it was, but at all events it remains in dispute to this day. The Reformation Churches almost unanimously reject it, and the Orthodox do not consider it so well founded as deliberately to strive for as low a number as possible of married ministers. This ecumenical fact ought not to be neglected, considering that the non-Catholic theological conclusions also are a *locus theologicus,* as Vatican II has clearly admitted.[3]

Finally, one must recognize that the affinity theory is weakened by the fact that a law was apparently needed in order to urge the "ideal." The idea of affinity was not by any means always spontaneously applied in practical life; accordingly, Church history does not reveal the existence of any unshakable conviction as to an inner connection between ministry and celibacy. The study of spirituality has brought out that, insofar as permanent uneasiness about the celibacy of the minister yields any clear opinion, that opinion seems to be markedly conditioned by the anthropological and ascetic thinking reigning at certain times and in certain places. Besides, the idea of so-called superiority also played its part, thanks to which the unmarried life was rated higher than the married, not in so many words perhaps, but in actual life and pastoral guidance. To this day, one can detect, in many ecclesiastical speeches and doings, a "virginizing" of the Christian ideal of chastity. It is not surprising therefore that, in proportion as this process of equating the moral virtue of chastity with sexual continence becomes subject to scholarly criticism, the theory of the supposed connection between ministry and unmarried life loses its cogency.

[3] Cf. *i.a. Lumen gentium* #15, and *Unitatis redintegratio,* on ecumenism, #3.

After this first appraisal of the relative value of the affinity thesis, we shall examine more closely how it is formulated, and gauge its theological tenability. Section 16 of the decree *Presbyterorum ordinis*[4] adopted by Vatican II constitutes a good starting point. It is common knowledge that this text could not be extensively debated, which diminishes its value considerably. But it can at least be considered as the formulation of opinions endorsed by many people to this day.

With respect to the priestly life, the Church has always held in especially high regard perfect and perpetual continence on behalf of the kingdom of heaven. Such continence was recommended by Christ the Lord and has been gladly embraced and praiseworthily observed down through the years and in our day too by many Christians. For it simultaneously signifies and stimulates pastoral charity and is a special fountain of spiritual fruitfulness on earth. It is not, indeed, demanded by the very nature of the priesthood, as is evident from the practice of the primitive Church and from the tradition of the Eastern Churches . . .

Celibacy accords with the priesthood on many scores. For the whole priestly mission is dedicated to that new humanity which Christ, the conqueror of death, raises up in the world through His Spirit. This humanity takes its origin "not of blood, nor of the will of the flesh, nor of the will of man, but of God" (Jn. 1:13). Through virginity or celibacy observed for the sake of the kingdom of heaven, priests are consecrated to Christ in a new and distinguished way. They more easily hold fast to Him with undivided heart. They more freely devote themselves in Him and through Him to the service of God and men. They more readily minister to his kingdom and to the work of heavenly regeneration, and thus become more apt to exercise paternity in Christ, and do so to a greater extent.

[4] We have chosen the text of *Presbyterorum ordinis* as a starting point, rather than the recent encyclical *Sacerdotalis caelibatus;* a conciliar document is more important than a papal encyclical. The ways in which each document approaches the problem are closely parallel, and therefore our remarks also apply to the encyclical. The encyclical does come up in Part III (pp. 250-253 in MS).

Hence in this way they profess before men that they desire to dedicate themselves in an undivided way to the task assigned to them, namely, to betroth the faithful to one man, and present them as a pure virgin to Christ. They thereby evoke that mysterious marriage which was established by God and will be fully manifested in the future, and by which the Church has Christ as her only spouse. Moreover, they become a vivid sign of that future world which is already present through faith and charity, and in which the children of the resurrection will neither marry nor take wives.

For these reasons, which are based on the mystery of Christ and His mission,[5] celibacy was at first recommended to priests. Then, in the Latin Church, it was imposed by law on all who were to be promoted to sacred orders. This legislation, to the extent that it concerns those who are destined for the priesthood, this most holy Synod again approves and confirms. It trusts in the Spirit that the gift of celibacy, which so befits the priesthood of the New Testament, will be generously bestowed by the Father, as long as those who share in Christ's priesthood through the sacrament of orders, and indeed the whole Church, humbly and earnestly pray for it.

This holy Synod likewise exhorts all priests who, trusting in God's grace, have freely undertaken sacred celibacy in imitation of Christ to hold fast to it magnanimously and wholeheartedly. May they persevere faithfully in this state, and recognize this surpassing gift which the Father has given them, and which the Lord praised so openly. Let them keep in mind the great mysteries which are signified and fulfilled in it.

It is hard to imagine that the text of this section would have remained as it now stands if comprehensive discussion had been possible. Its length alone leads one to suspect that its compilers found themselves constrained to illustrate, by means of an accumulation of arguments of differing value, a thesis that could not be supported succinctly and convincingly. We cannot go at

[5] The translation of this last clause is inaccurate in Abbott, and has been corrected here (Ed.).

length into each separate idea, but there are a few critical comments which should not be left unsaid.

It is claimed twice that the Lord himself counselled celibacy and Matthew is quoted in reference: "Let anyone accept this who can" (19:12). Read in the context of the complete peri-cope—the logion of Matthew 19:10:12—the text seems to mean that the special situation of being unmarried is defended rather than recommended. The expression used in the conciliar docu-ment, "praised so openly" (*tam aperte extollitur*), goes some-what further than the scriptural text allows for.[6]

Something else should be challenged too, namely the not quite justified use of other biblical texts. The "new humanity" which the priest is called to serve takes its origin from God, and is not generated by man. John is quoted here (1:13), not un-fairly, but the manner of it suggests that the new world will bear a distinctly virginal stamp. This does not follow from the scriptural text itself, which speaks of a process of salvation in which neither marriage nor continence have any part: only by accepting and believing in the name of the Lord can one be-come a child of God, not by remaining unmarried, as such. A similar reservation should be made as regards the "eschatological argument" used later, where the reference is to Luke 20:25-36. This text also is not about any inner-worldly distinction between marriage and celibacy, but maintains only that it is impossible to speak meaningfully of the next life in terms of earthly sex-uality. Not being married on earth is in itself no anticipation of the eschaton; it is only in belief and in love—as the text of the decree itself states—that the future world is already present. Being unmarried is at most a special and striking form of ex-pression of that belief and that hope, not that belief or hope it-self.

Nor would it seem reasonable to relate the celibacy of the

[6]For a commentary on Matthew 19:10-12, see J. Blinzler, "Eisin eunuchoi. Zur Auslegung von Mt. 19:12," *Zs. f.d. Neutest. Wiss.*, 48 (1957), pp. 254-270.

minister directly to the biblical text in which marriage is used as the image of the love between the Lord and his Church. That could give the impression that the minister is exclusively placed on "the side" of the Lord, and cast in "the man's part"; but the minister is also a member of the Church, and consequently is also cast in "the woman's part." However, it should above all be remembered that Scripture is simply using the image of marriage, not that of being unmarried. Seemingly, the compilers of the decree have failed adequately to realize that when Paul, in 2 Corinthians 11:2, speaks of the Church as a chaste virgin, he is not suggesting that a kind of "virginal marriage" has been concluded between the Lord and his Church, but he is speaking in the vein of the Old Testament, where unfaithfulness to Yahweh is styled adultery (Ezek 16; Hos 2:1, and 18): the Church is a virgin because and insofar as she has not given herself to other gods; but *in* her marriage to Christ, she loses her virginity to become the mother of all those who are redeemed. The celibacy of the minister cannot be illustrated or justified by these biblical images.

When, therefore, the conciliar text states that the celibacy of the minister is "based on the mystery of Christ and his mission," one may observe that the motives advanced do not warrant this conclusion at all. Moreover, in a formulation of this kind, the admission that celibacy is not demanded by the very nature of the ministry is again weakened to a large extent. It also implies that the early Church, as well as the Protestant and Eastern Churches who had and have married ministers, have not sufficiently realized this inner connection of ministry and celibacy; their practice is not condemned as unlawful, but seems, at any rate, less than ideal, a consequence of an imperfect understanding of the faith. Again, as far as the individual married minister is concerned, the attitude is hardly positive: he is someone who, "alas," has not grasped the biblical call, and can only be admitted exceptionally—for instance, when there is a shortage of ministers.

Another objection to the text is that an all-too-easy jump is made from desirability to precept, from charism to law. Celibacy is a charismatic gift of the Lord, a gift for which man can prepare himself by prayer and desire—since a man may strive for spiritual gifts (1 Cor 12:31, 14:1, 39). Man, however, cannot force God to bestow them, and it is therefore unthinkable that the ecclesiastical community and Church law prescribe that somebody remain unmarried; if this should happen, not only would human freedom be threatened, but also the state of being unmarried would no longer deserve the name of charismatic virginity, since imposed by a law. The danger is not at all hypothetical under the present legislation on celibacy. It does more than invite candidates to the ministry earnestly to consider whether they are not equally called to a life of continence; it also legally establishes the preference for the unmarried minister with the result that ecclesiastical ministry and celibacy must in fact go together. Celibacy becomes a criterion for admission to, or maintenance in the ministry, and is also represented as a professional duty resulting from the ministry. We shall revert later to this distinction, but must point out at once that the law on celibacy proceeds from the premise that the grace of celibacy is granted along with that of the ministry, and that the person concerned can and should pray that God bestow it on him. No objection can be raised to such a prayer, but as to the law, does it not provide as if God had guaranteed that he would always answer the request? That sort of optimistic understanding cannot be justified from Scripture.

In addition to these objections of a more scriptural nature, the text of Vatican II raises a serious one in the field of formal theology: direct relationship is established between the *life situation* of being unmarried and the *function* of ecclesiastical ministry. We have shown earlier, particularly in section 8, that the ecclesiastical ministry is primarily and formally a functional given. Both ecclesiastical ministry and unmarried life are forms of availability for the kingdom of heaven, and it is quite possible to combine them, as the history of the Church abundantly shows. But these two forms are not on the same level because, by definition, life situation and function are not analogous concepts. The statement that someone *is* a minister has an essentially different scope than the statement that someone *is* unmarried. That is true for every form of ecclesiastical ministry, but it is particularly evident, of course, as regards the so-called part-time ministry. If the requirement of celibacy does indeed derive from the theological given on the ecclesiastical ministry, it must apply also to one that would be exercised, for instance, during a short period of a few hours per year. These cases are not only conceivable in principle, they actually occur, as we saw in the eleventh section. Clearly, it is extremely difficult to show a real inner connection between such a minimal and incidental ministry and the "permanent" life situation of being unmarried; because the respective givens lie in planes too different, and are too widely separated

It appears that, for a multitude of reasons, the thesis of the inner affinity of ecclesiastical ministry and celibate life situation cannot be demonstrated. Even if one could show that in the majority of concrete cases the conjunction of ministry and celibacy is possible, meaningful, and desirable, it still could not be contended that the invitation to continue in celibacy springs from the fundamental given of the ministry *as such*. Our whole analysis, in the preceding sections, of the theological concepts concerning the ecclesiastical ministry precludes any endorsement of such a dogmatic theological affinity thesis. The origin of such a belief should accordingly be explained in terms of a theological approach, now no longer admissible, which considered ministry and life situation as largely coincidental, and did not sufficiently take into account the fact that "the ministry" does not exist; there is only a wealth of "ministries" in the Church, whose one common denominator is "the formal representation of the Lord."

It is worth repeating that in this reasoning the concrete conjunction of ministry and celibacy is neither rejected nor underestimated. Such positions would in effect be claiming that the ministry really includes an invitation to marriage, which is not demonstrable either. As it is, we can say a priori that the gift of celibacy, a gift that can be granted to every Christian, can also be in store for the minister, with the result that for him personally the unmarried life becomes "the better way" of spirituality. We can go a step further, however, and say that the individual minister—and with him the whole ecclesiastical community—can and may interpret this invitation as being connected with the concrete ministerial calling which has been attributed in concrete circumstances. We have already shown in the preceding section that it can be the case for a minister who is appointed to a religious community. But that is not the only possibility. The secular minister also may be so absorbed in his work for the kingdom of heaven that marriage for him becomes existentially meaningless. For the ecclesiastical ministry, although it is primarily a functional given, is most strongly concerned with the fundamental religious data of sin and salvation, of belief and expectation, of the profession of the supremacy of God over the whole of creation. It will never be enough for the minister simply to proclaim his belief in words; he must witness by the whole of his life, just as the Lord whom he represents was not content to express his message in words alone, but was the incarnation of it in his whole person. This puts the possibility of celibacy in a positive light. Charismatic celibacy—even if it is rather meaningless to call it a "higher life situation" in the objective sense—is a very striking admission and telling sign of belief in God as the absolute value and the highest, men can pursue. Ecclesiastical ministry and celibacy, therefore, do have something to do with each other, if not on formal theological grounds, at least for kerygmatic, practical reasons. It would be strange indeed if the very ministers who are so closely involved in "the holy," should step aside from involvement in "the

holy" that lies in celibacy. There is nothing abnormal, therefore, about the fact that a comparatively large number of ministers find themselves called to celibacy.

We have tried to show that a certain preference for the unmarried minister need in no way be unfair in itself, but it remains to be seen how strong this preference may and can be,
and how it can become operative. To answer these questions,
we shall go back to the distinction we have already briefly indicated, between *selection principle* and *professional obligation*.

We feel we must dismiss the question of celibacy as a professional obligation. No satisfactory scriptural or theological
arguments can be adduced in support of this concept, because
there is no essential connection between ministry and celibacy;
this is explicitly acknowledged in *Presbyterorum ordinis*. Being married and being a minister can go together, and therefore, marriage does not in principle render a person unfit for
the ministry, nor does the ministry render a person unfit for
marriage. The legislation of the Latin Church does not do adequate justice to this fundamental concept. Ordination after
marriage is recognized as valid, although it becomes lawful
only after the impediment has been lifted; but a marriage concluded after ordination is not recognized as valid unless there is
an explicit dispensation as regards the diriment marriage impediment constituted by the ordination. No objections can be
raised against the first provision, on theological grounds, but the
second must be simply rejected, because it lacks any biblical
support, conflicts with a sound doctrine on celibacy as a free
gift of grace, and robs man of his natural right to marriage, a
right that cannot be taken from him by any human ecclesiastical
law.

On the matter of celibacy as a selection principle, it is less
easy for a theologian to give a clear opinion. He can readily admit that the lawmakers may have serious reasons for explicitly
showing a preference for unmarried ministers, a preference
for which there is perhaps no explanation which is complete and

convincing for everyone, because it may be joined with a moment of intuition that will not lend itself to any exhaustive analysis. Furthermore, it is not the part of the theologian to give a final opinion on pastoral practical motives. This, however, does not alter the fact that he is interested in the explicit and implicit reasons invoked in defense of this preference, and in testing their validity.

He will, accordingly, ask himself if sufficient regard is paid to the freedom of man. One can say quite rightly that nobody is actually forced to accept the ministry plus celibacy, and that the freedom of the candidates is adequately tested. Whoever is not in favor of the preference of the Church need not apply for the ministry. But that does not exhaust the matter. For many feel that there is something like a "package deal" here; there is really no room for an independent choice of, respectively, the ministry or the unmarried life situation. A person who longs for the ministry may feel compelled to take celibacy into the bargain. It becomes dubious then to speak of a charism, because, as Schillebeeckx says, "as a charism celibacy can only be accepted freely; it can never be imposed, directly or obliquely, not even by the hierarchy." [7] The problem applies not only to the initial phase of the unmarried life, but also to its continuance: the decision, once freely taken, must be freely maintained. Legislation can be of service as a moral support and as a demand for fidelity, but the requirement of fidelity can also be experienced as an abuse when a person has personally outgrown the phase during which he could not existentially do other than remain unmarried. It is not only celibacy itself, but also the beneficial experience of it in conjunction with the ministry that is a charism; one cannot simply make the two identical.

A second question is this: is not the preference for the unmarried minister to be attributed to an attitude of mind that considers celibacy as a "higher" life situation? The question of whether celibacy is an "objectively higher" way—even if the

[7] E. Schillebeeckx, *Celibacy* (New York, 1968), p. 79.

answer were positive, which I seriously doubt—should play no part in setting the disciplinary policy of the Church. Vatican II, as we saw, has presented the superiority theme much more carefully than did Trent, but has not dissociated itself from it sufficiently. When it said in *Presybterorum ordinis* that through celibacy "the priests . . . consecrated to Christ . . . more easily hold fast to Him with undivided heart," a possibility that has often—but by no means always—been ascertained is generalized into a commonly valid, desirable requirement. For the theologian, this should be followed by a big question mark.

Finally, one may ask whether an outspoken preference for the unmarried minister is desirable from a kerygmatic point of view; in other words, if this preference does not express a concept of Church existence that is difficult to hold. The difficulty is recognized by the bishops of the Netherlands in a document published on March 13, 1967:

Confident that remaining unmarried for the sake of the kingdom of heaven has a positive value—even for our time—we feel, on the other hand, that the question of making the celibacy of secular priests optional deserves further study and research . . . Our first consideration is not—although we do not exclude this possibility—to answer the need of individual priests or to stem a possible shortage of priests, but by making celibacy optional, eventually to give the new form of the Church more distinct features, and bring out the characteristic significance of both the priesthood and the state of virginity.[8]

The problem stated in this passage is of the utmost importance, because its formulation goes beyond the practical issues, however important. In the light of the ideas we have developed in this study, it can be said without much hesitation that the question put by the Netherlands bishops can be answered in the affirmative for more reasons than one. The correct view of

[8] *Pastorale Beleidslijnen voor de Ambtsvervulling van de Priester in Nederland,* no. XI (Rotterdam, 1967).

celibacy as a charismatic gift, over which the institutional Church can only exercise a very restricted rule, is undoubtedly seen more clearly when there is no law which almost inevitably gives the impression that the free working of the Spirit is fettered by human decrees. The arguments that may eventually be adduced in favor of the maintanance of the celibacy of ministers will more easily emerge in their own independent forcefulness, and the unmarried minister will make a more convincing impression, once everybody knows that he has chosen his life situation in complete freedom and may give it up if he wishes to do so. Moreover, he himself will find in the fact that the choice is his own, the stimulus to live his calling consistently and to the best of his ability, unhampered by the worry that he may be doomed to adhere for life to a way of life that gives him little personal satisfaction.

But there is an even more important consideration. Any statement in defense of optional celibacy is not only, or even primarily, concerned with the possibility of marriage for those who have been ordained, but with the possibility of also opening the ecclesiastical ministry to those who are already married. This is a matter above all, of the new image of the Church. A Church which likes to insist on the fact that she is other than the world, that she stands somewhat "above" the world as a higher authority and a nuisance value, will prefer that her ministers, who are considered as a kind of nucleus in their work and in their lives, lead a life that underscores their being different; and, of course, abstaining from as vital a human relationship as marriage is a very striking way of doing it. But a Church which takes her incarnation seriously, and respects the value of the earthly reality and in principle entertains a positive attitude toward the tendency to secularization, will also wish to have her ministry shaped so as to relate to this world. Now that, in *Gaudium et spes,* Vatican II has given a provisional charter to the movement for commitment to the world, and the ministry has been rediscovered as a service to the world, it would be anomalous to maintain an obsolescent "celibacy line" for that ministry. It would mean that the incarnation mandate is still not being taken seriously enough, and that an adjustment of the centuries-old virginizing of the human Christian ideal of chastity is being rejected. The ministers would still be a group of "holy outsiders," respected and perhaps admired, but not considered as persons who, in the secular city where most people are married, perform a task of importance to mankind and bring it an indispensable message.

It would seem, therefore, that the question of the celibacy of the minister is no secondary matter; rather, it is the test which will determine the degree of self-knowledge of the Church and of the earnestness with which she will serve the world. New and serious reflection on the preference given to the unmarried minister, and on the legislation resulting from it, is for many reasons a matter of fidelity to the Gospel.

17. THEOLOGY OF THE "EXODUS"

Our critical analysis of the expression "a priest forever" was based, among other things, on the fact that there are many cases in which the ecclesiastical ministry is not exercised until the moment of death. We shall now examine the question of leaving the ministry somewhat more explicitly, not only because it is required if this study is to be complete, but also and particularly because the "premature" departures from the ministry have shown a marked increase in recent years, a phenomenon which has brought up questions of fidelity and loyalty, among others.

The enumeration in Section 11 of various causes of departures from the ministry shows that release from it is not always an abnormal, sad, or tragic event. Likely enough, it will usually be accompanied by a certain feeling of nostalgia, but that will often be offset by resignation and even thankfulness, because "it is all over!" Who will deny that the occurrence can be a real relief for the minister for whom the task has become too heavy, or for the community of the faithful that can no longer be particularly enthusiastic about the ministerial performance of certain individuals? Nor is it warranted to speak in all cases of disloyalty and dereliction of duty. It can happen that tendering one's resignation, or dismissal, is a moral duty, because it is better for the person concerned and the community, and because maintenance of membership in the ministry would be unjustified and harmful.

The question of loyalty arises, of course, mostly when the minister himself resigns without being able to invoke any of the reasons generally regarded as compelling. A step of this order seems to need a different kind of justification, because disinclination, a simple "I don't feel like it any more," is apparently not adequate. It may be useful in this connection to point out that any such reservation seldom obtains in the case of secular professions. Of course, there, it will usually seem strange that somebody should give up a function for which he has undergone long and intensive training and which enjoys social prestige, but disloyalty will not usually be suspected. People will, rightly so, see to it that current business is taken care of as well as possible and that, particularly when the responsibilities of the position involve other people, there is no vacuum which might frustrate reasonable expectations. But no further justification is required for such a step. Notice of the resignation can be given in advance and measures taken to cover the transition period.

It would seem that resignation from the ministry requires a special form of defense and that the process has much more emotional repercussions. It can be somewhat sensational, happens suddenly in most cases, and is not infrequently followed by a difficult period during which the person concerned must start a new life. The former minister is considered, if not exactly as a renegade and a traitor, at least as a failure and a pathetic individual. Because of the traditional condensation of the function into a state of life, resigning from it means not only a change in function, but also giving up an entirely special group of associates and sphere of life. And because the minister stands in the community as a sort of incarnation of the faith, as a basic figure of the Church and the image of Christian virtue, his departure can easily create an atmosphere of uncertainty and doubt among the faithful he leaves behind. This is particularly intense when leaving the ministry is coupled with leaving the Church or giving up the vaunted—and virginized—ideal of celibacy. It must be added that the legislation of the Church suggests this "doubtful" nature of a departure from the ministry: the discharge must be requested as a favor; it is seldom or never qualified as "honorable," and there are no structural measures, or obligations ensuing a positive support in the transition period. The ex-minister looks like a prodigal son, unfit for any further ecclesiastical work; one can only pray and hope for his return.

To clarify and judge this complicated reality, we should first state that a farewell from the ministry is not a farewell to faith and Church; it is renouncing a function within the community of the faithful, not renouncing that community. When leaving the ministry also involves leaving the Church, the combination is accidental. It seems fair to say that, if this distinction had always been clearly realized, many cases which led from a simple resignation from the ministry to a break with the Church could have been avoided.

We can gain a better understanding of the difference between "falling away" and leaving the ministry by distinguishing between the fundamental options of a man, his general design for living, and the decisions as to life situation and function situated within these fundamental options.[1] The compulsory character of both categories varies. We may say that the reconsideration of a decision involving man's fundamental life op-

---

[1] Cf. E. Schillebeeckx, "Roeping, levensontwerp en levensstaat," *Tijdschrift voor Geestelijk Leven*, 17 (1961), pp. 471–520.

tions, once they have been positively taken, is very difficult to accept as ethically justifiable. When a man renounces fundamental obligations after he has admitted their fundamental character, he betrays himself. For instance, since man does not finally dispose of his own life, we may conclude that suicide is never ethically justifiable. Because it is an essential obligation for man to live as man together with his fellows, he may never opt on principle for hatred, total egoism, and deliberate inhumanity. For the person who has been granted faith in the Lord Jesus Christ, this means that he may never give up on principle his call to live for God; faith, once it has been accepted, becomes a requirement of life, and perseverance in the faith, a condition of salvation. Naturally, it is possible for one's personal view of the content of these fundamental demands to change, and become objectively faulty, but it remains true that a person's conscience is his ultimate criterion, and that obedience to the guidance of conscience is the touchstone of his fundamental loyalty.

The problems related to leaving the ministry do not lie on this plane of fundamental options for human living. Otherwise, the community of the faithful, which can never release anybody from his fundamental baptismal obligations, could not ever dismiss a minister from the ministry either. The baptismal sphragis can never disappear, but the mark of the ministerial function can be deleted insofar as it contains a mandate to exercise an actual ministerial function. Of course, the ex-minister also remains a member of the Church, a man redeemed and called to salvation. The minister cannot be released from allegiance to his fundamental humanity and Christian vocation, nor can he release himself from it.

The ultimate question in regard to loyalty lies on the level of the functional options, the secondary choices situated within the frame of one's basic options. Loyalty can also play a part, because here, too, there can be a call and a divine invitation which can impose obligations that a man cannot set aside simply because he longs for a change. God has every right and reason to expect a faithful performance of the charismatic tasks he imposes, and the ministry is certainly one of these charismatic gifts. But here loyalty is far more extensively conditioned, because the changing life situation and the development of man himself play a greater role. The entire human ecclesiastical reality is calling here, the whole concrete situation is "the finger of God." The secondary calling can change as man discovers other possibilities and desires in himself, and circumstances invite him to a different kind of work. It is then that a decision can be taken to give up a previous calling because a new one is available.

All this applies equally to the ecclesiastical ministry. The call to represent the Lord takes on a different concrete form in each different minister's life. One is called to full-time ministry, another is led to part-time ministry because a smaller or larger part of his available time and energy is devoted to work in the framework of apostolic secularity, another again finds the attraction of apostolic secularity so strong and invigorating that he begins to think of giving up the ministry on this account. Allegiance to the earlier call and mandate makes way for another voice he is now listening to. This means that leaving the ministry may result from answering another invitation; for him, to work for apostolic secularity becomes "the better way." In a case like this, to speak of "degradation" makes little sense, because the ecclesiastical ministry, however exalted, is not, in an absolute sense, a higher mandate for every Christian. If we want to bring up the matter of loyalty or disloyalty here, the question is not one of loyalty or disloyalty in terms of public Church law, but of individual conscience and responsibility.

We have tried to show the possibility of a positive new opportunity occurring as an alternative to the vocation of the ministry. But such is not always the case in reality. Leaving the ministry can also assume a more negative aspect; interest in the ministry has declined to such an extent, or the difficulties in exercising it have become so great, that departure from the ministry has become a distinctly negative event, with no positive alternative to follow. Here again, loyalty and responsibility play their part, not only as regards the individual minister, but also the community as a whole, "the employer." The minister will have to ask himself whether, if the interest is less, it is perhaps also his own fault. Was he sufficiently committed to his work? Has he perhaps become discouraged because he overestimated the real difficulties? Has he kept himself informed on current tasks and problems so as to be able to handle them? Has he cultivated his spiritual life so as to keep an affinity for the work of the ministry? These are difficult questions to answer, and the outsider must certainly be extremely careful in the matter; but they are questions that must be put. Fidelity to the ministry does not mean an uncritical acceptance of that form of it which prevailed at the time of a person's appointment, but an evolving loyalty to an evolving ministry; it presupposes and demands development in the minister himself. But the question of loyalty is also a question of the conscience of the community. When there is a discrepancy between the personal disposition of the minister and the structural possibilities, it may not be excluded that the fault lies partly with the community which clings too tenaciously to the old ways, and gives too little scope for the minister's own initiative. When the minister comes to feel so oppressed by unsuitable forms that he feels he must give up the ministry, it is no longer a question of personal failure; his leaving becomes a protest, an act of criticism which the community should take as a very serious warning. Such a possibility is distinctly more than theoretical. In recent years particularly, many have left saying that they could see no reasonable possibilities in the existing situation, but longed for the day when they could rejoin a renewed ministry. They are not right a priori in the manner of their protest, but they pose a problem deserving earnest attention.

We have so far mentioned only the difficulties connected with the exercise of the ministry. But we must not forget that many of the difficulties that lead to leaving the ministry do not lie in that area, but in the field of personal spirituality and personal milieu. Celibacy is clearly the most striking factor here, but we are actually dealing with the whole question of the secularization of a life pattern that had become, in the course of centuries, uniform and monastic. The minister, especially one whose work lies among "ordinary people," often seems to experience an isolation of which the meaning is no longer clear either to him or to others, and that hinders rather than helps the effectiveness of his work and of the example he sets.

In considering the loyalty question, we may again say that the community must ask itself whether the functioning of the ministry is not impeded by an adherence to requirements theologically unfounded and by a sort of "package deal" that is not, or at least is no longer, justified. There are, in the lives of men, genuine dilemma situations: a person wants two things at once, but cannot have them both, is in fact compelled to choose one and—with some regret—renounce the other. The ecclesiastical community may not confront her minister with this kind of situation unless the dilemma has fundamental arguments in its favor. Otherwise—and we saw that they were practically lacking as regards the connection between ministry and life situation, and ministry and spirituality—the community, in maintaining the dilemma, goes beyond the limits of its competence, fetters human freedom, and complicates the work of the Spirit. This is not to say that the Church does not have the right to have an explicit preference for specific spiritualities, or for celibates. The point at issue is more the manner in which the preference can be effected. The community of the faithful is not responsible for an individual's inability personally to adopt the Church's preference, but she may not resent this inability and should with the greatest generosity, allow someone who can no longer accept celibacy or another form of spiritual life to resign from the ministry in all honor. To date, this has seldom or never been done wholeheartedly, because the theological understanding of the matter was not sufficiently developed, and also because it was feared that such a positive attitude would encourage departures from the ministry. Now that the theological position has become a little clearer, leaving the ministry on account of difficulties with its "spirituality" can no longer be described as questionable (loyalty, here, is exclusively a matter for the individual conscience). If it is feared that this more broad-minded attitude will bring about an increase in the number of people leaving the ministry, the only conclusion to be considered is that, possibly, the selection criteria have been too narrow. As long as this question remains open, it makes little sense to pray for more vocations.

As regards the departures from the ministry on account of the celibacy question, it is even truer that a new positive vocation can open up here: the intensive cultivation of love of a fellow man in God. Many seem to entertain the notion that leaving the ministry "on account of a woman" is even worse than doing it for other reasons. Our fresh understanding teaches us that the reverse can be true. A marriage contracted by someone who was unmarried before is no moral degradation and no "lower way"; to fall in love and marry is a new charism granted after that of virginity has gone: marriage also is a way to God, and it is not of less value than leading a virginal life. The thought of marriage is, as such, no "temptation" that the unmarried minister should reject out of hand; marriage can be a new vocation. All this, of course, is valid only insofar as it applies to a statement of principles. As to whether renouncing celibacy and contracting marriage is also "the better way" for an individual minister, that is an entirely different matter. The last word is up to his conscience, and the concrete situation prevailing at the time will play an important part in shaping that decision. But he should not wonder whether the ecclesiastical community and Church law will perhaps morally condemn his decision. They have no authority to do so. For the Lord himself has not forbidden his ministers to marry, or said that being married makes them less fit, or unfit, for their work in his service. If one of his Churches claims that she must make this prohibition, the burden of the proof rests with her, not with the individual minister.

Finally, one more question: is there a parallel between fidelity to the ministry or to celibacy on the one hand, and marital fidelity on the other? Is it true in both cases that what God has united, man must not divide and that once the hand is laid on the plough, no one who looks back is fit for the kingdom of God?

It must be emphasized first and foremost that whoever enters the ministry, or accepts the gift of celibacy, undertakes a serious task from which he must not let himself be turned away by fickleness or a brief sinking of his energy and courage. Leaving the ministry or ending one's unmarried life is not an everyday decision. But the ethical imperative of not looking back once the hand is laid on the plough is there no absolute requirement, because another form of service to Church and world, as well as a married life, may also be waiting for the plough. The comparison with marital fidelity hardly stands because, anthropologically and theologically, the foundations of marital fidelity go much deeper. A marriage contract establishes a relation between persons that is essentially different from the service that binds a minister to his community, because marriage creates an existential oneness, so that, as Scripture has it, the two become one flesh. The same Scripture shows the marriage bond as the image of the bond uniting God and his people, Christ and his Church. One could perhaps say that marriage is also one of these fundamental options that man may not go back on because in so doing he would be unfaithful to his essential call to community. And one might add that, when a weak man fails to remain faithful in all cases, and in fact and existentially can do little else but break the conjugal bond, such a step can at most be tolerated, but we cannot also say, as we can in the case of renouncing the ministry or giving up celibacy, that it is possible in principle to sense a new vocation in the decision. We cannot, within the framework of this study, go any further into the complicated problem of the indissolubility of marriage, a tenet that is probably less monolithic than it is often thought to be. All we want to show is that the parallel between fidelity to the ministry (*casu quo* fidelity to celibacy) and marital fidelity is not very clear. Indeed, what is true of all these obligations is that a decision once taken, a pact once concluded, must be confirmed every day: fidelity is a gift to chisel, not an immovable, once-and-forever fact. Whoever has married a woman must propose to her again every day, just as the minister must be ready again every day to listen to the voice of his Lord and the voice of his fellow man, and answer to the best of his understanding and ability.

PART III

❊·❊

THE MINISTRY OF THE FUTURE

1. THE MINISTRY IS CHANGING

In 1963, there appeared in the United States an article provocatively entitled "What Is Wrong with the Church: The Clergy." [1] The accusation, of course, is too sweeping to be altogether true, but the basic idea it expresses deserves unqualified attention.

For the Church of Christ did not fall into widespread disrepute because Christians were no longer disposed to serve their fellowmen and the world, but because many people could not or no longer recognize the forms and manner of the service as truly valid and effective. The willingness to serve was still there, but the actual ability to do so was apparently seriously impaired. One of the most important causes of the failure was, not unfairly, imputed to the ecclesiastical "cadre." There was usually no lack of good will, but rather a mistaken view of the true function of the Church in the world. When the Church is seen as a haven, a citadel in the land of the heathens, attention is understandably given first to her internal structures and relations, to the defense of the characteristic ecclesiastical position challenged from outside. The group of ministers can then come to

[1] P. Way, *Renewal* (1963).

be seen as the nucleus of the Church, the highest embodiment of the Christian ideal of holiness; the ministry becomes the object of veneration, a part of "the treasure of the faith," to be preserved whole and inviolate. It is awarded in particular and more or less exclusively, properties that belong to the whole Church: unity, holiness, catholicity, and apostolicity. Unconditional obedience to the ministry becomes the touchstone of membership in the Church, the ministers personify the objectified and permanently valid composition of Christian holiness, forms of belief and life are considered really Christian only if they have been authenticated by the ministry, and in the college of ministers lies the absolute guarantee that the Church of today is still exactly the same Church as the one founded by Christ. A Church heavily concentrated around the ministry finds it hard to relativize her own historic forms; since it is this concentration, and not faith, which made her appear as the unshakeable rock standing in the stream of human evolution. The stability of the ministerial patterns seems to be the condition and the guarantee of the imperishability of the Church.

The man of today is less open to so great a preoccupation with internal ecclesiastical life, and the more recent developments in ecclesiology support his attitude. While the secular world around him was forever changing, and his own human sensitivity was acquiring new forms, "the Church" seemed to remain a fixed given. Conflicts arose to the point where one could feel that membership in the Church hindered his development as a human being, and begin to wonder whether, in order to be true to his own human dynamic, he must not give up an obsolescent institution, or at least dissociate himself mentally from many practices and rules. He could hardly sense in his Church community the quickening spirit he felt blowing through the evolution of the planet. He began to find the Church was a brake rather than a source of inspiration.

The new image of the Church, which is now beginning to emerge, has awakened fresh hope and put a stop to widespread pessimism and mistrust. Even if everything is not yet clear, even if there is still a great deal of hesitation, it is once more possible to believe that the Church has a future. The changes in theological thought and ecclesiastical life patterns give renewed strength to the intuition of faith which senses that Christianity will perform its mission profitably in the world of tomorrow, although ecclesiastical forms and Christian life-styles will be altered.

It is in this stream of Christian and ecclesiastical evolution that the ministry also moves, and must move, if it is not to betray its own function. Although the ministry grew out of the past, it is not its job to stand in the Church as a symbol of rigid adherence to that past. It must be ready to serve the world of today and tomorrow, and should therefore itself be modern, and continue to be modern. The minister is not the personification of immutability, but the driving power of the human Christian evolution toward the fullness of faith and love. It is therefore characteristic of the ministry always to be changing, to experience crisis, to be reforming. Just as the Church must always be shaped anew, so also the ministry. Change is not a sign of decay, but on the contrary, of health and vitality.

To think of the ministry in terms of evolution does not come easily to us, anymore than it does to think in terms of change of the Church as a whole, of doctrine and ethics. We must draw on our imagination, not only because we cherish a past that we were satisfied with for so long, but also because the future is not clear. For the so-called realist, who refuses to consider anything but facts he can grasp (yesterday's and today's), this may be a shocking idea. He might stop to think that precisely those whom we usually call "tough realists"—the politicians, the economists, the captains of industry—are continually concerned with tomorrow because they know that without it, today makes no sense. The "children of light" have something to learn from them.

One might object that advocating evolutionary thinking is

like preaching truisms. Isn't it especially the Church which is bent on the future? Isn't she the first phase of eschatological salvation, and does she not long for the coming of the Bridegroom? Of course, that is true; the Church believes in a future. But her faith often seems to be a waiting faith, the expectation of a sudden event wrought "from above" and which in one movement will establish the new Time. That kind of faith may harbor the idea that all men's thinking and doing is mere patchwork, but it may also hide a dread of opening up new ways, a fear of taking one's life into his own hands. The Christian message may perhaps even be called revolutionary; the very least it is evolutionary. To have a sense of crisis—in the full sense of the word—and to be prepared for change are not minor matters but structural duties. Surely it is not without reason that in our day a man to whom life had brought wisdom showed the Church that her duty lay in *aggiornamento,* in being abreast of every moment of the history of man.

2. DEMOLITION AND CONSTRUCTION

When the Prophet Jeremiah was called to his office, he was commanded to tear up and to knock down, to destroy and to overthrow, to build and to plant (Jer 1:10). Renewal is not effected without destruction and suffering. When the seed sprouts, it tears its husk and opens up the soil; when a child is born, the mother endures pain: when a new building is to come up, the old is dismantled and torn down.

If we are going to refit the house of the ministry, we shall have to demolish parts of it. The wallpaper will have to go, doors and windows will have to be moved, and the heap of unusable materials will grow in the garden. In the middle part of this book, we have perhaps inflicted a good deal of damage on the familiar house of the ministry: the painting of the sacred hierarch went from the wall and his altar was moved to a room less often used; the name plate reading "priest" was unscrewed and replaced with an ordinary card saying "servant"; the baroque front was made to look simpler, so that the house stands out less among the homes of the worldly; the heavy oak portal with the double lock has gone, and a swinging door been put up instead: anybody may come in; the warning "men only" has been pulled up and the former bachelors' rooms now have double beds; the residents have been told that their stay will not necessarily be permanent, and that they may have to do a great deal of their work outside their quarters. But the dismantling has made the house more liveable; it has, among other things, improved the acoustics, so that the voice of Scripture can be caught more clearly, telling of the underlying unity of the people of God, brotherly service to all, and apostolic concern for the salvation of the whole world. No longer is the house of the ministry strictly private, reserved for a select group of people; it has now become a community center for the world, and a base for outgoing action.

Some might claim that the main emphasis of our study is on tearing down, on disposing of all that has become superfluous or trying, and that it suggests few new departures in replacement. That is true, but isn't that also the usual way of things? In the majority of cases, houses that have been rebuilt and reconditioned look rather bare, but why? Because we had become used to the clutter; after living awhile with the spaciousness, we realize that something else has replaced the old after all: light, a better over-all view, and freedom. These are not negative things: their function is only different from that of big pieces of furniture and heavy draperies.

3. THE BREACH OF THE DEMARCATION LINES

To characterize the program for the reconstruction of the house of the ministry succinctly, we could say that its main point must be tearing down dividing walls and erasing demarcation lines; demolishing, not so much the needless partitions inside the house as the barriers which turn the ministry and ministers into a little world of their own, cut off from the rest of God's people and the profane world. In the course of our study, we made a critical appraisal of the use and need of the traditional lines: the clergy line, the professional line, the sex line, the regulars line, and the celibacy line. The need for them is no longer clear, and only after we have levelled the ground will the roads to the future make good going.

One of the most fantastic gifts the Lord granted his followers is the belief in the oneness and equality of all men. For him, there is no man or woman, slave or freeborn, Jew or Gentile, colored or white; and even as to distinguishing between good and bad, he taught us to be extremely careful: the harvest will show the weed. Why then should his community make needless distinctions between "hierarchy" and laity, clergy and people, heads and subordinates, holy and "ordinary" Christians, sticklers and accommodating fellows?

If the ecclesiastical ministry really wishes to serve the one community of God and promote the unity of all mankind, it must not itself be a source of disruption; it must not dig trenches, but build bridges. The minister, while exercising to the full his own specific mission, the representation of the Lord, should embody this mission and live it, not as an outsider but as a member of the people of God, marked off as little as possible from those for whom he is appointed. He will have to ask himself if the whole historical condensation of the ecclesiastical ministry into a clerical life situation is really in conformity with the evangelical warning of the Lord who became a man among men: You, however, must not allow yourselves to be called Rabbi, since you have only one Master, and you are all brothers. You must call no one on earth your Father, since you have only one Father and he is in heaven. Nor must you allow yourselves to be called teachers, for you have only one Teacher, the Christ. The greatest among you must be your servant. Anyone who exalts himself will be humbled, and anyone who humbles himself will be exalted (Mt 23:8-12). Being a minister is always a small aspect of anyone's Christianity; what binds a minister to his fellow Christians is always more than what separates him from them.

Both from a theological and a practical point of view, one can only welcome the present trend toward a declericalization of the ministry and of the person of the minister. The disappearance of clerical garb, the participation "as layman" in the celebration of the Eucharist, the criticism of celibacy, the desire for "secular work" attributed on the basis of recognized professional training: these are not phenomena to be tolerated, but various expressions of a fundamentally correct intuition. "Crisis phenomena" of this kind point to a readiness for inner divestment, for kenosis; they indicate that the ministry is on its way from "authority" to "service." The ministry is once again being merged with the community from which it had become isolated.

Theologically, we can also welcome the developments taking place in the ministry as a whole. The pyramidal shape of the governmental structure is disappearing; an all-too-monarchical papacy is being counterbalanced by a renewed and improved conciliar theory of episcopal collegiality; at the regional and provincial levels of ecclesiastical structure, forms of management and mutual consultation are beginning to take shape which will correct the excessive autonomy of local bishops, and the singularity of any given diocese; and within the diocese, efforts are being made toward the establishment of a more collegial and horizontal relationship between the bishop and his fellow workers ensuring a readier use of the leader and team terminology than of the words authorities and obedient servants.

4. FROM AUTHORITY TO SERVICE

As the demarcation lines are erased, the whole ministerial institution acquires a different character. As long as the ministry stands above the community, it is tempted to reign and give orders, consider objections and criticism as illegal, and absolutize its own ideas. But let it stand among the faithful, and allow the community to ask questions and suggest things to be done, and the ministry becomes humble service. When this happens, there will be no need to wonder whether respect for authority is perhaps in danger, or the rightful authorities are possibly being bypassed; then, the first and last standard of efficiency of the ministry will be: is as much room as possible being made for the saving works of the Lord of the Church? Hierarchical relationships become service relationships, structures spring up or go, according as they are needed or superfluous, and the ministry as a whole changes from a static power factor into a dynamic source of inspiration.

The change from power to service will be primarily a change in mentality. Once the service idea has become part and parcel of every minister's attitude, the most important condition for a renewal of the ministry will have been met. At the same time, however, we must have the beginning of a reappraisal of structures, based on the new concept of the unity and collective responsibility of the whole people of God. The structures of the ministry will have to merge, as much as possible, with the general Christian structures, remaining outside those that are designed for the joint endeavors of minister and laity on behalf of the salvation of world and Church only when it is inherently required. During the 1920's and 1930's the concept of the responsibility of the laity expressed itself in the various forms of Catholic action, which were often considered as a help to the "hierarchic apostolate" and were quite definitely supervised by the ministry. Nowadays, the question to be considered is the fusion of the respective structures of the ministerial and the lay apostolate.

In this field, Vatican II has opened up possibilities that must still be thought through and worked out. It has initiated integration, while remaining hesitant as to a radical reform. In the decree *Apostolicam actuositatem,* on the apostolate of the laity, a good piece of work in itself, the reasoning, as in *Lumen gentium,* still proceeds from an inadequate understanding of the difference between minister and layman. The same applies to the councils of priests and the pastoral councils advocated by Vatican II: the division between laity and ministry has not been sufficiently leveled off. Laity and ministers are responsible together for the whole life of the Church, and consequently the specifically ministerial task is to be carried out within mixed structures. The minister, however, does not function as the authority who obligingly listens to advice, only to take the final decision alone later, but as the recorder who registers and authenticates the collective deliberation and joint decision. The final stage will have to be the pastoral council, composed of ministers and laymen; priests' councils and other kinds of ministerial bodies will in the long run have to become merely complementary structures. They could perhaps even disappear to a large extent after they have helped, during the transition period, to bring to full growth the idea of the oneness of God's people and of the ministry as service.

5. THE PHILOSOPHER OF THE CONSTRUCTION GANG

There was a construction worker, about forty, who knew his job and was a nice fellow, always ready to help with some festive occasion or to go along with a prank. But he had something else besides. The others did not know exactly how to describe it; the best they could do was to say that he was "such a swell guy." He had a sort of quiet wisdom and a humorous sense of proportion that made him a kind of leader. Not in the sense of a union leader, because he was not really aggressive; he was not for standing on "his rights" so much, and he did not worry, or not too much, about making a dollar more, or less, a week. He was no scholar either, for he had not gone beyond technical school, and when he had driven around in France during a previous vacation, his ignorance of the language had once or twice landed him in real difficulties. The other men knew that he read the papers and occasionally went through a serious book. He knew how to use his wits—you could see that from the way he took part in discussions; he did not shout, but the remarks he made regularly made you say, "Well, that's something to consider too." He was the philosopher of the group; not the stuffy puzzle-headed kind, but one who always made you want not to be too brash, because he'd give you to understand in passing that there were more things between heaven and earth than you had thought out for yourself. He always saw a little more, grasped a little more, had a feeling for the relative value of things. If someone turned up in the morning feeling blue because his wife had been a pest or his motorbike had broken down, he would have a bit of a laugh like anybody else; but he would not go on teasing, for he had a good memory, and knew that the same thing had happened to him a couple of days earlier and that he might find himself in the same situation on the next day. In this way, he was a sort of counsellor; you could go to him to borrow a claw hammer and at the same time casually mention a "life problem" and try to find out what he thought about it; and you knew that he would keep the matter to himself.

All this was somehow connected with his faith. He was a Catholic, he did not hide the fact, but that did not seem to make him pious or soft. He was a churchgoer, but he was not forever on the pastor's doorstep. He thought that the separation of the Churches was idiotic, and was not so certain there was any need for a Catholic Party; he thought that the pope just should not bother with the size of families, and objected somewhat to the fact that the Church was rather often on the side of the rich. He tried to be a good Christian, read the scriptures sometimes, and thought that Jesus and Pope John and Bishop Bekkers were fantastic people. He belonged to a discussion group on the Council, and liked to speak about it. Some of the men enjoyed listening then, because they felt that what he thought was important, must really be worthwhile.

Sometimes, to tease him, the others called him "the pastor," but there was nothing insulting about it; instead, the word was a token of respect. They made him a spiritual guide, because that is what he had really become over the years. In the group, he functioned as the philosopher, as the man of God; not as a "religious leader" and still less as a manager of an organized Church, but as a colleague. He himself realized quite well that he must use his charism very carefully, that he had to wait till the time was ripe; he knew too that he could be accepted as a man of God only because and insofar as he was accepted as fellow man, and continued to be accepted as such. He was able to say things about God and about faith because he made it plausible that God and faith had something to do with himself, with those around him, with the work and with the whole of their life.

His talking about God and faith also had something to do with his Church. She functioned more in the background. But they never felt her presence as a threatening foreign authority, because their "priest" never used her as an authority; he found inspiration in her, and interpreted that inspiration fairly freely, so as to apply it to an actual situation. The others had no objections that the Church should officially approve and support the work he did with them, provided he did not become a sort of delegate of this Church, because then he would be less one of them. He gave them what they needed from time to time, a little support to help them behave well, a little feeling for relativity, the belief that one could be simultaneously a Christian and a human being. And sometimes he would have them all together in the evening after work, or during a weekend, tell the children something about being good, try to settle quarrels, have a meal with them, and expand their being together into a commemoration of Jesus who is as indispensable to men as food and drink.

6. THE MEN FROM THE TRAINING CENTER

This man was no human or religious genius who could do everything alone. He did not know everything about his faith, nor was he an all-round psychologist or teacher. His work was directed and supported by others, experts whom the Church put at his disposal. He corresponded with them, explained his problems to them, received advice from them, and he sometimes invited them to come and do things that he did not quite know how to handle. This group of experts, under the leadership of a person who coordinated and supervised these activities, belonged to the training center; proficient in theoretical and practical sciences, they constituted the backbone of its staff; sometimes they sat at their desks to prepare the plans and the counselling, at others they were in the field to help the local workers and check whether their plans and projects were really practicable.

The head of the training center occupied a position of the utmost importance. He enjoyed a special kind of authority, not so much as an expert in every field, but because he, together with the heads of the other training centers, had received in a very special manner the task of preserving unity and giving to all the workers the assurance that what they did conformed indeed with what Jesus had indicated in his day, and which had been explained originally by the first overseers, the apostles. The philosopher of the construction gang knew that it was only by keeping continually in touch with the head of the center that he could make his own work fruitful, and that only by referring to him would his words and deeds acquire something of the power of Jesus Christ.

7. ONE MINISTRY, BUT A THOUSAND FORMS

The concrete ecclesiastical ministry is built around the needs of the community; if these needs change, the ministry must grow with them. It is therefore impossible to give a complete picture of tomorrow's ministry; it will be different from day to day, because the world is different every day. But one can nevertheless sketch an outline of it.

The nucleus of the ecclesiastical ministry will prove more and more to lie in the episcopate. After Vatican II, this is no rash statement: the collegial ministry is the ministry par excellence because it is the unifying and coordinating ecclesiastical office both as regards the Church as a world entity, and as regards the Church at the local level. The universal Church is centered round the apostolic college; the local Church, round the bishop's see. The bishop gathers together all the services existing in the local Church; that is why the difference between the bishop and the other members of his Church is more fundamental than that separating subordinate ministers and the laity: it is under his guidance that they all work for the sanctification of the world, although in different ways. The bishop is first and last the one who represents the Lord in his Church. The heavy emphasis laid on the episcopate does not, however, mean that the bishop becomes a kind of local autocrat; his office is in essence a supervisory service, and the one he represents is not the glorified Lord of the kingdom to come, but the Son of man, working among us in humility; the bishop receives the gifts of the Spirit in a special manner, but as the Spirit comes to all the members of the Church, the bishop always remains the colleague and fellow Christian of all those for whom he exercises his pastoral office. The collegial bond between the bishop and all those under his supervision, all those who are covered by his ultimate responsibility for the continuance of Christ's work, is at least as important as the collegial horizontal link that binds the bishops among themselves.

The reasons for distinguishing between laity and "lower" ministers will change increasingly from a matter of principle to that of situation. The lay apostolate under strict hierarchical management becomes a Christian apostolate in which everybody works together on the basis of equal responsibility. The status of being a layman will grow; correspondingly, that of being a minister will diminish, until a level is reached of a new unity and an equal value. When a specific ministry is needed as participation in that representation of Christ which is primarily embodied in the bishop, some will be appointed and ordained either for a long period of time or for incidental work.

The difference between those who serve the community directly and full-time, and those who are chiefly concerned with apostolic secularity and devote only a part of their time to strictly ecclesiastical work, will be greater than the difference between minister and laity. At first sight, this might seem to be the beginning of a new form of clericalization, because the full-timers could, in the long run, turn into a specific and "higher" ecclesiastical group into a nucleus Church. However, there is no need to fear this too greatly, provided the full-time functions continue to be considered as down-to-earth "services," and are not given too great a dignity suggested by excessively sacralizing and mystifying forms of vocation and appointment. It will also be important, of course, to do away in earnest with the traditional condensation of the ministry into a life situation. The full-timers, the men and women from the training center, will derive their professional status primarily from their professional ability, and not from some kind of ordination that sets them apart; possibly, it will become apparent that there are not so very many ecclesiastical activities for which this ordination is necessary per se. And because professional satisfaction stems mainly from the quality of the specialized work, rather than from the somewhat mysterious atmosphere which surrounds it, recruitment for functions of this sort may perhaps also be less difficult in the long run.

The possibilities of the part-time ministry warrant an even greater optimism. During recent years, and particularly owing to the impetus given by Vatican II, the layman has shaken off the passivity engendered by his isolation, and enormous good will is apparent everywhere, a readiness to think together about, and work together for, the Church of the future. Considering

can therefore spend much, if not the greatest part, of his time in the service of apostolic secularity, which largely removes the danger of any clericalization of the person of the deacon. As to celibacy: Vatican II apparently still found it impossible to give up the traditional coupling of ecclesiastical office and celibacy; actually, a sort of celibacy law was also introduced for the deacons; only with a certain hesitancy is the diaconate conferred on "men of more mature age, living in the married state"; and the celibate deacon may not marry after ordination. It is known that 839 of the 2,203 bishops voting (about 40 per cent) were prepared not to require any celibacy rules as regards the diaconate.[1] In all likelihood, therefore, we shall have a large number of married deacons, providing a certain familiarity with the married minister, and a chance that a thorough discussion of the celibacy of the presbyters, which will have to take place in any case in the none-too-distant future, can be more profitably undertaken.

The "reinstatement" of the diaconate, however poor the reasons for it, does at least show that there is a priori no desire to maintain the traditional structures of the ministry only, and consequently no rejection of an *aggiornamento* of the ministry.

9. THE CELIBACY OF THE PRESBYTERS AND BISHOPS

The recent encyclical *Sacerdotalis caelibatus* has been a disappointment to many, and even roused many people's indignation. And rightly so, for it is, theologically considered, a very weak piece of work and certainly no example of an intelligent pastoral policy.

The weakness of the encyclical does not lie in its exposition of the virginal state of life as such. Aside from some reservations one may have as to the virginizing of the Christian ideal

---

[1] Cf. R. Bunnik, "Het zielzorgelijk tekort. Concilie en Celibaat," *T.E.U.,* 13 (1966), pp. 137-151; see in particular, pp. 139-141.

of chastity, which can again be detected,[1] the tribute paid to the virginal state of life is acceptable. But the encyclical fails completely to make any sound examination of the essential questions regarding the connection between ministry and life situation, or give any real justification for the *law* on celibacy. It shows no advance at all on section 16 of *Presbyterorum ordinis* and its theology of the ministry is out of date and simplistic. No account is taken of the views on ministry and celibacy of other Churches, nor does one get the impression that the law of celibacy is yet seen as a structural problem of the Church; the legitimacy of enacting legislation on a charismatic state of life that must be freely chosen and continued remains as doubtful as before.

The publication of *Sacerdotalis caelibatus* will not, therefore, herald the end of discussions on the celibacy of the ministers. Rather, these are likely to become sharper, because what had remained a more or less open question—for it was not seriously debated by Vatican II—can, it would seem, no longer be argued, thanks to an utterly inadequate encyclical in which the objections against mandatory celibacy are hardly taken seriously. This cannot be admitted on grounds of either theological understanding or pastoral consideration. Future discussions will inevitably center on the legality of a law on celibacy, and on the extent to which ecclesiastical authorities and the community of the faithful are competent so deeply to interfere in the personal life pattern of a minister.

Theologians today do not differ fundamentally on the value of virginal life, and apparently there is a widespread willingness to consider on what grounds the state of being unmarried can be recommended to the ecclesiastical minister. But the jump

---

[1] In some places, the unmarried state of celibate priests is qualified in the encyclical as "perfect chastity." The unmarried state as such is no virtue of chastity, but merely a situation in which Christian chastity can acquire a characteristic feature; we examined earlier, on pp. 148-149 and p. 167, whether this is, or not, a "higher" form of chastity.

from recommendation to legal regulation is no longer acceptable to a growing number of serious people; this is a matter of principle, regardless of the reservations one might entertain concerning the tenability of the traditional arguments of a more practical nature. By its failure to respect the personal freedom of man, the encyclical enhances once again the danger of a concept of the ministry that will emphasize ruling rather than serving, and as a result, it looks as if the big battle over the radical change in principles which the ministry must effect, from authority to service, will be joined precisely in the field of the celibacy of the ministers.[2] The selection of this "battlefield" is nothing to rejoice about, because so much personal happiness is at stake; but history seems to make this inevitable.

The introduction of a large scale married diaconate may bring about a favorable climate for this radical change in principles. Vatican II, by creating the possibility of a married diaconate, has recognized that an optimal number of ministers is more important than an all-too-rigorous adherence to a preference for unmarried ministers. Here we have a development on which there is no going back: the same thing will have to be said about the presbyterial and episcopal ministries. Surely, calling married people to the presbyterate will have to be the first practical step. Once this has become accepted practice, marriage after ordination should also become acceptable without too much difficulty, for then no one will be prepared to admit that somebody who was a good minister as a celibate suddenly loses this quality by contracting marriage. That the married person makes as good and as useful a minister as the unmarried is a matter that cannot be debated a priori, although the experience of other Churches would seem to point in that direction; only

[2] This applies in particular to the theological views on the practical functioning of the papal office. Cf. H. Küng, *The Church* (New York, 1967), pp. 388-480.

after a goodly period of practice shall we be able to establish the validity, in the long run, of a certain preference, in practice, for the unmarried—a preference however, that is not urged by legal prescripts.[3]

10. THE WOMAN MINISTER

As long as the law on celibacy is in effect, and the minister is not allowed to have a wife as helpmate, it hardly seems indicated to insist on making the ecclesiastical ministry accessible to women. But the question should all the same be considered even now.

In the thirteenth section we saw that, in principle, there is no reason to exclude women from the ecclesiastical ministries, and that one is justified in thinking that her presence would profit the ministry and thereby make more fruitful the service of the Church to the world. This assumption cannot be verified from experience, but reasons for experimenting can already be found. In fact, women have never been completely shut out, for from the very earliest times, they were, whether or not they openly exercised the ecclesiastic function of deaconess, active in religious instruction, for instance, or ecclesiastical social work. At this time, other possibilities are in sight: theology, participation in discussions within the Church and in pastoral councils, administrative functions; and nuns can already perform such liturgical functions as conducting prayer services and dispensing the Eucharist. To date, these developments can only be interpreted as performance of functions, still lay in essence, although very important. Vatican II, as we have said already, took no steps toward any "ministerializing" of these actual activities.

One may wonder whether such a "ministerializing" and formalizing is indeed necessary at a time when the functions of the

[3] For several other practical suggestions, please turn to *De Wan*, vol. 1, 1966-1967, no. 7 (also published in *Kath. Archief*, vol. 22, 1967, col. 528-541).

ecclesiastical ministry are being so strongly declericalized. That is partly true: if a greater or lesser number of women were permitted to cross the sex line, and nothing else were to change, little would have been gained. But on the other hand, it is also true that there is a real difference between minister and layman, a difference that can be formally defined and determined by law. Never may declericalization lead to a total disappearance of the ecclesiastical ministry, and therefore, if woman is really going to be fully involved in the total life of the church, the sex line will have to be crossed explicitly, and woman will have to be called and formally ordained. Several Reformation Churches show us a way here: they formally open their ministries to women and so seem to hold the view that a gradual declericalization of the ministry is not sufficient in order to do full justice to woman's contribution to the life of the Church.

This is a clear invitation to the Catholic Church; the ordination of women is a test case of true ecumenical disposition and readiness to review, for the sake of unity, historical practices that are not necessary.

11. VOCATION AND TRAINING

Much has been written and said in the last years about the reform of priestly formation and new ways of recruiting candidates. Traditional recruitment methods were no longer adequate and the results of professional training and spiritual education no longer satisfactory. As regards the theological and pastoral education of full-time ministers, important changes are presently under way: greater centralization, less waste of manpower, and higher standards of training.

But all this leaves one question unanswered: what exactly is it we are calling people to, and what are we training them for? For one's vision of the ministry of the future determines to a large extent the methods of calling and forming. The changes effected to date still derive very much from the traditional idea of a full-time and permanent ministry, though one can, it is true, detect some notion of the possibility of early specialization, and the field of recruitment is still almost exclusively limited to young men who have reached the age when they must choose a profession.

Since we assume that the forms of the ministry of the future will be extremely numerous, we must ask ourselves whether the reforms being effected at present, however necessary, are yet radical enough, and whether we do not require a reorientation that goes much deeper. One question is particularly valid in this connection: should the matter of what is usually called late vocations not be studied much more extensively, keeping in mind, above all, the part-time ministry? The contemporary structures of priestly formation, even when modernized, still bear the stamp of a certain mythologizing of the ministry that makes of it a kind of exalted specialization combined with a form of expert authority, whose validity is questionable. By this we do not mean to criticize the present reforms; they are desirable and necessary. We only wish to indicate they are no cure-all, because they are restricted to one form of renewal of the ecclesiastical ministry.

Our philosopher of the construction gang had first developed into a mature person and mature Christian, and only after that, and through it, gradually grew into one form of ecclesiastical ministry. For ministers of this type, part-timers and "late vocations," completely new methods of education and training must be developed: evening and week-end courses, something like those for which workers are picked and in which they are trained to become labor leaders.[1] This approach would yield a great deal of manpower, because contact with the person's own milieu can be maintained and there is no need to fear any estrangement from his own circle due to a long and isolating period of

[1] The existing open courses in theology—some of which are a little like secondary teacher training courses qualifying for religious instruction—could perhaps be developed and made to serve the needs of part-time ministry formation.

formation. A part-time ministry will be more attractive because it requires far fewer "sacrifices" socially, psychologically, and perhaps also economically.

But it may also be useful to direct even many of those who apply for the ministry when they are still young toward the part-time ministry. Besides being formed for strictly ecclesiastical work, they will also have to be trained for a "profane" profession, possibly in the social field (teaching, social work, mental health), but equally perhaps for more technical tasks. This will ensure that they remain or become to a maximum integrated in the ordinary life of society (which will improve the efficacy of their work as ecclesiastical ministers), that they need struggle less with the problem of their professional standing, and that they can resign more easily from the ministry when there is some reason or other for them to do so.

A third group will have to be constituted, full-time ministers with a highly specialized and preferably academic education. They make up the diocesan staff and are also eventually leaders or members of the local pastoral working group. Their number will depend on existing needs, and it is not necessary, of course, for all of them to receive a formal ministerial appointment to the function. For the distinction between minister and nonminister must not necessarily coincide with the difference between full-timer and part-timer. That applies to all branches; as we have seen, neither proclaiming, nor theology, nor liturgy, nor pastoral management are specifically ministerial tasks by reason of their content.

12. TOWARD AN ECUMENICAL MINISTRY

The Churches once so sadly divided are, in our time of grace, slowly coming to a new oneness in the Lord. The numerous ecclesiastical ministries of today and tomorrow also partake in this growth toward unity. That is why the ministries of tomorrow will be ecumenical, mutually related in the richness of their differentiations, just as the pluriform Church of tomorrow will be one and at the same time varied.

Bringing the ecclesiastical ministry up to date is therefore not an internal concern of the Catholic Church. It must be handled in close relationship with the other Christian Churches. We have not been able to develop this ecumenical aspect in the course of this study, but we hope that the reader was aware of its continuing presence in the background. The abolition of the lines separating ministry and nonministry will contribute toward the elimination of the boundaries separating the Churches.

There is much to be said for the contention that what separates Christians most from each other is ecclesiology, their different understanding of the life and function of the Church. If the ecumenical mentality demands extensive discussion of the views on the Church, it follows that the ministries of the various Churches must also be examined.

In the Church of tomorrow, pastors and clergymen are going to look very much alike. If the reader of this book has begun to wonder whether there still is a properly "Roman" ministry, he has grasped one of the author's important meanings; for the author has often looked with some envy at the Reformation which has already had four centuries in which to work at the *aggiornamento* of a too strongly clericalized ecclesiastical ministry.

13. THOSE WHO BELIEVE KEEP GOING

There is an old saying to the effect that those who believe do not hurry. And it is a fact that when the message of salvation is delivered too hastily, without proper assurance that the field is ready to receive the seed, it works more harm than good.

But this kind of saying cannot be used as a guideline for every action of the Church. One may rightly contend that man's haste must not try to hurry the tempo of the Spirit, but it is just as true that man must believe that the tempo he considers right is the tempo that the Spirit has put before him. Warning against too great a hurry can also hide an unwillingness or an inability to take on one's own responsibilities.

Bringing the ecclesiastical ministry up to date is an urgent matter, and it must be undertaken by us, members of the Church of today, as the Spirit wills it and with his help. What the ministry of the future will look like, nobody knows exactly, and what is said about it in this book is only an attempt at preliminary orientation; but it springs from the certainty that tomorrow's ministry, however much it continues that of today, must be different, otherwise it would no longer be a living ministry. The risk of a possibly inaccurate grasp is less than the risk of immobilism and ossification. "To live is to change, and to be perfect is to have changed often."

SELECTED READING LIST

The following is not an exhaustive bibliography, but a list of what the author considers to be the most important and easily available relevant studies, many of which contain further elaborations on the subjects discussed in the present work. From the period before Vatican II, only a very few basic studies have been mentioned; for this English edition a number of recent titles have been added. The material is indicated in its original language, or, in the case of foreign titles, in English, whenever we have found a translation in that language.

ON ECCLESIOLOGY IN GENERAL

Baraúna, G., ed., *De Kerk van Vaticanum II*. Bilthoven, Nelissen, 1966, 2 vols.

Baum, G., "Het leergezag in een veranderende Kerk," *Concilium*, 3 (1967), n. 1, pp. 64-80.

Congar, Y., "De Kerk als Volk Gods," *Concilium*, 1 (1965), n. 1, pp. 5-16.

Fries, H., *Aspekten der Kirche*. Stuttgart, Schwabenverlag, 1963.

Goddijn, H. and W. Goddijn, *Sociologie van Kerk en Godsdienst*. Utrecht, Spectrum, 1966.

Hoekendijk, J., *The Church Inside Out*. Trans. by I. C. Rottenberg. Philadelphia, Westminster Press, 1966.

Lubac, H. de, *Méditation sur l'Eglise*. Paris, Aubier, 1954.

Küng, H., *Structures of the Church*. Trans. by S. Attanasio. New York, T. Nelson, 1964.

———, "De charismatische structuur van de Kerk," *Concilium*, 1 (1965), n. 4, pp. 40-58.

———, *The Church*. New York, Sheed and Ward, 1967.

Mulders, J., *Het Mysterie der Kerk*. Tielt, Lannoo, 1965.

Philips, G., *De Dogmatische Constitutie over de Kerk "Lumen Gentium,"* Vol. I. Antwerp, Patmos, 1967.

Rahner, K., "Das Charismatische in der Kirche," *Stimmen der Zeit* 82 (1957), pp. 161-186.

——, *The Church and the Sacraments*. Trans. by W. J. O'Hara. New York, Herder and Herder, 1963.

Röper, A., *Die anonymen Christen*. Mainz, Grünewald, 1963.

Smulders, P., "Sacramenten en Kerk," *Bijdragen*, 17 (1956), pp. 391-418.

GENERAL WORKS ON THE ECCLESIASTICAL MINISTRY

Anciaux, P., *Het Ambt in de Kerk*, Tielt, Lannoo, 1963.

Antweiler, A., *Der Priester Heute und Morgen*. Münster, Aschendorf, 1967.

Beeck, F. van, "Thoughts on an ecumenical understanding of the sacraments," *Journal of Ecumenical Studies*, 3 (1966), pp. 57-112.

Bellet, M., *La Peur ou la Foi, une analyse du prêtre*. Paris, Desclée, 1967.

Bogers, H., et al., *Essays en Interviews over de Priester*. Utrecht, Ambo, 1965.

Boon, R., *Apostolisch Ambt en Reformatie*. Nijkerk, Callenbach, 1965.

Bouchette, H., *Ambt en Mythe*. Bilthoven, Nelissen, 1966.

Brunot, A., et al., *Prêtres, pourquoi?* Paris, Ed. Ouvrières, 1965.

Chalendar, X. de, *Les Prêtres*. Paris, Ed. du Seuil, 1965.

La Collégialité Episcopale. Histoire et Théologie. Paris, Cerf, 1965.

Colson, J., *L'Episcopat Catholique*. Paris, Cerf, 1963.

——, *Ministre de Jésus-Christ ou le Sacerdoce de l'Evangile*. Paris, Beauchesne, 1966.

Congar, Y., *A Gospel Priesthood*. New York, Herder and Herder, 1967.

Coste, R., *L'Homme-prêtre*. Paris, Desclée, 1962.

Davis, Charles, *A Question of Conscience*, New York, Harper and Row, 1967.

Delmotte, J., *Ik wijd U*. Tielt, Lannoo, 1966.

Denis, H., *Le Prêtre de Demain*. Tournai, Casterman, 1967.

Denniston, R., *Part-time Priests? A Discussion*. London, Skeffington, 1960.

Duquesne, J., *Le Prêtres*. Paris, Grasset, 1965.

Fichter, J., *Priest and People*. New York, Sheed and Ward, 1965.

————, *America's Forgotten Priests—What They Are Saying*. New York, Harper & Row, 1968.

Goddijn, W., "Le rôle du prêtre dans l'Eglise et la société," *Social Compass*, 12 (1965), pp. 21-33.

Grelot, P., *Le Ministère de la Nouvelle Alliance*. Paris, Cerf, 1967.

Haarsma, F., "Pastoral-theologische beschouwingen over de priester," *Tijdschrift voor Theologie*, 5 (1965), pp. 272-295.

Haneveer, P., *Beheerders van Gods Geheimen*. Bruges, Desclée, 1962.

Hebert, A., *Apostle and Bishop. A Study of the Gospel, the Ministry, and the Church-community*. London, Faber, 1963.

Heenan, J., *Council and Clergy*. London, Chapman, 1966.

Hurley, D., and J. Cunnane, *Vatican II on Priests and Seminaries*. Dublin, Scepter Books, 1967.

Illich, I., "The Vanishing Clergyman," *The Critic*, 26 (June-July), 1967.

James, E., *The Nature and Function of Priesthood*. New York, Barnes & Noble, 1961. London, Thames and Hudson, 1955.

Johnston, R., ed., *The Church and Its Changing Ministry*. New York, 1961.

Kirk, K., ed., *The Apostolic Ministry*. London, Hodder & Stoughton, 1946.

Lash, N., "Priesterschap, kerkelijk ambt en intercommunie," *Tijdschrift voor Theologie*, 7 (1967), pp. 105-126.

Leclercq, J., *Le Prêtre devant Dieu et devant les Hommes*. Paris, Casterman, 1964.

Leslie Newbigin, J., *The Ministry of the Church, Ordained and Unordained, Paid and Unpaid*. London, Edinburgh House Press, 1953.

Maranache, A., *Prêtres à la Manière des Apôtres pour les Hommes de Demain*. Paris, Centurion, 1967.

Monjardet, A., *Autre Prêtre, Autre Englise*. Paris, L'Epi, 1967.

Niebuhr, H. R., *The Purpose of the Church and its Ministry*. New York, Harper & Row, 1956.

Paton, D., ed., *New Forms of Ministry*. London, Edinburgh House Press, 1965.

Les Prêtres dans la Pensée de Vatican II. Paris, Centre National de Vocations, 1966.

Rahner, K., *Vom Sinn des Kirchlichen Amtes.* Freiburg, Herder, 1966.

——, *Knechte Christi.* Freiburg, Herder, 1967.

Robinson, J., *The New Reformation?* Philadelphia, Westminster Press, 1965.

Rogé, J., *Le Simple Prêtre. Sa Formation, Son Expérience.* Paris, Casterman, 1965.

Romaniuk, C., *Le Sacerdoce dans le Nouveau Testament,* Le Puy, Mappus, 1967.

Salaün, R. and E. Marcus, *Qu'est-ce qu'un Prêtre?* Paris, Seuil, 1966.

Schelkle, K., *Jungerschaft und Apostelamt. Eine Biblische Auslegung des Priesterlichen Dienstes.* Freiburg, Herder, 1957.

Sykes, N., *Old Priest and New Presbyter.* Cambridge, Cambridge University Press, 1956.

Volk, H., *Der Priester und Seine Dienst.* Mainz, Grünewald, 1967.

Weber, H.-R., *The Militant Ministry.* Philadelphia, Fortress Press, 1964.

Weitzel, E., ed., *Pastoral Ministry in a Time of Change.* Milwaukee, Bruce, 1966.

World Council of Churches. Commission for the Study on Patterns of Ministry and Theological Education, *Ministry. Working Papers.* Geneva, 1965.

Wulf, F., "Stellung und Aufgabe des Priesters in der Kirche nach dem zweiten Vatikanischen Konzil," *Geist und Leben,* 39 (1966), pp. 45-61.

Zimmermann, H., *Die Hohepriester-Christologie des Hebräerbriefes.* Paderborn, Schöningh, 1964.

THE COMMON AND THE SPECIAL PRIESTHOOD; THE RELATIONSHIP
BETWEEN LAYMAN AND MINISTER

Bouchette, H., *Leek en Ambt.* Amsterdam, ten Have, 1963.

Cadet, J., *Le Laicat et le Droit de l'Eglise.* Paris, Ed. Ouvrières, 1963.

Congar, Y., *Lay People in the Church.* Trans. by D. Attwater, Westminster, Md., Newman Press, 1957.

Dondeyne, A., *Priester en Leek.* Antwerp, Patmos, 1962.

Duss-von Werdt, J., "Wat kan de leek zonder de priester?" *Concilium,* 4 (1968), pp. 99-107.

Gibbs, M. and T. Morton, *God's Frozen People*. Philadelphia, West-minster Press, 1965. London, Collins, 1964.

Heimerl, H., *Kirche, Klerus and Laien*. Vienna, Herder, 1961.

————, "Het begrip 'leek' in de constitutie over de Kerk van Vati-canum II." *Concilium*, 2 (1966), n. 3, pp. 127-144.

Kraemer, H., *A Theology of the Laity*. London, Lutterworth Press, 1958. Philadelphia, Westminster Press, 1959.

Neill, S. and H.-R. Weber, ed., *The Layman in Christian History*. Philadelphia, Westminster Press, 1963.

Rahner, K., "Ueber das Laienapostolat," *Schriften zur Theologie II*. Einsiedeln, Benzinger, 1955, pp. 339-373.

————, "Weihe des Laien zur Seelsorge," *Schriften zur Theologie III*. Einsiedeln, Benzinger, 1956, pp. 313-328.

Schelkle, K., *Ihr alle seid Geistliche*. Einsiedeln, Benzinger, 1965.

Schillebeeckx, E., "Dogmatiek van ambt en lekestaat," *Tijdschrift voor Theologie*, 2 (1962), pp. 258-292.

Semmelroth, O., "Het priesterlijk godsvolk en zijn ambtelijke leid-ers," *Concilium*, 4 (1968), n. 1, pp. 86-99.

Vorgrimler, H., "Das allgemeine Priestertum," *Lebendiges Zeugnis*, Heft 2-3 (November, 1964), pp. 92-113.

Weinzierl, E., "Die Funktion des Laien in der Kirche," *Der Seel-sorger*, 36 (1966), pp. 229-240.

SPIRITUALITY. THE CELIBACY OF THE MINISTER

Audet, J.-P., *Structures of Christian Priesthood. Home, Marriage and Celibacy in the Pastoral Service of the Church*. London, Sheed and Ward, 1967; New York, Macmillan, 1967.

Bailey, D., *The Man-woman Relation in Christian Thought*. London, Longmans, 1959.

Bunnik, R., "The question of married priests." *Cross Currents*, 15 (1965), pp. 407-431 and 16 (1966), pp. 81-112; also in *Social Compass*, 12 (1965), pp. 53-100.

————, "Het zielzorgelijk tekort. Concilie en Celibaat," *Te Elfder Ure*, 13 (1966), pp. 137-151.

————, "De theologische studie van virginiteit en ambtscelibaat," *Tijdschrift voor Theologie*, 6 (1966), pp. 148-182.

Catholicus, *Um den Zölibat*. Nürnberg, Glock und Lutz, 1966.

Cattin, P., *Spiritualité sacerdotale. Documents pontificaux sur le sacerdoce, de Pie X à Jean XXIII.* Fribourg-Paris, 1964.

Concilium, 1 (1965), n. 9, and 1 (1966), n. 9 (Special issues devoted to the question of spirituality).

Cooman, L. de, *Le sacerdoce et l'état de perfection.* Paris, 1963.

Fesquet, H., *Trois questions brûlantes à Rome.* Paris, Grasset, 1964, pp. 69-94 and 121-138.

Frein, G., *Celibacy, the Necessary Option.* New York, Herder and Herder, 1968.

Görres, I., *Is Celibacy Outdated?* Westminster, Md., Newman Press, 1965.

Hayot, P., *Prêtre au milieu du monde. Réflexions sur la vocation et la spiritualité du clergé séculier.* Tournai, Centre Diocesan de Documentation, 1963.

Hermand, P., *The Priest, Celibate or Married.* Baltimore, Helicon, 1966.

Hesse, P., ed., *Jungfräulichkeit und Zölibat.* Vienna, Herder, 1964.

Lea, H., *A History of Sacerdotal Celibacy in the Christian Church.* New York, Macmillan, 1907, 2 vols.

Legrand, L., *The Biblical Doctrine of Virginity.* New York, Sheed and Ward, 1963. London, Chapman, 1963.

Matura, Th., *Célibat et communauté. Les fondements évangeliques de la vie réligieuse.* Paris, Cerf, 1967.

O'Neill, D., *Priestly Celibacy and Maturity.* New York, Sheed and Ward, 1965.

Ons Geestelijk Leven 43 (1966-1967), pp. 321-364. (A special issue on celibacy containing articles by A. Brekelmans, G. Bouwman, and A. van Rijen.)

Oraison, M., *Le célibat, aspect négatif, realités positives.* Paris, Centurion, 1966.

Pfliegler, M., *Celibacy.* London, Sheed and Ward, 1967.

Priesterlicher Lebensstil in der Gegenwart. Würzburg, Echter Verlag, 1965.

Rahner, K., "Theologie der Entsagung," *Schriften zur Theologie* III. Einsiedeln, Benzinger, 1956, pp. 61-72.

———, "Ueber die evangelische Räte," *Geist und Leben,* 37 (1964), pp. 17-37.

————, "The Celibacy of the Secular Priest Today," *The Furrow* (Feb.), 1968.

Schillebeeckx, E., *Celibacy*. New York, Sheed and Ward, 1968.

Spicq, C., *Spiritualité sacerdotale d'après Saint Paul*. Paris, Cerf, 1954.

Thurian, M., *Marriage and Celibacy*. London, S.C.M. Press, 1959.

Vogels, H., *Zur Ehelosigkeit der Priester der Lateinische Ritus*. Freiburg, 1963 (Privately printed).

Weber, L., *Mysterium Magnum. Zur innerkirchlichen Diskussion um Ehe, Geschlecht und Jungfräulichkeit*. Freiburg, Herder, 1963.

Wulf, F., "Priestertum und Rätestand," *Geist und Leben*, 33 (1960), pp. 109-118 and 247-261.

————, "Der Zölibat des Weltpriesters und die Jungfräulichkeit des Ordensstandes," *Geist und Leben*, 35 (1962), pp. 51-55.

————, "Ist das Zölibatsgesetz heute noch angebracht?" *Geist und Leben*, 40 (1967), pp. 301-306.

THE IMAGE OF THE PRIEST. VOCATION AND FORMATION

Brothers, J., "Social change and the role of the priest," *Social Compass*, 10 (1963), pp. 477-489.

Carrier, H., *La Vocation. Dynamismes psycho-religieuses*. Rome, Presses de l'université grégorienne, 1966.

Chalendar, X. de, *Pourquoi pas? Lettres sur la vocation sacerdotale*. Paris, Fayard, 1964.

Cordes, P., "Zur Priesterausbildung: Gedanken über die Erhaltung des Berufswillens," *Geist und Leben*, 39 (1966), pp. 62-70.

Crottognini, J., *Werden und Krise des Priesterberufs*. Einsiedeln, Benzinger, 1955.

————, "Ausbildung und Erziehung der Theologiestudenten heute," *Theologie und Glaube*, 54 (1964), pp. 251-271.

Dellepoort, J., ed., *Die europäische Priesterfrage*. Vienna, Herder, 1959.

Griesl, G., *Berufung und Lebensform des Priesters*. Innsbrück, Tyrolia, 1967.

Herklots, H., et al., *Preparing for the Ministry of the 1970's*. London, S.C.M. Press, 1964.

Hofman, H., *Making the Ministry Relevant*. New York, 1960.

Hostie, R., *The Discernment of Vocations*. London, Chapman, 1963.

Jedin, H., "Die Bedeutung des Tridentinische Dekretes über die Priesterseminäre für das Leben der Kirche," *Theologie und Glaube*, 54 (1964), pp. 181-198.

Klostermann, F., "Priesterbild und Priesterbildung. Ueberlegungen für übermorgen," *Der Seelsorger*, 35 (1965), pp. 299-316.

————, "Entmythologisierung des Priesterbildes und der Priesterberufung," *Der Seelsorger*, 36 (1966), pp. 10-29.

Lindner, T., L. Lentner, and A. Holl, *Priesterbild und Berufswahlmotive*. Vienna, Herder, 1963.

Picard, P., and E. Emrich, *Priesterbildung in der Diskussion*. Mainz, Grünewald, 1967.

Priesterroeping en Seminarie. Haarlem, Gottmer, 1964.

Schreuder, O., *Het Professioneel Karakter van het Geestelijk Ambt*. Nijmegen, Dekker & van de Vegt, 1964.

Stenger, H., *Wissenschaft und Zeugnis. Die Ausbildung des Katholischen Seelsorgeklerus in psychologischer Sicht*. Salzburg, Müller, 1961.

LEAVING THE MINISTRY

De Crisis in het Ambt. Visies en Verwachtingen van Uitgetreden Priesters. Hilversum, Brand, 1967.

Davis, C., *A Question of Conscience*. London, Hodder and Stoughton, 1967.

Kavanaugh, J., *A Modern Priest Looks at His Outdated Church*. New York, Trident Press, 1967.

Kuin, J., "Van priester tot leek," *Te Elfder Ure*, 11 (1964), pp. 49-71.

Willemse, J., ed., *Te Pas en te Onpas. Brief van een Theoloog*. Hilversum, Brand, 1967.

CONCELEBRATION AND PRIVATE MASS

Danneels, G., "Het probleem der concelebratie," *Collationes Brugenses et Gandavenses*, 9 (1963), pp. 160-189.

Fransen, P., "Dogmatische beschouwingen over concelebratie," *Tijdschrift voor Liturgie*, 47 (1963), pp. 337-362.

Häussling, A., "Ursprunge der Privatmesse," *Stimmen der Zeit*, 90 (1965), pp. 21-28.

————, "Die Konzelebration. Ein Modellfall der Liturgie-reform," *Stimmen der Zeit*, 92 (1967), pp. 334-343.

Häussling, A., and K. Rahner, *Die vielen Messen und das eine Opfer. Eine Untersuchung über die rechte Norm der Messhäufigkeit*. Freiburg, Herder, 1966.

Roguet, A., "Pour une théologie de la concélébration," *La Maison-Dieu*, n. 88 (1966), pp. 116-126.

THE DIACONATE

Bouchette, H., *Het Oude Diaconaat in de zich Vernieuwende Kerk*. Bilthoven, Nelissen, 1966.

Colson, J., *La fonction diaconale aux origines de l'Eglise*. Paris, Desclée, 1960.

————, "Les diacres à la lumière de l'histoire," *La Vie Spirituelle*, n. 537 (1967), pp. 442-467.

Hornef, J., "Der Diakon kommt wieder—Möglichkeiten der Verwirklichung," *Theologie und Glaube*, 55 (1965), pp. 98-106.

————, "Diakonat und Oekumene," *Stimmen der Zeit*, 90 (1964-1965), pp. 697-711.

Rahner, K., "Die Lehre des II Vatikanischen Konzils über den Diakonat," *Der Seelsorger*, 36 (1966), pp. 193-200.

Rahner, K., and H. Vorgrimler, ed., *Diaconia in Christo*. Freiburg, Herder, 1961.

Winninger, P., Y. Congar, et al., *Le Diacre dans l'Eglise et le monde d'aujourd'hui*. Paris, Cerf, 1966.

See also the articles by A. Kerkvoorde and P. Winninger in *De Kerk van Vaticanum II*, edited by G. Baraúna, vol. II, pp. 216-265 and 266-281.

WOMAN AND THE MINISTRY

Concerning the Ordination of Women. Geneva, World Council of Churches, 1964.

Eyden, R. van, "Die Frau im Kirchenamt," *Wort und Wahrheit*, 22 (1967), pp. 350-362.

Gössmann, E., "*De vrouw als priester*," *Concilium*, 4 (1968), n. 4, pp. 108-117.

Govaart-Halker, T., "Ceterum censeo," *Kultuurleven*, 34 (1967), pp. 564-579.

Hannon, V., *The Question of Women and the Priesthood. Can Women Be Admitted to Holy Orders?* London, Chapman, 1967.

Heinzelmann, G., ed., *Wir schweigen nicht länger. Frauen aussern sich zum II Vatikanischen Konzil.* Zürich, Interfeminas Verlag, 1964.

Meer, H. van der, *Theologische Ueberlegungen über die Thesis: "Subiectum ordinationis est mas."* Innsbrück, 1962 (ms.).

Peters, J., "De vrouw in de ambtelijke dienst van de Kerk," *Concilium*, 4 (1968), n. 4, pp. 118-129.

Schüszler, E., *Der Vergessene Partner.* Düsseldorf, Patmos, 1964.

Thrall, M., *The Ordination of Women to the Priesthood. A Study of the Biblical Evidence.* London, S.C.M. Press, 1958.